BOLD
TYPES

BOLD
TYPES

BOLD TYPES

How Australia's First Women Journalists Blazed a Trail

PATRICIA CLARKE

CELEBRATING

NATIONAL LIBRARY
OF AUSTRALIA
PUBLISHING

50 YEARS

Published by National Library of Australia Publishing
Canberra ACT 2600
ISBN: 9781922507372
© National Library of Australia 2022
Text © Patricia Clarke 2022
Introduction © Amy Remeikis 2022

The National Library of Australia acknowledges Australia's First Nations Peoples—the First Australians—as the Traditional Owners and Custodians of this land and gives respect to the Elders—past and present—and through them to all Australian Aboriginal and Torres Strait Islander people.

First Nations Peoples are advised that this book contains names of deceased people, and content that may be considered culturally sensitive.

Images: (front cover) Barbara Joan Isaacson, *Caroline Isaacson and a Party of Australian Female Photographers and Journalists*, courtesy Australian War Memorial, P05161.007; *Woman at the Government Printing Offices*, c.1930, nla.cat-vn6334791; (back cover) *Patricia Clarke*, supplied by author; *Anna Blackwell*, supplied by author; *Portrait of Jessie (Tasma) Couvreur*, 1889, nla. cat-vn3049072; *Flora Shaw*, alicemag.ng/flora-shaw; *Edith Dickenson*, commons.wikimedia. org/wiki/File:Edith-Dickenson; *Alice Henry*, c.1920, State Library Victoria, H36114; *Jennie Scott Griffiths*, supplied by author; *Stella Allan*, halloffame.melbournepressclub.com/article/stella-allan; *Frances Taylor*, supplied by author; *Government Bank Thrift Organiser Janet Mitchell*, c.1930, nla.cat-vn6255949; Barbara Joan Isaacson, *Caroline Isaacson Boarding a Douglas C-47 Aircraft*, 1943, courtesy Australian War Memorial, P05161.013; Barbara Joan Isaacson, *Connie Robertson and Australian Female Journalists Boarding a Douglas C-47 Aircraft*, 1943, courtesy Australian War Memorial, P05161.012; Barbara Joan Isaacson, *Iris Dexter Standing under a Douglas C-47 Aircraft*, 1943, courtesy Australian War Memorial, P05161.017; Barbara Joan Isaacson, *Henry Steele, Caroline Isaacson and Patricia Knox Boarding a Douglas C-47 Aircraft*, 1943, courtesy Australian War Memorial, P05161.014.

Publisher: Lauren Smith
Managing editor: Amelia Hartney
Editor: Irma Gold
Cover designer: Nada Backovic
Internal designer: David Potter
Image coordinator: Jemma Posch
Printed in Australia

Find out more about NLA Publishing at nla.gov.au/national-library-publishing.

A catalogue record for this book is available from the National Library of Australia

Contents

Introduction

by Amy Remeikis

Be smart but not intimidating, approachable but not a pushover. Be assertive (as long as it isn't aggressive), one of the boys but always a lady. Women journalists should ask the hard questions but not interrupt. We are to be truth telling but never difficult, passionate but never angry, enthusiastic but not overly excitable. And never, ever 'shrill'. A woman can care (as long as she isn't too 'emotional'), she can explain (as long as she doesn't lecture). And some things, even after all these years, are still considered best left to the boys. More than a century after Edith Dickenson reported from the Boer War by sea mail, unable to access the almost-instant cable transmission available to male correspondents (it was deemed too expensive for women's work), the boys' club remains alive and well.

And yet, women continue to break new ground, smashing not just the ceiling, but the walls, windows and doors that try to contain us in a narrow view of what journalism should be.

From the first 'inky wayfarers' and 'penny liners' to the political editors who lead the Australian press gallery today, women have always been a crucial part of journalism. 'Anonymous' may have been a woman, but there were many others watching history unfold under a by-line, analysing and explaining it through their own lens—all while hearing how they couldn't possibly understand the significance of the events they were both witnessing and living. But it is precisely women's experiences, as distinct from men's, our views and, yes, *emotions* that not only set us apart, but help to tell the stories history, and men, have missed.

Patricia Clarke began her journalism career in 1951, not long after the final story told in this book. Seven decades later, Pat is still telling stories, still shining a light into parts of history the patriarchy left dark, giving those women back their voices. Pat has stood sentry over an unfolding history we don't like to acknowledge in the media, given the industry's penchant for considering itself an overall progressive force. She was part of a workforce that pushed not only for equality, but respect, a push that eventually snowballed into the end of the 'women's pages' and saw women's by-lines take their rightful place alongside their male colleagues'. From police stations to Parliament House, Pat has both recorded history and helped make it.

Bold Types is just part of Patricia Clarke's professional legacy, which began when she first stepped into a newsroom 71 years ago. The stories she tells here are timeless, made richer by her own experiences and understanding of both the differences and commonalities. Having lived and contributed to the changes, Pat is perhaps one of the only voices in Australian journalism who can tell you these stories—as well as let you know just how much there still is to change.

There have been gains. And wins. And defying the odds. The women in this book, through their fight and determination, paved the way for the women editors, correspondents and media leaders we know now. There is no Katharine Murphy, Laura Tingle, Patricia Karvelas, Fran Kelly, Leigh Sales, Samantha Maiden or Karen Middleton without Stella Allan, who, despite being refused a seat in the (then all-male)

New Zealand parliamentary press gallery, became the first woman parliamentary reporter in either Australia or New Zealand—from the special cubicle where she was segregated.

There is no Avani Dias or Isabella Higgins or Zoe Daniel (in her incarnation as a foreign correspondent) without Janet Mitchell, who watched as Japanese troops marched into the Chinese province of Manzhou (Manchuria), capturing the moment many now see as a precursor to the Second World War in letters to her family, which she later turned into a series of broadcasts for the ABC upon her return to Australia. Maxine McKew, Pru Goward and now Daniel are part of a long line of women journalists who saw an opportunity to better create change by joining politics, instead of just reporting on it, which owes a debt of gratitude to Alice Henry, a woman who resigned her rather constricting position in Australian journalism to fight for women's suffrage, not just in Australia, but in the United States.

There is no Lenore Taylor, Michelle Grattan, Gay Alcorn, Lisa Wilkinson or Lisa Davies without Jennie Scott Griffiths, the first female editor of a weekly women's paper. Scott Griffiths had already worked as the 'unacknowledged, unpaid' editor of the *Fiji Times* when it had been under her husband's stewardship. In 1915, she was able to put her name to her editorship of the *Woman's Weekly*—two years after she had been given the job. Pat will tell you the rest of that story.

But the more things change, the more they stay the same. For every step—or shove—forward, there have been just as many steps—and shoves—back.

The boys' club may not be as acceptable today, but it still exists. It dwells in the editors' and chief editors' rooms, in the boardrooms of media organisations, the rarefied places where women still do not have access (The Australia Club, which counts the most influential powerbrokers among its membership, remains stubbornly male-only in 2022), the golf clubs, whisky bars and country pubs. Men by and large still hold the most powerful positions in Australian media, are promoted faster, paid better and offered more opportunities than their women counterparts, who still have to work twice as hard to receive even half the credit. Women still find our careers stymied by childcare and labour within the home, and even those without children can find themselves overlooked for overseas postings, promotions or more responsibility because they could one day have children.

The term 'sexual harassment' may not have existed when Stella Allan (one of Australia's greatest trailblazing journalists regardless of sex) began her career, but a lack of legally recognised phrases didn't mean it didn't happen. Then, it was just one of the costs of a woman doing business in a man's world. We know sexual harassment and abuse still happens, but there is at least a pathway (thorny as it is) for justice in the modern era, although much of what the women in this book experienced would ring true to women in media today. Women still report harassment and abuse on the job far more than our male colleagues, and others are still at risk within their own workplace. The whisper network spoken of in *Bold Types*, where women warned other women of men to watch out for in their building, or on news rounds, existed for women entering the federal press gallery in the 2020s.

Sharing a cab with a male contact or colleague is still enough to set tongues wagging about exactly how she got that job/story/promotion, while dining with a male contact—an occurrence so common for male journalists they barely blink an eye—is often turned into a small group event, lest anyone wonder what that dinner is for.

While men are considered presentable as long as they are in a suit or something suitable for the terrain, women journalists working for commercial television networks are still expected to have perfect hair and makeup even when covering natural disasters. Stories abound of women covering human tragedy in all its forms, sleeping where they can, facing all Mother Nature can throw—and then receiving phone calls from irate senior producers about their hair. Wearing florals or prints or having too dark hair (or too light) can have you pulled from air until the issue is rectified. Viewer complaints to television news stations often focus on how a woman journalist looked or sounded, or how someone didn't like her blouse. And yet one of the most high-profile men in Australian television journalism wore the same suit on air every day for a year and no-one noticed.

Women in the media get more than our fair share of criticism, receiving sexual assault and death threats for the sin of asking tough questions to a politician a viewer or listener likes, accused of being shrill or hysterical for daring to have a voice above a tenor. Women's voices are often bemoaned for our 'vocal fry' by viewers and listeners alike, unwilling or unable to hear a higher pitched voice without perfect elocution. If the woman is Indigenous, Asian, Muslim, Black, Brown, gay or trans (for example), you can add a racist, homophobic or xenophobic slant to the misogynistic insult.

Women, particularly marginalised women, could write entire books on it (and do). But most just get on with the job the best they can—an example set by the women in this book. In doing so, they're changing our world.

When sexual assault allegations rocked the federal parliament in 2021, it was women journalists who not only broke the story, but ensured it stayed on the national agenda, prosecuting each and every loose end, unanswered question and wilfully ignored thread. It was women journalists, digging into their own personal experiences and the experiences of those around them who kept pushing until the government of the day had no choice but to react. Women kept the focus where it was needed, ensuring the men in power—in both parliament and the press gallery—not only paid attention, but ceded space. It was women journalists who took the lead in explaining a universal national pain and shame, elevating the voices of those who needed to be heard in order to address it.

While the men may have offered their empathy, their discomfort was clear. It wasn't a topic anyone wanted to speak about, which women knew had always been the problem. So they filled the vacuum with story after story, call after call, until it had to be heard. News Corp national political editor Samantha Maiden became the first journalist to win the Canberra Press Gallery Journalist of the Year and the Gold Walkley in the same year. But she also had to fend off a public attack by a prime minister who was scrambling to respond to an issue she, and senior women gallery colleagues, would not let drop.

There was no bigger story at the time, and yet women journalists often have to fight against notions our stories 'just aren't as big'. This is not new. Alice Blackwell, a poet, translator and, as this book lays out, master observer and talented writer, had her work dismissed as 'gossip'. Other women profiled in this book were forced to take lower profile beats, writing specifically for women on 'women's issues'. Even when taking on meatier rounds (either through circumstance or desperation) and proving their worth, they were soon shuffled back to the shadow of the men, who were paid more, often, to do less. As Pat observes, it has never been easy. But that doesn't mean it hasn't been worth it. Or fun.

I became a journalist because I had seen the power of telling individuals' stories up close. My father was a refugee, who arrived in this country around the same time Pat was starting her journalism career. He learnt about his new home from listening to the news. Many decades later, he began teaching his children what we could learn about life from the news, not just in our own country, but around the world. I spent my breakfasts listening to Radio National and becoming increasingly agitated by the injustices it would report, the questions it would raise. My father, a staunch conservative, would give his interpretation of what we had heard, which taught me the value of a diversity of voices and opinions. Those mornings and evenings, bookmarked by ABC news openings, lit a fire in me to tell some of those same stories, to help explain Australia, as I see it, to others. It hasn't always been easy. There are times I have been left painfully aware of my gender. There has been harassment and unwanted advances, touches and comments, dismissals and missed opportunities. There have been inequities, including in one job where I was given stewardship over two male colleagues who both earned more than me. But there have been wins and rushes and times when my experiences helped shaped stories that led to real change. It's that which keeps you going, keeps you fighting, keeps you reporting.

The 2022 election saw a Coalition government swept from power, in large part by women.

Women did not see themselves reflected in their government, or in their local parliamentary representatives. And while big-ticket election issues played out on the campaign—culture wars and gaffes and the politics of the 'economy'—women journalists saw the anger that had risen over the previous 18 months and the reckoning that was coming, and they reported on the discontent within electorates. Women voters turned against the government, in enough numbers to change that government. There was a time such a story would have been missed. This time around, it bubbled away as an undercurrent, eventually growing to a roaring tide, which swept away those who had tried to ignore it.

Women journalists, then and now, battle entrenched power their entire careers and, more often than not, ensure that truth prevails. They doggedly expose corruption, wrongs and long-ignored injustices, which have led to law and industry changes and, in turn, better our world. Women have led the battle for gender equality, yes, but they have also pushed for more attention and change for those in aged care, with disability, minorities and Australian First Nations peoples.

Shirley Stott Despoja never took a job with any 'women's pages', demanding and eventually triumphing in her ambition to be a general news reporter with the Adelaide *Advertiser*. She was the first woman employed on its general news beat, helping to change the city as its Arts editor. Caroline Jones, the first woman reporter on the former ABC current affairs show *This Day Tonight*, as well as the first woman to anchor *Four Corners*, continued mentoring and supporting young women in media up until her 2022 death, with scholarships named in her honour. Yvonne O'Keefe became the first woman to anchor a State of Origin rugby league broadcast, a media domain that until recently was still seen as the bastion of men. Nas Campanella was the first blind newsreader in the world to read and operate a studio for herself, live to air. Brooke Boney was the first Indigenous woman to be named as part of a commercial network breakfast television team. Avani Dias is the only Australian journalist for an Australian network covering South Asia. Of course there are more contemporary trailblazers. And there will be still more to come.

Because there is still so far to go. When it comes to race, religion, gender and disability, there always is—particularly when there is any intersectionality. For all its gains, there is still a stunning lack of diversity in media and, as women have shown, a diversity of voices and experiences makes our national story richer. It can be easy to forget how far we have come when looking at the state of the profession for women today. But the pioneering battle of the women Pat profiles, these bold types, is the reason we are here to carry it on.

Then, women were often defined by the men in their life—fathers or husbands—and bound by the strictures of a society that was not yet ready to embrace their multitudes. It would be easy to think of them as extraordinary, but they were probably just bemused and exhausted—a recognisable state for any woman. The hidden and unpaid labours of child-raising and -care, housekeeping and life administration still fall more often to women than men no matter our profession or hours, and those ties make the juggle more difficult than it needs to be. But that is part of what makes ordinary women extraordinary. They just keep on getting on with the job.

Then, and now. And always.

Preface

Bold Types has a long history. It began when I started work as a journalist in the early 1950s, a bygone era that is now part of media history. Women journalists were scarce and usually employed in the lower grades of the organisations I worked for.

Most women journalists worked on the women's pages of newspapers. They were usually paid at the lowest level, with only the few who held great responsibility even approaching the salary levels of male journalists with less responsibility. This festered in my mind through the female liberation movement that began in the 1960s until I left full-time journalism and started to have books published. My third book, *Pen Portraits: Women Writers and Journalists in Nineteenth Century Australia*, published in 1988, is a forerunner of *Bold Types*. When I re-read chapter one of *Pen Portraits*, I found my description of the work of women journalists in the 1890s still applied in the 1950s.

The fight by women journalists for gender equality continued to nag at me, and over the years I wrote many articles that were published in media, historical and cultural affairs journals. Some of these articles were earlier versions of chapters in *Bold Types*, and emphasised different aspects of the women's lives.

The women journalists whose stories are told here ventured far and wide in their search for relevance and female equality, and were adventurous and independent. They variously lived through wars and depressions—from the constraints of the nineteenth century to the First World War, the heady euphoria and freedom of the 1920s, the hard times of the 1930s Great Depression to the fear of invasion and the grating restrictions of the Second World War. The society through which they moved defined the limits of what they could achieve. Yet, theirs is a story of tenacious determination against the forces of the patriarchy. The chequered journey of this fight, from 1860 to the end of the Second World War, is the focus of *Bold Types*. Together, individual experiences reveal the range of gains women journalists made in this period of close to a century, and the setbacks they encountered.

The advent of fast cable transmission of news in 1872 was a giant step forward for journalism. This was, however, a step back for early women journalists who were increasingly confined to the long 'society' columns that were judged not worth the cost of cabling. In contrast, male reporters—who were regarded as more mobile, adaptable and worldly-wise—sent more immediate news by cable. Similarly, the explosion of illustrated advertising—an important milestone in creating many more jobs for women journalists—saw a great expansion of women's pages in both the broadsheet and tabloid press. This had the effect of relegating most women journalists to work on these pages and not on the broader fields open to male journalists, which ranged from court reporting and police rounds to sport to war. The women's pages came to be regarded as the only work women journalists could do.

Women journalists were a particular challenge to society because they chose to work in an overwhelmingly male profession. During the period covered here, most women were locked into marriage, and the legal system was loaded against women seeking divorce. In 1860, women had no property rights, or rights over their children. Even after these rights were won, most women remained financially dependent on male breadwinners. Contraception was increasing available, but all methods had a degree of uncertainty and anxiety. Abortion was illegal, although many women in the twentieth century were aware of gossip about access to illegal abortion, ranging from specialists in Macquarie Street, Sydney, or Collins Street, Melbourne, to backyard operators. Among the journalists included in this book, some were unmarried, a few had conventional marriages of varied compatibility, two were divorced, and others had relationships that were unconventional at the time, from extramarital to veiled lesbian.

The journalists in *Bold Types* were a particularly ground-breaking group given the societies in which they were living. The earlier journalists wrote thousands of words in longhand using quill pens. They ventured into muddy battlefields, down mines, and into slums and prisons in their crinoline-style, ankle-length dresses. Many of their words remain in print while more ephemeral cable news sent by male correspondents was submerged by subsequent events. Women who reached positions of standing and power could suffer the full brunt of gender discrimination either publicly or subtly. They also had to ignore the ethos of a society that disapproved of middle-class women working at all, much less in a such a public job as journalism.

The women journalists who followed in the twentieth century were no less intrepid as they defied gender barriers and fought against the taboos and the economic conditions of the eras in which they lived. Their great journalistic achievements did not save many of them from the effects of the Great Depression when women found permanent jobs in journalism almost impossible to find. There is statistical evidence that women journalists were particularly hard hit by loss of employment in depressed financial conditions.

All women journalists found social and patriarchal influences were pervasive and hard to resist. Apart from the small minority employed on socialist publications, they worked in a press environment for proprietors who ranged from being moderately to deeply conservative. Journalists had to conform to their paper's policy. Those who did not had to find work elsewhere or lose their hard-won jobs.

Many women chafed at their confinement to the women's pages, some for their entire working lives. The alternative was to resign, rather than submit to a life of writing 'society' columns. The overriding need for an income dictated that most conformed. Several individual stories in *Bold Types* illustrate this dilemma that continues to dog journalists—whether to stick with their views or keep a job. This affected women journalists more than men, particularly a century ago when their mere acceptance in the profession was problematic. For many years, protecting women's alleged innocence and inability to handle the tougher aspects of life was often the excuse for preventing them from reporting on wars, doing police rounds or reporting law courts. The few who ventured into male territory were the subject of extraordinary antagonism from male journalists who openly expressed their disdain of female journalists.

Even during the Second World War, the government actively prevented women correspondents from leaving Australia. When Australia was under threat from advancing Japanese forces, women were confined to writing about life on the home front, close to the headquarters of the papers they worked for. Even reporting on the work of nurses and ancillary staff employed at overseas bases was done by male war correspondents. The only concession came when the persuasive skills of women journalists were needed to publicise a government campaign to get recruits for the women's services.

I chose for this book women journalists who were remarkable for their independence and courage, who travelled to many countries in their search for stories, and whose lives made an important contribution to the history of women in journalism. Each journalist's story contributes to the uneven fight for gender equality—a unique part of the mosaic that is still unfolding today.

The story begins with Anna Blackwell.

Anna Blackwell

First female foreign correspondent for Australia

In 1860, when Anna Blackwell was appointed Paris correspondent for the Sydney Morning Herald, *she was one of only a handful of women with any journalistic association with an Australian newspaper, and there were not many more in Britain or other countries. She was the only female among the foreign correspondents appointed to represent the paper in Europe, the United States and Britain—a remarkable move by the conservative Fairfax family, who even a century later relegated women journalists to outdated women's page journalism. Anna's account of her escape from Paris in 1870, as the Prussian Army was about to besiege the city, was the high point of her 30-year career with the paper. Her early life in an activist family prepared her for her role as an international correspondent.*

Anna Blackwell began representing the *Sydney Morning Herald* in Paris in 1860 when the only method of communicating news to Australia was by handwritten dispatches sent by boat—a journey halfway around the world, which took at least four months. Ten years later as she fled Paris, Anna still had to send her dramatic dispatch on the Franco-Prussian War by sea mail, even though cable transmission was available to correspondents sending urgent news in short dispatches. Male reporters, who were regarded as more agile, wrote the more important cabled news, while Anna and the women who followed her were increasingly confined to human interest and social gossip columns, which continued to be dispatched by sea mail. This meant women journalists remained on the lower rungs of the journalistic hierarchy with low incomes. Anna's meagre remuneration, which she decried later in life, is a stark example of this situation.

The popularity and longevity of Anna's columns indicated that Australians—many of whom were migrants who arrived during the huge influx of the gold-rush years—were avid for news from abroad and appreciated her light, satirical style. In her peacetime columns, she combined news of social and political movements with entertaining stories from the capitals of Europe. Australians preferred her columns to the serious style of other correspondents.

Anna reports Franco-Prussian War

Once the Franco-Prussian War began, the tone of Anna's dispatches changed as she emphasised the seriousness of the French situation. Ostensibly, the war began on 17 July 1870 over Prussia's push to have an ally appointed to the throne of Spain over French opposition. This goaded the French Emperor into declaring war, expecting that a quick victory would boost his sagging popularity. Prussian Chancellor Otto von Bismarck welcomed this move, taking the opportunity to build support from other German states.[1] In a dispatch on 18 August 1870 covering the first weeks of the war, Anna reflected a general air of complacency in official sources in contrast with the effect of the war on ordinary people:

> The sweeping up of the young, able-bodied males, is going on at such a rate that one involuntarily wonders if ordinary life here will not come to a standstill. Your butcher has gone; your milkman is going; your grocer has lost one or two of his shopmen, and he fears lest he too, may not be made to follow them to the front; your greengrocer's son went last week, his nephew goes tonight; and your bread was brought to you by a poor woman, whose tears flow fast as she explains that her husband has been 'called for' and that she is forced to take his place at the baker's to get bread for her children.[2]

In later parts of this long dispatch, Anna recorded that the 'wild excitement of Paris was calming down', while one million men on either side prepared 'to tear one another to pieces' in a war 'desired and determined beforehand' by the French Government and while 'the singing of "patriotic songs" proceeded at the opera'. By 12 August, she reported that, although only sketchy accounts of three main battles had reached the capital, 'the utter incapacity of the French forces to cope with the Prussians' was becoming apparent as they dug in at Metz. Meanwhile, the French Government seized English publications as they arrived in France, which Anna interpreted as 'the French having experienced some new reverse'.

Anna's next dispatch mirrored the change in mood from the expectation of an easy and quick victory to the encirclement of almost the entire French Army—an event so inconceivable that at first it was not believed in Paris. There was such a lack of reliable news in the capital, that Anna wrote of victory for the French, even though the French forces of a quarter of a million men—led by Emperor Napoleon III and the Army chief—had already surrendered to the Prussian Army. One historian described the lack of news as 'a plethora of incredible rumours which, since no one could refute them, the Paris Press printed with avidity'.[3] The complete and sudden destruction of French military power was so unprecedented and the Prussian success so complete that it 'astounded the world'.[4]

As Parisians moved from complacency to alarm, Anna described the latest developments on 19 and 25 August 1870. Then, on 31 August, she wrote a graphic account of her departure from Paris ahead of the invading forces. After she reached Boulogne, she wrote the final part of her story. It was an account of a war that was so fast moving it was over in seven weeks.

Dramatic escape from Paris

Anna's personal experience of escape and the vividness of her words added to the drama of her report. She decided to escape after she read a placard on the city walls warning that 'all foreigners and useless mouths' would be ejected from the city when the Prussians arrived because of the difficulty authorities foresaw in feeding even its own citizens. For Parisians, the problem of getting enough food into the city, a problem that 'proved to be worse than even the Government had suspected',[5] overshadowed their shame at surrendering and any relief they held that the fighting was over.

The warning on a placard, Anna wrote, 'determined your correspondent to follow the example so generally set by the foreign residents, and to seek residence in the "English colony" [Boulogne]'.[6] She did this even though her instinct as a journalist would have been to stay and record this extraordinary event in world history. As she left, she described the 'grave and anxious faces and the vague and dubious bits of intelligence given out by the anxious authorities'. Peasants from surrounding districts, who had been ordered to send all their grain, hay and flour to Paris, piled their families and belongings on top of their wagons and joined the huge numbers of people moving to the centre of the city preparing to withstand the siege. Anna wrote:

> The train by which your correspondent quitted the capital was delayed three hours on the road by the enormous crowding of the line, train after train, of interminable length, bringing stores of grain, flour, provisions, cattle, sheep, forage, coal, &c, to the city so soon to be beleaguered by the foe. It really seemed, as the long lines of laden wagons went by, as though all France were being drained for the last scene of the sad drama in progress. All night, before I left Paris, the

bleating of sheep and lowing of cattle filled the streets, reserves for living food being created in all the vacant lots within the fortifications.

As she travelled nearly 300 kilometres through the countryside to Boulogne, she recorded:

At every station, even the smallest, was a group of people eagerly waiting for news, and a squad of country bumpkins being drafted off to war. It was heartrending to see all the young faces, all the figures, generally small, going off thus to form 'flesh for cannon', according to the saying of the first of the now extinct 'Napoleons', for whatever else may be the results of this war, the downfall of Empire is sure to be one of them.[7]

On the day that Anna's story—posted as usual by slow sea mail—arrived in Sydney, crowds surged around the doors of the *Sydney Morning Herald* because of the coincidental arrival from Honolulu of a ship carrying mail with more recent news that had travelled part of the way by cable. Although Anna's story was well behind agency cables, it was still highly valued because it was an eyewitness account by a known correspondent. It was published on pages two and three, demonstrating its importance to her loyal readership, and the value the *Sydney Morning Herald* placed on her personal account. After her forced departure from Paris, Anna sent a dispatch covering what news she heard from Paris during October, but by November she was in England and her opinion on what news she could garner from France was of little interest.[8] She stayed in England, where several of her sisters lived, until the Franco-Prussian War and its aftermath were over. When Anna returned to Paris, she again began sending dispatches of European news to her wide-flung outlets. She wrote the first of her new columns for the *Sydney Morning Herald* on 16 January 1874. It was published on 18 March 1874.

Early life and background

Anna Blackwell's early life in an exceptional family of engaged activists prepared her for life as an international correspondent. She was born in Bristol, England, on 21 June 1816, the eldest of nine surviving children of Samuel and Hannah Blackwell. One of her sisters, Elizabeth Blackwell, became famous as the world's first qualified female doctor. In 1832, when Anna was 16, the family migrated to the United States, partly for financial reasons and partly so that Samuel could further his interest in the abolition of slavery. At first the family lived in New York, where the older daughters campaigned for women's rights and supported the anti-slavery movement, then in Newark, New Jersey, and Cincinnati, Ohio, where Samuel died in 1838.

As the eldest child, Anna took teaching jobs to help support the family and taught, along with some of her sisters, in a school her mother and aunt started. By the early 1840s, she had begun writing articles for papers and magazines.[9] In 1845, she joined the Brook Farm utopian community, a short-lived experiment in communal living in Massachusetts, which adopted some of the theories of French utopian socialist and philosopher Charles Fourier, whose works she later translated.[10]

By 1860, Anna was well established as a foreign correspondent in Paris, sending dispatches to newspapers and periodicals in the United States, India, South Africa and Canada. Her columns, which were signed 'Fidelitas' for most of her outlets, consisted of lively news items that combined the reporting of political and international events with accounts of life in Paris and other European capitals. She described her columns as 'either purely gossip, purely political or mixed', according to what the editor required in each of the 11 papers to which she was contracted. When John Fairfax decided to make the *Sydney Morning Herald*'s 'columns the receptacle for cosmopolitan news gathered by its own correspondents', she was the only female correspondent among those appointed in England, the United States, St Petersburg, and other Continental centres.[11] Anna was also a poet and translator. A collection of her poems was published in England in 1853 and, in addition to translating Fourier, she also translated the works of Allan Kardec on spiritualism and a novel by Georges Sand.[12]

Distinctive style

One of Anna's first columns for the *Sydney Morning Herald* on 24 October 1860—signed 'Stella', the pseudonym she used for the *Herald*—consisted of six full-length columns of closely packed type covering many European countries. It was dispatched, as was all overseas news, by sea mail and appeared in the paper on 18 December 1860, nearly two months later. Typical of many columns that followed, it contained political, social and trade news, accounts of activities of British and European royalty, and interesting sidelights on food, the weather and social morality. There were mentions of such diverse subjects as Garibaldi's progress in the liberation of Italy and the intricate manoeuvres between Garibaldi and Cavour, a leading figure in the unification of the country; Queen Victoria's recent visit to Hesse; the abnormally cold European weather plus a theory about the correlation between weather conditions and moral health; the acceptance of potatoes as a food by the French; the French Emperor and Empress' tour of Algiers, Lyons and the south of France; British free-trader politician Richard Cobden's negotiations for a treaty with the French Government; and several examples of the Serbian Prince's harsh rule.

The beginning of the Serbian item is a good example of Anna's chatty style as she shared confidences from the capitals of Europe with her readers in far-off Australia. One cleverly written sentence conveys that her source was an important public figure and sets Serbia in its place as a country Austria desired, even though Serbia was under Turkish influence. The sentence ends with a snippet on the Serbian ruler. Anna may have been exaggerating the importance of her source, and her knowledge of geopolitics may have been superficial, but it was information that was engaging and informative. The item read:

> A highly intelligent Frenchman, who has for several years occupied an important public post at Bucharest, and who is intimately acquainted with all the region which Austria would so much like to add to her dominions at the expense of Turkey, has curious particulars of the late Prince Milosch, and the way in which he governed.

Among the incidents that followed was one in which the prince ordered a bishop to be buried alive for allegedly fleecing his flock.[13]

'Miss Blackwell is much appreciated': James Fairfax

Early in 1865, when the proprietor of the *Sydney Morning Herald*, John Fairfax, was travelling to England, his son James Reading Fairfax wrote telling him he could pick up a copy of the *Sydney Morning Herald* in Paris from their correspondent 'Miss Blackwell'.[14] James and his elder brother, Charles, had been partners in John Fairfax and Sons since 1856 when their father took them into the firm.[15] Later that year, in a further letter to his father, who had reached London, James praised Anna's dispatches in the context of the appointment of a London correspondent. He wrote:

> It would be an advantage to have an English correspondent who would give us English news in the pleasing way in which 'Stella' gives

us Continental ... Miss Blackwell, I think, is much appreciated & if a person could be obtained at a reasonable salary, articles of a similar character on English affairs would be attractive to our readers.[16]

Praise like this ensured that Anna continued in her position without challenge.

In the 1870s, Anna's relatives saw her long-standing involvement in spiritualism as a sign of eccentricity,[17] but there is no evidence that it affected the quality of her columns. Her dispatches continued to cover an extraordinary range of subjects in her usual engaging manner, as a dispatch published in August 1880 shows. Over four tightly packed columns, she moved seamlessly from celebrations in Portugal for the country's great poet Camoes and navigator Vasco da Gama to the Fine Arts Exhibition in Turin and an exhibition of flowers and birds in Madrid organised by the Spanish Society for the Protection of Animals. Here, she paused to draw attention to the paradox that almost all the attendees at the exhibition also attended bullfights. She continued with the Mediterranean Regatta and the wine produced from Italian, French and other European vineyards. Then there were plans for the International Congress of Geography in Venice the following year and festivities in Rouen to commemorate the entry of Henry II into the city in 1550. She also described a military funeral in Paris carried out with all the splendid pomp of which 'the Catholic Church and the military' were capable.

Without a pause and scarcely a break in the long paragraphs, she was back to Italy where she reported the opening of the Mount Vesuvius Railway, followed by reflections on the effect of telegraph communication and the cost to France of its failure to clear 5 million wild wolves that ravaged the countryside. Anna followed this up with details of negotiations of a projected plan to restore the Kingdom of

Israel in an area said to be 'inhabited only by a few nomad tribes'. She concluded with a lengthy item on the increased cultivation of flowers in France before she diverted to the design of famous gardens. This 6,300-word dispatch, sent on 11 June 1880 from Paris, covered two-thirds of page seven of the *Sydney Morning Herald* when it was published on 24 August. This left only one column on the foreign news page for a story on China as a market for Australian wool, and a sixth column of advertisements.

Altogether during that month, Anna had three dispatches published totalling 15,646 words. This was not an unusual example of her output. Her lively and slightly ironic style appealed to readers in New South Wales who appreciated news that could range from the contemplative or provocative to the bizarre. It is probably safe to say that not much newsworthy activity or European event escaped Anna's eagle eyes.

Meagre pay

More than 20 years after they first began appearing in the *Sydney Morning Herald*, Anna's columns remained as popular as ever. There had been some talk among the Fairfax executives about changing their emphasis, but on 4 June 1881, James Reading Fairfax, who had become head of the company following the death of his father in 1877,[18] wrote to Anna reaffirming her role:

> *Since writing to you respecting your correspondence we have been reconsidering the matter and think it better that you should continue the monthly budget as formerly and not trouble to write upon politics more than you used to do ... We think it better for our readers here to have a special letter from Paris from a correspondent devoted more especially to the political aspect of affairs. So please, consider the arrangements for your continental gossip undisturbed. There appears*

to be some probability of my being in Europe towards the end of the present or the beginning of next year when I shall do myself the pleasure of seeing you.[19]

Fairfax's reference to Anna's column as 'gossip' is a marker to the start of the long era when women journalists were increasingly confined to the women's pages, often referred to derogatorily as social notes or gossip columns. Alice Henry resigned when an effort was made to confine her to 'fashions, frills and frivolities' on the *Australasian*. Other women journalists in a similar situation persevered, often managing to differentiate their columns by their emphasis on particular intellectual pursuits in which they were expert, for example literature, music, art or philosophical theories.

In her later years, Anna became involved in some implausible money-making schemes, including one aimed at digging up treasure supposedly buried in seventeenth-century France by the fleeing James II. These schemes ruined her financially.[20] At the same time, changes in world conditions and greater access to news drastically reduced her newspaper outlets until only two remained from an original eleven. Then a Montreal paper dispensed with her column in 1885, leaving her with only the *Sydney Morning Herald*. Apart from £100 a year that she received from the *Herald*, her only other source of income was £100 a year from her brother Henry Blackwell.

In 1890, the *Sydney Morning Herald* raised her fee from £100 to £125 a year. This, she recorded, gave her no pleasure as she believed they should have raised her payment 25 years earlier. On 9 March 1888, Anna wrote the last column under the by-line 'from our Special Correspondent "Stella"'. This column was published on 16 April. She continued to write further columns using the by-line 'our correspondent' until the early 1890s. By then, she was in her late seventies and decided to retire instead 'of working herself to death' to pay for what she described as her 'coming cremation'.[21] She moved to Hastings where she lived with an invalid sister, Marian, in the same area as her sister Dr Elizabeth Blackwell, who lived with another unmarried sister.

Anna died on 4 January 1900, aged 84, after an attack of influenza and bronchitis.[22] The *Sydney Morning Herald* did not note her death at the time it occurred, but the obituary writer remembered her when the more famous Blackwell sister Dr Elizabeth died ten years later. Belatedly, on 4 June 1910, the *Sydney Morning Herald* wrote about its veteran correspondent:

[Anna] *was almost as distinguished in the world of literature as her sister was in the world of medicine. She was a contributor to the columns of the* Herald *at the time of the Franco-Prussian War and was compelled to leave Paris during the siege. Upon the termination of hostilities, however, she returned to her duties, and continued to act as the Paris correspondent of this journal.*[23]

Anna was appointed when women journalists were rare. Her vivid style of writing and her diverse subject matter continued to hold the interest of readers and the approval of the Fairfax family for 30 or so years.

The subject of the next chapter, Jessie (Tasma) Couvreur, who was later to hold the prestigious position of Brussels Correspondent for the London *Times*, began her career in Europe in the later 1870s posting articles by sea mail to the weekly *Australasian* for which she was paid per line only after publication.

Jessie (Tasma) Couvreur

London *Times* Brussels correspondent

The climax of Jessie Couvreur's career came when she was appointed Brussels correspondent for The Times, *London. The position was hard won after she proved her worth over a nerve-wracking period when she was paid only for the cost of the telegrams she sent. Even after she was appointed in 1894, Tasma, as she was known, came under constant criticism and scrutiny in ways that male recruits did not. Her vindication came the following year when the Netherlands— previously without a* Times *correspondent—was added to her territory. Jessie joined Flora Shaw, whose unique appointment to the powerful position of Colonial Correspondent occurred a few years before. During the previous two decades, Jessie had gained great success not only as a journalist and highly acclaimed novelist but as a public lecturer, for which she had been honoured by the French Academy and the King of the Belgians.*

Jessie Couvreur's journalistic career began in 1877 when her first article, 'A Hint to the Paris Commissioners', was published in the *Australasian*, the weekly stablemate of the Melbourne daily, the *Argus*. This article came about due to her natural ability combined with an urgent need to make herself financially independent after separating from her first husband, Charles Fraser. Nearly 20 years later, her appointment as Brussels correspondent for *The Times* occurred when she needed to earn money after the death of her second husband, the Belgian statesman Auguste Couvreur. Her early life in Australia and her cosmopolitan life in Paris and Brussels equipped her to report for an Australian audience the social, political and philosophical trends sweeping Europe in the later 1870s and the 1880s.

Early life and background

Jessie Catherine Huybers was born on 28 October 1848 at Southwood Lodge, Highgate, then lived on the northern outskirts of London. Her Anglo-French mother, Charlotte (nee Ogleby), ran a small boarding school in their home. Her Flemish-born father, Alfred Huybers, was a clerk in a merchant's office, and later an agent for imported wines. When Jessie was four, she sailed for Hobart with her parents, her elder brother, William, and a younger brother, Robert, who died during a scarlet fever epidemic soon after they landed. Charlotte, a dominant figure in her children's lives, was shocked at her new home. She saw Hobart as a small and primitive town where convicts in chains still walked the streets and hangings were held in public view. She was never happy at being anchored in a colonial outpost, far from the treasures of Europe, and her attitude had a deep and lasting effect on almost all her children.

Five more children were born in Hobart, where Alfred was soon a leading merchant and wine importer. Charlotte had arrived ready to school her children in the artistic, literary and cultural education available in Europe. She taught her daughters entirely at home and her sons, in their younger years, using the extensive library that she brought to the colony. It included 300 volumes in French of the great French novelists, dramatists and philosophers, and the complete works of English writers from Shakespeare to George Eliot, in addition to volumes on history and the arts. Her children grew up intellectually curious with a love of learning, an openness to new ideas, a great attraction to intellectual argument, and with vivid imaginations and unusual talents in many of the arts, particularly drawing, painting and writing. Jessie was her mother's prize pupil and as she grew older she took over teaching the younger children.[1]

When she was 18, Jessie married Charles Fraser, 25, against her mother's wishes. They were two strikingly handsome young people from prominent Hobart families. The Fraser family had strong military traditions, a close association with the authoritarian convict system and links with conservative politics and the squattocracy. Charles' brother-in-law was Melbourne-based flour miller and station owner William Degraves, on whom her husband depended for a job. Charles had the glamourous aura of a splendid horseman, and he never disguised the fact that his great interests were breeding and racing horses, and betting on them. Jessie left behind a home where wide-ranging, intellectual and stimulating conversation raged.[2]

In the early part of their marriage, the Frasers lived at Carlsruhe, near the Victorian town of Kyneton, in a large, bluestone mansion, Montpellier, built by William Degraves as a residence beside his flour mill. The house was so grand that he offered it to Victorian governors as a summer residence. Charles managed Degraves' flour milling and agricultural interests while also indulging his passion for breeding and racing horses. When Degraves fell into serious financial problems, the young couple were separated for long periods while Charles prepared his brother-in-law's stations, located from northern Victoria to North Queensland, for sale. They lived briefly at Oakville, a heavily mortgaged farming property south-east of Melbourne, but Jessie spent long holidays with her family in Hobart and several members of her family visited her for extended periods. While Charles buried himself in the racing pages and rode several winners at Melbourne racetracks, his mother-in-law flooded his home with talk on subjects that did not interest him. Degraves' financial difficulties and the uncertainty about their future livelihood added stress to a childless marriage that was already showing many signs of incompatibility. Once the properties were sold, Charles and his horses were homeless. He had no employment and little money, and Jessie returned to her family in Hobart, before sailing with them for Europe.[3]

Culture in Europe

On 4 March 1873, Jessie Fraser, aged 24, left Hobart with her mother and four of her siblings on the barque *Windward* travelling via Cape Horn to London. As she sailed through the mountainous seas of the Southern Ocean, her identity as Charles Fraser's wife slipped away. She became again Charlotte Huybers' eldest daughter, responsible for the education of the younger members of the family. She maintained a routine of lessons, teaching literature, history and art from the books that they had brought with them. She led them in reading Shakespeare, French novels, and the *Iliad* and the *Odyssey*. It was as though the past five and a half years of her life had barely existed. In the diary she kept on the *Windward*, she mentioned it only once: 'No one could imagine how different my life was this time last year'.[4]

The diary reveals nothing of her inner life, her views on her marriage or her husband, but it was her first disciplined attempt at writing, and it developed her skill at observing, recording and interpreting characters, events and scenes. It was valuable practice for her later career as she described interactions among her family and fellow passengers, all confined to a very restricted space.

As they arrived in London, Jessie ended her diary with the ironic touch that became a feature of her novels. She was 'winding up', she wrote, 'like the Author of a 3-volume novel, with heaping on us all every imaginable and unimaginable benefit'.[5] She had escaped for a time from an incompatible marriage, she was about to see those long-imagined and talked-about treasures of European civilisation, and she had started to write. She had also begun the process of repositioning herself from a colonial housewife to an independent woman.

During nearly three years in Europe, the Huybers family spent a short time in London, some months in Paris and nearly two years in Brussels. In London, Jessie sought out events and people that nurtured her developing independence and feminism. At a meeting on the 'Female Education Question', she discovered she held more advanced views on the right of women to education than the distinguished male speakers on the platform. She also discovered female businesses that were employing only women, such as the Victoria Press founded by women's rights advocate Emily Faithfull. She agreed with Faithfull's ideas on the importance of women gaining independence through paid work.[6]

In Brussels, Jessie immersed herself in the city's art galleries, operas, concerts, lectures and sites of architectural and historical significance. The city was to have a lasting effect on all the Huybers family—some were to return there many times, some lived there for long periods, and two died there. For Jessie, Brussels began the long road towards maturity and independence that was to separate her from Australia and her husband. But for the present she was tied to Charles Fraser. Divorce was not only almost unattainable legally, but carried a social stigma few dared incur. In Europe, Jessie acquired the cultural knowledge and became acquainted with the philosophical theories that would inform the rest of her life.

Before returning home there was a further six months of concentrated learning in Paris. Money was scarce so they all had to eat sparingly and walk everywhere. Jessie enrolled at the free *Ecole professionnelle pour jeunes filles*, where she learnt drawing, engraving, etching, wood carving, and fan and porcelain painting.

While these were traditional ladylike accomplishments, Jessie believed the school taught valuable skills that young women could turn into lucrative employment.

On 27 December 1875, with her head full of stimulating experiences, Jessie arrived back in Melbourne. She returned to her former life as Charles Fraser's wife, this time in a small, basic homestead at Pemberley, a property Charles had leased near Malmsbury, which, like nearby Kyneton, was a horseracing centre. The following year their wary reunion was shattered when Jessie learned from her husband that he had had a relationship with a servant and fathered a child.[7] This news affected her deeply, no doubt partly because it involved such a public display of unfaithfulness.

Published author

The breakdown of her relationship reinforced her determination to become independent by establishing a literary and journalistic career. She was fortunate that at about this time her mother, who had separated from her husband, Alfred Huybers, in Hobart, moved to Melbourne, where she rented Blairgowrie, a historic home in South Yarra. During frequent visits to this desirable location, Jessie established contacts with publishers, particularly Gowen Evans, a director of the *Argus* and *Australasian*. The first of her many articles and stories, 'A Hint for the Paris Commissioners', was published in the *Australasian* in November 1877 under the name of Tasma. Written in an essay style that gradually led to the main topic, it had many of the characteristics of her later work. The wide-ranging opening was so extensive that the subject, the *Ecole professionnelle pour jeunes filles*, was not named until more than halfway through. This was followed by its relevance to the *Exposition universelle* in Paris, where the work of Victoria's finest artists and artisans was displayed. By contrast, a growing number of women in Victoria seeking paid work needed practical instruction in skills that had money-making potential. Jessie advocated for a similar school to the Paris *Ecole* that she had attended. She wrote:

> For let there be Mrs Somervilles, George Eliots and Harriet Martineaus, it is to finger work, not brain work, to which the mass of women turn by instinct from their doll-dressing to their bonnet-trimming days ... there are unemployed girls of all classes waiting to be benefitted ... [By] the introduction into Victoria of porcelain and faience painting, the colony would be so much the richer by the amount of ingenuity turned into a useful channel.[8]

Jessie followed with many other articles on diverse subjects, ranging from reviews of the latest French novels to articles that raised daring subjects such as advocating cremation, an avant-garde idea that was associated with radical thought and opposed by most Christian religions. In the context of a review of a book by Alexandre Dumas Jr, she wrote a vehement defence of women who killed husbands or lovers after being mistreated over long periods.[9]

From the beginning of her writing career, Jessie was published under the name Tasma, a move that predated by a decade the adoption of 'Melba' by the famous operatic soprano Nellie Mitchell. Some of Jessie's stories appeared first in annuals and edited collections, others in the *Australasian*. Some were so popular they were reprinted many times in anthologies. 'Concerning the Forthcoming Melbourne Cup' and 'How a Claim was Nearly Jumped in Gum-Tree Gully' appealed because of their celebration of Australian life. Others, such as 'Malus Oculus', appealed because of their exotic locales and unusual subjects.[10]

By the time Jessie left Melbourne on the steamship *Sobraon* on 28 February 1879 to join her mother and some siblings who had returned to Paris, she had an established reputation as a writer in Victoria. Philip Mennell, the editor of *Australian Wilds*, one of seven publications in which her most popular story, 'Monsieur Caloche', was published, described her as a 'universal favourite'.[11] Jessie 'intends to extend her literary connexion', her brother Edward wrote. He was confident she 'ought soon to make a name for herself'.[12] In Europe, she did just this, not only as a writer for an Australian periodical but as a renowned lecturer, a highly praised novelist and as a foreign correspondent for *The Times*.

Correspondent in Europe

Over the next few years, Jessie had a constant stream of articles published in the *Australasian*. They covered the latest developments in European art, literature and theatre; social and philosophical controversies; charitable works among poor people; and radical issues including experiments in collectivist living, communism and moves towards reform of the divorce laws and acceptance of cremation. Whenever possible she related the subjects to Australian experience. When she described an experiment in communal living in Guise, she wrote that there was no need for such experiments in Australia 'where eight-hour champions carry broidered banners along the public streets'.[13] In reporting social issues she made a point of gaining personal experience of conditions, for example, by spending time in a night shelter for destitute men in Paris before writing about it. The shelter was a challenge to her antagonism to the French Clerical (Catholic) Party. She found that although it was run by 'some of the richest and most influential of the clerical party', it was 'immeasurably superior to ordinary workhouses or refuges'. It accepted 'every beggar or vagabond who presented himself before half past nine', provided lodging for three days and found work for the men. In the three years it had been operating, the night shelter had housed 36,000 men. Among its clientele, Jessie wrote:

> It is sad to see, that among civil engineers, officers, and lawyers—in very small numbers—sadly 200 teachers and professors have inscribed themselves as paupers ... [M]any a despairing waif has been saved from suicide by the knowledge that there was at least a comfortable bed open for him to reflect in ... It is in works like this that the clerical party maintains its influence in France: 'les clericales' has almost passed into a term of contempt, but charity appeals to every shade of feeling. Even one of the most vehement of the antagonists of the church—a 'bonnet rouge' gave his franc towards it.[14]

Jessie also displayed her sense of justice and the advantage of being an outsider in her description of a decree prohibiting Jesuits teaching in France as 'very like persecution'.[15]

Not until the advent of the internet have Australian readers had the opportunity to read so consistently and in such depth about the intellectual life of Europe. Her comments were always informed by her strong social conscience, her concern for the plight of the poor and workers, and her understanding of the oppressiveness of dictatorships—but she kept her readers engaged by adding some lighter content. When she wrote from Hamburg, Berlin, Dresden, Prague, Vienna and Budapest, she interspersed her articles with lively accounts of street life. From Berlin she wrote that 'despite its Protestantism and its propriety', happy families crowded the city's gardens on Sundays, lamps glittered in leafy alleys, bands played and the people 'dine, sup, smoke, laugh and flirt as though there were no conscription and no Bismarck'. She advised Australia to borrow some European customs, such as continental Sundays.[16]

Pioneer public lecturer

Jessie also found another unusual career. Less than two years after her return to Europe, she became a celebrity lecturer—a career for which there were few female models in Europe. In the United States, women had begun lecturing in the 1850s, almost invariably as advocates of women's rights, anti-slavery or one of the other great issues of the day. In a novel published much later, *A Knight of the White Feather*, Jessie expressed the unusual nature of the role of lecturer through her character Linda Robley. Linda's suitor is shocked when she addresses a public meeting in country Victoria on positivism, his shock caused as much by her 'having the face to do it' as by the subject.[17] Jessie may have wished to lecture on subjects close to her heart—women's education and independence, literature, art and philosophical theories. Instead, in the heyday of colonialism, when most European countries looked to conquests and markets, she found enthusiastic audiences for talks on the geography, history, industries, culture and social progress of Australia.

Her success was so great and so unusual that in a short time she became a highly regarded public figure. She was invited to speak to the *Société de géographie commerciale de Paris* following publication of her article on the prospects of emigration to the fruit-growing districts of Tasmania in *Nouvelle Revue*, a periodical begun by feminist Juliette Adam.[18] Her lecture on 20 July 1880, on *'L'Australie et les avantages qu'elle offre a l'émigration française'*, was the first time a woman had addressed the society, and it was an enormous success. She learnt her speech by heart and spoke in French with an accent which was regarded as beguiling. For the occasion she discarded both her maiden and married names and was introduced as 'Mme Jessie Tasma'.[19] Like her speeches that followed, it was a publicity talk highlighting the best attributes of Australian life and glossing over its faults. A colonial agent-general could hardly have equalled her enthusiasm. It was a revelation to an audience that knew little of Australia.

Following this success, Jessie was asked to speak in many cities and towns in France and Belgium, finishing each lecture with a magic lantern show. Everywhere she spoke the halls were crowded. At Bordeaux, she was presented with a silver medal specially struck by the Geographical Society in her honour.[20] During a tour of Belgium, as reports of her speeches at Ghent, Marchiennes and Bruges appeared in the press, interest developed to a crescendo. When she spoke on 16 March 1881 at Antwerp to the Artistic, Literary and Scientific Circle, a crowd of 1,200 attended. One newspaper described the reason for the great crowd at Antwerp simply as 'Mme Tasma' and remarked on her fluent French and her charming accent.[21] On one occasion she acknowledged these 'sugary amiable' comments,[22] recognising the patronising, sexist overtone that emphasised her attraction as a young and beautiful woman in an unusual role.

Jessie's lecture tour of Belgium created such a sensation that King Leopold invited her to a private audience at the Palace at Laeken. Her report published in the *Australasian* disclosed that the main subject of their discussion was the need for a direct shipping link between their two countries.[23] She has 'come out as a "*conferencière*" with much success', her brother Edward wrote. He added that she ought 'to find the path to fame clear & easy'.[24]

During these years, Jessie worked to earn as much money as possible, sending a stream of articles to the *Australasian* from Paris and from several central European countries, as well as continuing on the European lecture circuit, which, as she wrote, paid its lecturers handsomely, unlike organisations in Britain.[25] In France, her lectures were so admired that she was accorded the singular honour of being named *l'Officier d'Académie*, a decoration awarded by the President of the Republic to persons 'who had rendered exceptional service in the field of education or in influencing French culture'. At the time, it 'was rarely given to foreigners and even more rarely to women'.[26]

Divorce, marriage and freedom

In June 1883, Jessie returned to Melbourne to pursue a divorce from Charles. It was an unusual move given that the restrictions of the law and the need for an expensive Supreme Court case deterred most. When Fraser v Fraser came before the Court in December 1883, it was one of 37 applications that year and one of a record 25 granted.[27] While Charles bore the brunt of the accusations, he had a monetary advantage as he engaged no lawyer, leaving the case undefended. Jessie had to pay her fares to and from Australia, and spend about nine months away from Europe, her main source of income. She also had to pay fees to the prominent lawyer she engaged, Dr (later Sir) John Madden.[28] She returned to Europe 'unfettered by any tie'.[29]

Although she had established a close relationship with Belgian statesman Auguste Couvreur, she hesitated for well over a year before marrying again. Auguste was one of the most distinguished, highly decorated and best-known political figures in Europe. He had been a member of the Belgian Chamber of Representatives since 1864 and from 1881 was vice-president of the chamber. He was a journalist and economist, and an advocate of free trade and European federalism. In Belgium, he worked tirelessly for universal state education, improvement of conditions for the working class, and expanded educational opportunities for women. To Jessie, he was not only a distinguished man of the world, but he also had many interests and ideals that were compatible with her own. His anti-clericalism was similar to her own views; she had the same enthusiasm for education and for improving educational opportunities for women, and at least as much sympathy with the plight of the working class. She also had an interest in promoting free trade as there was no protection for the agricultural and pastoral products that Australia exported. Moreover, both she and Auguste earned their living by writing for the press.

Her marriage to Auguste on 7 August 1885 at the Paddington Registry Office, London,[30] removed Jessie's immediate need to earn a living, giving her time to write the novels that made her a famous novelist of the day. When her first novel, *Uncle Piper of Piper's Hill*, set partly in Kyneton, her home when she was first married, and in Melbourne, was published in London in time for Christmas 1888, it was hailed as '*the* novel of the season' and brought her fame 'in a single week'. More effusive tributes followed.[31] After publication of her second novel, *In Her Earliest Youth*, in 1890, a London *Times* critic wrote that she was 'surpassed by few British novelists'.[32] More books followed quickly but to less acclaim. *A Sydney Sovereign*, a collection of her stories previously published in periodicals, appeared in 1890, *The Penance of Portia James* in 1891, *A Knight of the White Feather* in 1892, *Not Counting the Cost* in 1895 and *A Fiery Ordeal*, posthumously, in 1897.

Jessie's novels appeared at a time when the injustice of laws restricting women's rights were the subject of sustained attack, with radical female reformers criticising the institution of marriage. She introduced the 'deeply serious inquiry and impassioned debate over central questions of moral and social behaviour' at a time when conservatives believed they were witnessing the breakdown of the rules of society.[33] In her personal life, from the time she left Charles until she married Auguste, Jessie lived the life of an independent woman, free to travel as she chose, free to choose her male friends and free to earn a living. Only remnants of this freedom remained during her second marriage. In her diary she wrote, 'I am not born with a wife's instincts', after her husband insisted that she abandon her horse rides with Charles Buls, the Burgomaster of Brussels, following gossip by 'Mrs Grundy'—the generic name for a priggish woman. In Jessie's case, her hypocritical sisters-in-law Delphine and Victorie Couvreur were the spreaders of gossip.[34]

Brussels correspondent

Towards the end of 1893, only two years after he had been appointed the *Times* correspondent in Brussels, Auguste became seriously ill. As Jessie nursed him, she wrote and filed his dispatches to *The Times*, at first under his guidance and later on her own initiative. Her husband's death after a decade of marriage presented immediate financial problems but it also renewed her freedom to choose her own way of life and to grasp an opportunity to fill another unusual role. Jessie believed she was capable of undertaking the extremely demanding and prestigious position of foreign correspondent for *The Times*, which employed only one senior woman, its renowned Colonial Correspondent, Flora Shaw. In accounts of Jessie's life her appointment as Brussels correspondent is often dismissed in a sentence, but it was her most extraordinary achievement.

The Times regarded its foreign correspondents as an elite group and jealously guarded their standing and reputation. Jessie came to the position after achievements in several fields but nothing had prepared her for the work of foreign correspondent. Her writing for newspapers had been confined to feature articles and short stories written in a lengthy essay style. As a foreign correspondent she had to send succinct news reports on subjects that required a wide background in European social and political movements, and in rapidly changing developments.

In order to gain employment on *The Times*, she began by writing to the manager, Charles Frederic Moberly Bell, who offered her a trial during which the paper would pay her only for telegrams she sent of interesting news items.[35] Her first dispatch appeared in *The Times* on 14 May 1894. She followed this with an avalanche of reports that appeared almost daily over the following month. Many dealt with parliamentary proceedings, which were of considerable international interest since a general election was to be held later in the year with voting extended to all male adults. Moberly Bell saw enough worth in her dispatches to offer her a definite, though not generous, financial arrangement of £200 a year plus expenses to represent *The Times* in Brussels.[36]

The Foreign Manager, Sir Donald Mackenzie Wallace, had control of her work. In a stream of letters, he praised, criticised, berated and instructed her as he undertook her education as a *Times* foreign correspondent: 'a *métier* [profession] to be learnt', he told her.[37] He stressed the need for conciseness, on one occasion telling her 'to plunge at once *in medias res* [without preamble] is a good old maxim'.[38] He also set about changing her from a partisan reporter to a detached correspondent. Most correspondents held strong personal opinions, but Jessie had not developed sufficient subtlety to prevent hers from intruding too obviously. Wallace explained why one of her articles on Belgian politics was not suited to publication:

> *There is a tinge of rhetoric in the tone and the despatch reads rather as it if it was a leader in a party organ. Our Correspondent should be a calm, dispassionate observer who appears at least to belong to no party.*

He softened the blow with the slightly sarcastic politeness that was usual in his letters. 'Forgive me my giving you this little hint,' he wrote. 'It may be useful to you in future.' [39]

Jessie's frequent reports, sometimes reduced by a sub-editor to a few sentences, continued to appear in the lead-up to the October election. She also reported on developments in the Congo and fighting on the Upper Nile and she covered the Congress of Free Thought, the International Peace Congress, and the International Science Congress. Soon after her reports of the indecisive election appeared, Moberly Bell, hearing that she intended to visit London, telegrammed inviting her to dinner with Sir Donald Wallace.[40] She may well have felt that she had been accepted into the *Times* establishment.

Back in Belgium, she sent off a flood of stories on the second round of the election and the meeting of the new parliament. When she complained that some of her stories were not used, Wallace reassured her, 'Don't be unnecessarily worried ... It is the common lot of correspondents ... Of late Belgium has had more than its fair share of space'. He asked for a short, graphic account of the political changes following the election of the new conservative government. Her article met with his approval, and he told her he was trying to get the editor 'to find space to publish it *in extenso*'.[41] This was just one indication among many she received from Wallace of the tremendous pressure on space in the *Times'* colonial and foreign news section. News from all the countries of Europe, America and Asia and colonial territories in Africa, Asia and Australasia vied for space. In a favourite phrase, Wallace referred to the non-publication of stories as 'the massacre of the innocents', as he counselled her to send less. But she remained aware of competition from the Reuters correspondent in Brussels if she missed anything that was newsworthy.

When her major article on the political situation in Belgium appeared in full over two columns on 27 December 1894, she was vindicated. 'Your work has been excellent,' Wallace told her. 'You are fairly entitled to a month's holiday.'[42] When she returned to work, he steered her away from political news to wider questions, particularly the future of the Congo, as the Belgian Parliament debated annexing the territory, which had been a personal domain of the Belgian King since 1885. When Jessie sent a major article on the Congo, Wallace advised her that if space could not be found for it, it might be used as a leader, and this occurred on 4 June 1895 when a lengthy *Times* leader based on Jessie's article was published. On her next visit to London, Wallace said he was 'delighted' to see her, and she was invited to dinner with Moberly Bell and the Colonial Correspondent, Flora Shaw, at which she apparently made a good impression on both.[43]

Reporting from The Hague

When the Netherlands was added to her territory, her monthly payment increased because of her 'enlarged diocese'.[44] Not long after, Wallace was disturbed that she had left The Hague without informing him. He wrote:

> As I told you I wanted to have you at our disposal for a month it is a little wicked of you to remove yourself from the end of the cable! ... I want you to remain at The Hague until further orders—In fact as you force me to be explicit, The Hague is the place at which I wish you to be useful to us.

Flora Shaw had previously provided sealed instructions to Jessie on the background to proposed moves in the Transvaal, but Moberly Bell, ever cautious, did not disclose his reason for wanting her at The Hague in his accompanying letter.[45] Towards the end of 1895, his strategy became clear. Unknown to Jessie, this was to ensure that she would be strategically placed to report Dutch reaction to the attempted overthrow of the Boer Government in the Transvaal. Cecil Rhodes had secretly organised this overthrow with the veiled knowledge and support of Flora Shaw, *The Times* hierarchy and the British Colonial Office. While he was giving Jessie instructions, Moberly Bell also sent correspondents to other capitals so that *The Times* would have dispatches from strategic centres as soon as action began in South Africa. This occurred near the end of December when commander Leander Starr Jameson led his force of 500 towards the Transvaal in a move planned to coincide with a rising of Uitlanders in Johannesburg. When this rising failed to take place, Jameson's force was surrounded by Boers and forced to surrender on 2 January 1896. Jessie reported the extremely hostile Dutch reaction to the unsuccessful raid.

Jessie's articles were often placed prominently in the foreign news section, but the added burden of reporting from two countries, her stressful and fraught relationship with *The Times* and a deterioration in her health led her to an occasional practice that Wallace warned her against. Instead of giving 'the *essence* in your own words', he told her, she relied too much on quotes from the Belgian press. A worse journalistic transgression—copying material from another newspaper without attribution—landed her in serious trouble. On 10 November 1896, *The Times* published her dispatch, previewing the speech given by the king at the opening of the Belgian Parliament, which she had copied from another paper not realising that it was a skit on the government's proposed program.[46] It is hard to believe she would have made this error in normal circumstances, particularly when she had been warned a number of times. The extraordinary demands on her time and energy, her commitment to the high standards of *The Times*, the constant advice and polite criticism from Donald Wallace and the intrigue behind being sent to The Hague were stress enough. But several family members in various stages of crisis had also arrived in Brussels. To Jessie, her family was pursued by 'a continuous and relentless fate', as she watched them 'deliberately shipwreck their lives'.[47] Her brother Edward—a brilliant but unstable man—moved in with his wife and children. Soon after, he accepted the position of Brussels correspondent for the London *Daily Chronicle*, apparently oblivious to the problem he was creating in two correspondents for rival London papers living in the same house. The situation was only reluctantly accepted by *The Times* after management consoled itself by considering its superior position.

During the latter months of 1896, Jessie became ill with heart disease, causing what her brother described as 'a collapse of her system sad to witness'. As a previously healthy woman, there seems little doubt that it was related to her stressful professional life and family challenges. During the following months, she suffered continuing attacks of severe angina. She died on 27 October 1897 from cardiac failure, aged only 48. In accordance with her wishes, her body was taken to Paris where, unlike in Belgium, cremation was permitted.

Jessie's evolution to short story and non-fiction writer, acclaimed lecturer and famed novelist, and her appointment to such a prestigious position on *The Times*, remains remarkable. In fact, it could be ranked as the greatest achievement by an Australian female journalist in the nineteenth century. In the next chapter, Flora Shaw provides a contrasting glimpse into the security that can flow from an establishment British background and an indomitable sense of self-worth.

Flora Shaw

Reports from colonial Australia

Immediately after British journalist Flora Shaw returned to London in 1893 from a tour of the British colonies, she was appointed Colonial Correspondent on The Times, *with the responsibility for choosing correspondents in the colonies and organising their work.[1] No woman journalist had ever reached such a level of influence. Flora's job placed her at the centre of decision-making on the imperial policies of a newspaper that 'shaped the opinions of the educated classes who ruled the nation'.[2] Her salary of £800 a year made her the highest-paid female journalist in London. With influence came great responsibility, as she discovered in 1897 when* The Times *sent her to defend the paper at a House of Commons Select Committee inquiry. She was the first woman in British history to give evidence at such an inquiry.*

In October 1892, a 'Lady from London' appeared at the shearing shed on Portland Downs, a huge sheep station on the Barcoo River in western Queensland. To the shearers, she was a remarkable sight. They rarely saw any women while shearing in the outback, much less a woman of 'style and dress' from London.[3] Their visitor was Flora Shaw, on assignment from *The Times*, who was travelling vast distances by buggy to write articles on the Australian pastoral industry. The stations she reached—stretching from Ilfracombe through Blackall and Tambo to Charleville—were often a day's ride apart. Earlier she had travelled by coastal steamer from Cairns to Rockhampton, stopping at each port to write about the sugar industry, the separation of the colony into north and south, and the employment of 'coloured' labour. She also made inland trips to Charters Towers and Mount Morgan to write about gold mining and visit cattle-fattening stations and irrigated plantations on the Burdekin delta.

Despite their obvious value to *The Times*, Flora needed to write her dispatches in longhand, making sure she posted them in time to catch the next ship to London. Even for *The Times*, cable transmission would have been too expensive. She was in Australia as part of a tour of British colonies arranged by the manager of *The Times*, Charles Frederic Moberly Bell, so that she could gain firsthand colonial knowledge before he appointed her to the high position of Colonial Correspondent. Flora shared the conviction of the *Times* hierarchy that the British colonies should remain inextricably linked to Britain politically and economically through trade and investment.

Early life and background

Apart from her gender, Flora Shaw had the establishment background suited to a *Times* journalist. She was born on 19 December 1852 into an influential family, the fourth of 14 children of Captain (later Major-General) George Shaw, Royal Artillery. She was the granddaughter of Sir Frederick Shaw, who had represented Dublin in the House of Commons and was Recorder of Dublin (1828–1876), a judicial office in pre-independent Ireland. Her mother, Marie Desfontaines, was the daughter of the French governor of Mauritius. Flora was educated at home—at her grandparents' house in Dublin and in France through the aristocratic connections of her mother. After Marie's death and her father's remarriage, Flora sought an income to gain financial independence for herself and some dependent sisters. Her first foray into writing was as the author of works of fiction beginning with a popular children's novel, *Castle Blair*.[4]

Freelance correspondent

Flora's newspaper career began in the only way possible for a woman in the nineteenth century—as a freelance correspondent submitting articles. She had the advantage of being in a succession of newsworthy places, and her family connections oiled her way. Her first opportunity to write marketable articles came in 1886, at the age of 34, when she accompanied friends on an extended visit to Gibraltar. Before she left, she approached William T. Stead, the editor of the *Pall Mall Gazette*, who agreed to consider any material she might submit. Her article on Zebehr Pasha, who was being held in Gibraltar by the British as a political prisoner, was a front-page sensation in the *Gazette*.[5] Before the final part of her expanded series on Zebehr Pasha was published in the *Contemporary Review*, the British Government had released him and allowed him to return to Cairo. Her biographer wrote that Flora arrived in Gibraltar 'an amateur' and returned 'a professional with a reputation as a serious and capable journalist'.[6]

She was again fortunate when she had the opportunity to visit Egypt, a newsworthy trouble spot. Before she left England, she met the editor of the *Manchester Guardian*, Charles F. Scott, and as a result she arrived in Cairo in December 1888 as an accredited correspondent of the *Pall Mall Gazette* and the *Manchester Guardian*. In Egypt, she made an extraordinary impression on the long-established *Times* correspondent Moberly Bell. Both were strong imperialists who shared 'a conviction of the civilising influence of the British people'.[7]

A colonial expert

In March 1890, when Moberly Bell was recalled to the *Times* headquarters, he engaged Flora to write fortnightly columns on colonial subjects, although initially he did not reveal her gender to his colleagues.[8] For guidance on Australia she turned to Sir Robert Herbert, the Permanent Under Secretary at the British Colonial Office, who had been the first premier of Queensland following its separation from New South Wales in 1859. Herbert's advice and guidance were central to Flora's emergence as a specialist writer on colonial subjects thoroughly indoctrinated with the views of the British Government. She also began to study the politics of Africa at a time when European countries were dividing the continent and claiming colonies. She established a friendship with the British imperialist Cecil Rhodes, soon to be Prime Minister of Cape Colony. Rhodes gained her support for his view that it was 'the destiny of Britain to spread throughout the heart of Africa'.[9] Their views became so similar that they met whenever he was in London, fuelling rumours of a very unlikely romance.

During the next year, writing for three papers, Flora became well known as an imperial and colonial affairs expert. It was at this point that Moberly Bell arranged for her to tour the colonies. Aged 40, she set out for South Africa, continuing after several months to Australia. She landed by ship in Hobart on 15 September 1892, conscious that time pressed—if she were to visit north Queensland before the cyclone season there was no time to lose.[10]

Queensland Government welcomes Flora

The Queensland Government welcomed Flora because of the potential for her articles to increase British migration and investment, both vital to the economy in the aftermath of the 1890s depression. Soon after she arrived, the premier, Sir Samuel Griffith, and other ministers called on her, and from then she was given VIP treatment. The government arranged the best ship cabins and special train compartments. She was met on arrival, whether at ports, railway stations or bush outposts, and a driver was always on hand to drive her to her next destination, if necessary, by relays of horses. She had meetings with local civic leaders, senior public servants, technical experts, representatives of political organisations, and employer and labour groups.

Her tour of Queensland began with a four-day orientation train trip to farms and plantations within easy reach of Brisbane. In an apparently officially arranged situation, Flora found herself in a train compartment with the eccentric misogynist, land-owning millionaire James Tyson. The contrast between the pair was extraordinary— the rough, uncouth bushman, untutored in speech, and Flora, the delicately nurtured, well-groomed, urbane woman, with her precise, upper-class English articulation. Unexpectedly, they discovered that they agreed on fundamental values. By the time they parted, Tyson had told Flora he intended to leave her his money and possessions. In Queensland Government circles, it generally became known that she was to inherit his millions. Flora made up her mind she would use the money to run a line of steamers to link the British colonies of Australia, Canada and South Africa, in unbreakable ties with each other and the mother country economically and in trade. Although this was their only meeting, rumours of a developing romance swept through Brisbane. Like the rumours regarding Cecil Rhodes, these reflected society's need to see an attractive woman married, rather than competing in a male field. The death of James Tyson was an anticlimax. He died intestate in 1898 and his fortune was divided among relatives in whom he had taken no interest.

Challenges in the Far North

From Brisbane, Flora set off by coastal steamer to visit the northern part of Queensland. Her aim was to write about the sugar, mineral and pastoral industries of the colony, and explain the important political and economic issues to her readers in London. Flora's *Times* articles were highly regarded at the time. Now, they are evidence of the passions held long ago about questions that have long since been resolved or shelved. More interesting now are her letters to her sister Lulu in London, in which she records her travel experiences—coping with hazards, dangers, and immense discomfort in the long dresses of a fashionable lady—and in her frank word pictures of people she recorded in her diary. Her letters and diary are preserved in the Bodleian Library, Oxford. This is the first time that sections written in Australia have appeared in book form.[11]

Her movements on the northern section of her trip were dictated by the weekly arrival and departure of the coastal steamer, allowing her only a day at each port except when a week's travel inland had been arranged. She reported to her sister her first night on board as she travelled from Cairns to Geraldton (the original European name of Innisfail):

> *Little coastal steamers are not sumptuous. The night unfortunately for me became wet a little later on with gusts of wind that made it necessary to shut the ports. It was intensely hot, big cockroaches were the only things stirring beside the screen and not all the philosophy of which I was master could surmount the sense that if I went to sleep one of them would crawl over my face. Briefly I didn't go to sleep and was therefore fairly tired when a night of gentle touring brought us at about seven o'clock into the mouth of the Johnstone River and up between fringing palms and sugar fields to the steps of Goondi plantation.*[12]

The following night, back on the steamer to travel from Geraldton to Ingham, she escaped cockroaches by sleeping on deck and, from four in the morning, watched as the steamer entered Hinchinbrook Passage.[13] During long days in stifling heat, she visited large plantations at Cairns, Geraldton, Ingham, Ayr and Mackay, inspecting the quarters of South Sea Islander indentured labourers and their families. She also talked with large- and small-scale planters and inspected mills, some run by international sugar companies, others set up as local co-operatives. At Ingham she had a frightening experience travelling on a cane train while inspecting the Colonial Sugar Refining Company's Victoria plantation:

> It was very near being the last of the career of this particular Times correspondent. We were travelling at midday upon a tram-car behind a very puffy locomotive. The sun was bearing down upon us, the grass was like tinder all round, even the white linen coats of the gentlemen were hot and as for me I was hot through and through like dry toast. At last it seemed nearly too hot to be borne. I moved my dress away from my feet. As I did so there was a little cloud of white smoke and my skirt was in flames. I had nothing on but a thin silk dress and a silk petticoat. Both being so hot were like tinder and but for the courage and promptitude of my host who sat beside me I think I must really have been burnt to death. There was absolutely nothing to put the fire out with. The gentlemen's coats were all of white linen, the car we were in was made for coolness of open laths, to have jumped, as I had the flash of a thought to do, on to the ground to try and crush it out there would have been only to set the dry grass in a blaze.

The quick actions of her escort, Mr Farqhuar, saved her as he burnt his hands 'to the bone' crushing out the flames. Flora escaped, she wrote, 'with nothing worse than the loss of part of my dress and petticoat' while she upheld 'the dignity of the Times in the person of its correspondent by holding my truncated garments together as respectably as I could'. Travelling with little luggage and unable to vary her itinerary to buy new clothes, she had to continue the journey in her damaged clothing.[14]

Throughout her northern trip, Flora discussed the live political issues of separation of north Queensland as a new colony and the continued importation of South Sea Islanders as indentured labour for the sugar industry. Although she was conscientious in interviewing opposing sides in any controversy, the influence of the Queensland Government's policies was apparent in her articles. Like Sir Samuel Griffith, Flora favoured the development of small acreage cane farms as a way of encouraging British migration. She advocated the expansion of the British Empire through the migration of labour and capital. However, she saw the ultimate ideal as imperial federation of British colonies with representation in the United Kingdom parliament, an idea Griffith favoured.[15] 'I never thought of my work exactly as journalism,' she wrote, 'but rather as active politics without the fame.'[16]

At Mackay she met Englishman John Vincent Chataway, a brother-in-law of her mentor, *The Times'* Moberly Bell. This encounter would be important for her career. She found that Chataway—who was proprietor and editor of the Mackay *Daily Mercury*, a prominent lobbyist for the sugar industry, and a supporter of north Queensland separation and the importation of South Sea Islanders—shared her political views.[17]

Flora's article on the mineral wealth of Queensland was based on visits to mines at Charters Towers and Mount Morgan. She travelled by train from Townsville to Charters Towers where, at the end of a day at the mine, she wrote to her sister:

I went down three mines and climbed duly on my hands and knees down unfinished shafts and looked on while the width of strips was widened and found to my surprise that even at a depth of 1,200 feet I felt fairly cool while the gentlemen who accompanied me were in a condition of impromptu shower health. After the mines I went over crushing mills. You can picture to yourself the state of dirt in which I finally returned to the hotel.[18]

It is impossible not to admire Flora's stamina in what must surely be the only instance of a woman journalist of that era chasing a story down a mine. None of this material appeared in her *Times* articles, which were based on facts and statistics; it appears only in this personal letter.

After this extraordinary day at the mine, Flora found the editor of the local paper waiting to interview her, but she refused, as she did other local interviews, preferring to keep her views for her *Times* articles. Late that night she was still at work, poring over a geological map with the Queensland Government geologist Logan Jack, and talking with locals to get 'the feeling of a mining centre on separation and coloured labour'.[19] From Rockhampton she made a shorter and easier visit to Mount Morgan, then the world's richest gold lode. It had made its major shareholder, Rockhampton solicitor William Knox D'Arcy,[20] a millionaire who became a noted figure in London society.

Pastoral industry

At Rockhampton, her last coastal stop, Flora prepared for her journey to study the pastoral industry in western Queensland, which was of major interest to her readers in the aftermath of the 1891 shearers' strike. As always, she listened carefully to both sides. She met two labour leaders—William Kidston and James Stewart. Kidston was a principal figure in supporting the shearers and later became premier of Queensland. Stewart became a member of parliament for Rockhampton North and then a Labor Senator for Queensland from Federation until 1917. Flora was far from impartial. She was unable to entertain any argument in favour of collective bargaining for improved wages and conditions because it deprived employers of the right to negotiate individually with workers.[21] Flora's support for the squatters' demand for freedom of contract—the reason for the bitter shearers' strike was opposition to freedom of contract—was even clearer in a later conversation with a union organiser. She said, 'We people in England lost all sympathy with you when you began to dictate to the employers whom they should employ'.[22]

During their meeting with Flora, Kidston and Stewart described the life of shearers who averaged only four to five months work a year and spent the rest of the year tramping the bush in search of work.[23] She heard the squatters' view at length from station owner George Fairbairn, who accompanied her on the train journey west from Rockhampton to Ilfracombe, the stop before the end of the line at Longreach. She found the isolation and monotony of the countryside depressing. The townships she glimpsed had 'no redeeming' features, and the bush inn where she stayed at Ilfracombe was 'hideously ugly'.[24]

Western sheep stations

Flora came to the western sheep stations at a volatile time in the shearing industry, just a year after the 1891 shearers' strike. It was still a recent and bitter memory for the shearers, some of whose leaders were still in jail. The strike was a defining event in Australian history, leading to the founding at Barcaldine of the Australian Labor Party.

During the next two weeks, Flora made a journey of over 800 kilometres in an open buggy in temperatures often over 40 degrees. When rain did not make the tracks impassable or stop her crossing the flooded Barcoo River, she left each morning as soon as the horses could be rounded up, travelling a distance of about 80 kilometres, but occasionally up to 120 kilometres, to the next station. She heard views from station owners and managers about the industrial situation and the economics of running huge stations. The first of her two articles on the pastoral industry contained detailed accounts of the operation, finances and costs of employing and housing station hands and shearers on huge stations. Meeting shearers was a more awkward experience. At Portland Downs, she watched about 70 shearers, 'bare-armed and dirty', gather round a table to eat 'copiously of joints, stews, bread, pickles, jams and cakes' with their only utensils—tin plates, mugs and knives:

> It was a hugger-mugger of food on dirty boards, just one step removed from the well-filled troughs of swash and potatoes round which I have seen pigs crowd at home.[25]

She judged shearers materially much better off than English labourers; they were 'well paid' and 'extremely well fed', but far beneath them in decency of surroundings. She attributed 'a good deal of labour agitation' to the roughness of shearers' lives and a 'lack of wholesome pleasure'.[26] In support of this view she cited the well-publicised figure of shearers drinking away the cheque they had received from one employer before moving on to the next shearing job. When she saw the windowless shacks with mud floors, iron roofs and furniture made from packing cases, she wrote—in some surprise—that some of the station hands living in these shacks were 'the sons of English gentlemen!'[27]

Flora was invited to a meeting in the shearers' shed organised by the union delegate Drake Wood, whom she portrayed in her diary in extremely derogatory terms:

> One-eyed hare-lipped with the narrow brainless forehead of degraded races, false teeth prominently white in a countenance naturally sullen, bloated [and] reddened by circumstance. The very scum of the earth

he looked and when he began to talk with the snuffle of a country street preacher his misplaced meaning nil and English so ridiculously misemployed that it was difficult to maintain a decent gravity ... He could not answer a question he could not put a sentence together in English which conveyed a meaning of any kind. [The meeting] was wasted in everything but the insight it gave me into the conditions of labour agitation. This idiot with neither brains, eloquence nor character is a paid 'representative of labour' ... I learnt more contempt for labour agitation in those two hours than ever before in my experience.[28]

She was more restrained in her published article in which she described Wood as a man who was 'absolutely inept' and 'mouthed big nothings'.[29]

Wood's account of the meeting, published on the front page of the *Worker*, which began in satirical mode, went on to reject Flora's strongly held position that shearers must abandon their stand against freedom of contract and revert to individual bargaining. When the question of parliamentary representation arose, he explained the problem for itinerant workers who were unable to register to vote because they had no fixed address. He also argued against Flora's view of the need to increase British migration.[30]

Flora's mammoth journey in extraordinary heat continued as she collected information from station after station. After a massive journey of 120 kilometres in a single day from Northampton Downs, she reached Listowel in the late afternoon where the temperature was 41 degrees on the shaded verandah. At the shearing shed the next morning she watched shearers notch some record tallies before leaving for Minnie Downs, 80 kilometres away. She made few comments on these rides except in relation to the shearers she saw tramping the outback:

They are never long in one place but in the intervals move over the country with their 'swags' on their backs looking for employment demanding rations at any station to which they may chance to come and more often than is generally realised wandering away to die of thirst and exhaustion in the wild. In driving from station to station we often met them in pairs or encampments in which one or two were cooking the rations they had obtained. They look upon their rations as their right and will not be content with less than two or three lbs of meat, a pound of flour and a couple of ounces of tea and sugar.[31]

At Tambo a group of shearers Flora described as 'red radicals and enthusiastic socialists' gathered at the blacksmith's forge to talk with her. She was impressed by the 'very decent and intelligent' group, although in her view they were 'of course ignorant of facts on every subject and therefore not in a position to draw just conclusions'.[32] Paradoxically, she reported that every forge and shearing shed had copies of books on economics and politics. The shearers read the American political economist Henry George, internationally famous for his espousal of a single land tax and author of *Progress and Poverty: An Inquiry into the Causes of Economic Depressions*. They also read the English politician Henry Hyndman, author of *Socialism Made Easy* and founder of the Social Democratic Federation, and Edward Bellamy, who wrote a utopian novel, *Looking Backward: A Romance of 2000 AD*, in which he envisaged a future of equal distribution of wealth. Flora did not connect this reading with their passion to change political and social structures and she found 'pathetic' their opinion that Bellamy's theories could be realised.[33]

Towards the end of Flora's journey, it became a race to make up time lost by impassable tracks and the flooded Barcoo River. While travelling to the railhead at Charleville, she had to scramble from the buggy when it overturned at a crossing. She wrote in her diary that throughout the west she was struck by the absence of pleasure and its civilising influences. The life was 'distinctly brutalizing in its tendency, nature rebels, the men take to drink and gambling, the masters become boorish'.[34]

Return to Brisbane

On 6 November 1892, Flora caught the 9.45pm train for the long journey back to Brisbane. The Colonial Secretary, Horace Tozer, joined her at Ipswich for the last part of the journey. It was 10pm the following night before she reached Government House in Brisbane and the hospitality of Governor Sir Henry and Lady Norman. Many pioneer women made extraordinary journeys in buggies and other bush contraptions, making camp each night. Many had numerous children to care for, sometimes through illness and epidemic diseases, and some gave birth on the way. Flora's journey was more comfortable, with no worry about a meal and a bed for the night. Nevertheless, it was a considerable effort for a woman unused to such travel or to extreme summer heat. Flora told her sister her journey through the west had been 'rougher' than anything she had ever experienced and towards the end she 'began to feel that I was, much against my will, knocking up'.[35] It took such a toll on her health that she arrived in Brisbane exhausted and suffering bouts of illness. Her weakened condition remained for the rest of her Australian visit.

Escaping from Government House and meetings with Queensland politicians, Flora spent the next two weeks in the cooler climate of Toowoomba at the Blue Mountain Hotel. Despite often being ill, she was able to write and post her articles to *The Times*. Her six articles on Queensland were so successful that within a year they were published in book form.[36] While in Toowoomba she heard the disturbing news that her father had died, leaving her unmarried sisters in England dependent on an unsympathetic stepmother. She wrote long letters suggesting various relatives and friends they could visit until she returned and could arrange to provide a home for them.[37]

Southern colonies

In December 1892, Flora continued her journey through the southern colonies. When she arrived in New South Wales she had not fully recovered from her illness and did not venture outside Sydney. Instead, she relied on interviews with the government statistician Timothy Coghlan, members of the Employers' Federation executive, the Ship Owners' Union and executives of the Amalgamated Shearers' Union. From these she wrote articles covering finance, labour and the Federation movement.[38] By the time she reached Melbourne on New Year's Day 1893, Flora was ill again, and yet she undertook strenuous journeys in the intense heat of summer to study Victorian rural industries. Getting material on the fruit industry involved ten hours of rail travel and five hours of driving through farms. Studying the butter industry meant a further two days in temperatures that reached 43 degrees, while at vineyards the temperature remained over 38 degrees overnight.[39] Her article on Victorian finance stirred the most controversy of her tour. Flora wrote that the devastating depression of the 1890s, usually attributed to the collapse of the land boom and bank failures, was the outcome of Victorians 'leaning against posts instead of ... standing upright'.[40]

In South Australia, as well as writing articles on the Barossa wine district, she made an even more demanding three-day trip by train to Broken Hill, accompanied by Lady Downer, wife of the South

Australian premier, Sir John Downer. Her report on how miners were pioneering a culture of trade unionism resulted from this journey.[41]

Views on southern states

The articles Flora wrote on her Australian tour were limited to local political questions and their relationship to imperial governance, trade and migration. They were based on her evaluation of economics, labour/employer relations, trade and immigration prospects in the agricultural, pastoral and mining industries. She saw all these subjects through the prism of her prejudices, which were influenced by her privileged upbringing and reinforced by the similar views of her employer at *The Times*. Her articles were aimed quite clearly at politicians, investors, traders and manufacturers in Britain, and they aligned with the views of conservative colonial politicians. She was far from being an even-handed journalist.

Although Flora visited every major centre in the northern coastal area, and travelled inland to mining sites and western sheep stations, she only mentioned women as unnamed providers of meals, or as an unidentified wife of a sugar planter or station owner. The female suffrage movement did not exist in her world. Instead, she gave the impression of a talented woman in a powerful position who was proud to be operating in a man's world.

Her only mention of Aboriginal people came after a comment on the work of pioneer settlers ringbarking 'lifeless trees' in 'their sylvan graveyards', which represented to her 'the death and burial of primeval Australia'. She likened this death to what she saw as the Indigenous Australians dying out. In her eyes the British race had triumphed. The young Australia she saw was 'infinitely more interesting than anything which it has had occasion to displace'.[42]

Later career

Flora returned to London late in 1893 to wide acclaim. She was appointed *The Times* Colonial Correspondent,[43] an extraordinary achievement for a woman, placing her at the centre of *The Times'* decision-making on imperial policies. Through her columns, her views on colonial, economic and political issues reached leading policymakers. She grew into the role, becoming highly influential in the counsels of *The Times* and the Colonial Office, and playing 'an active political role, not merely reporting events'.[44] She discovered, however, that a woman was expendable when trouble arose. In 1897, there were persistent rumours that *The Times*—through Moberly Bell and Flora, and the Secretary of State for the Colonies, Joseph Chamberlain—had been involved in a conspiracy to overthrow the Boer Government in the Transvaal, masterminded by Cecil Rhodes. The action, known as the Jameson Raid, failed within a few days when the small invasion force, led by Dr Leander Starr Jameson, was forced to surrender.[45]

On 30 July 1896, the House of Commons set up a Select Committee to inquire into what was regarded as 'the most sensational event of the time'.[46] *The Times* decided that Flora would defend the paper before a House of Commons Select Committee. When Flora was called to give evidence on 23 May 1897, it was a historic occasion—she and the sister who accompanied her were the first women ever admitted to the Commons committee room at Westminster Hall. *The History of the Times* recorded that she 'faced calmly what would have been an ordeal for most women'.[47] *The Times* editor, James Buckle, was blatant about Flora's 'duty' to the paper:

> What I am most concerned for is the reputation of The Times, and its interests. I am convinced it is of the utmost importance to keep, if possible, [the Managing Director] Mr Bell's name out of the matter.[48]

He gave her detailed instructions on how to avoid answering questions and urged her to take all responsibility and 'at all costs keep *The Times* and its personalities' out of the inquiry.

> You are a journalist dealing with Colonial subjects and therefore bound to be informed on important Colonial matters. But not one engaged in getting up this plan though you subsequently approved and, I fear, we must say, aided it.[49]

Flora was questioned closely on the telegrams that she sent to Rhodes in December 1895 telling him delay was dangerous and that Chamberlain wanted the uprising to occur immediately. Her answers ensured *The Times* and the Colonial Office escaped censure and she was praised for the way in which she answered questions. 'Without her keen sense of loyalty to her colleagues and her discretion, much embarrassment might have been caused to the "people" of *The Times*,' the paper conceded.[50]

The limits to gender equality

Flora's employment in such a senior position on *The Times* was a gender-defying achievement in the 1890s, but it came at a cost. She believed implicitly in the imperial policies of the paper and was active in formulating them. However, she found *The Times* management was prepared to sacrifice her to save itself and its more senior men when it was under threat. Buckle's instructions remained a nagging memory casting a shadow 'never wholly lifted'.[51] According to several accounts of her life, her appearance before the parliamentary inquiry coincided with the end of a seven-year relationship with Sir George Goldie that she had hoped would lead to marriage. Goldie organised the Royal Niger Company, which had established British rule on the Niger River. Flora was responsible for the name 'Niger', which she first published in *The Times* early in 1897. When Goldie's wife died, and Flora realised there would be no marriage, she became ill.[52] In 1901, she resigned from *The Times* and the following year, at the age of 50, married Sir Frederick Lugard, later Lord Lugard, a British imperialist and colonial administrator in East Africa, Uganda, Hong Kong and Nigeria. During the First World War, Lady Lugard, as Flora was then known, was made a Dame of the British Empire for her work as a founder of the War Refugees Committee, which found accommodation for Belgian refugees. She died in 1929 after a lengthy period of ill health.

Flora Shaw was a remarkable woman who broke through gender barriers to gain financial independence and influence in a profession that was, and remained for at least a century, a difficult environment for women to achieve important positions.

Edith Dickenson

Australia's first female war correspondent

Edith Dickenson was appointed to report the Boer War when there were few women journalists in Australia and very few women war correspondents anywhere in the world. She was 'the only duly accredited lady writer in the field on behalf of an Australian paper'.[1] Although constrained by censorship and the transmission of her dispatches by sea mail, Edith was an intrepid, tenacious and empathetic reporter. Her dispatches were distinguished by her even-handed reporting of the devastation caused by both sides— the British and the Boers—and her compassionate reporting of the effect of imprisonment in British concentration camps on Boer women and children. Edith was a forerunner of Australian women war correspondents and was not equalled for many years.

In March 1900, Edith Dickenson arrived in Durban, South Africa, from Australia to report the war for the Adelaide *Advertiser*. The paper's editor and proprietor, Sir John Langdon Bonython, proposed to the Melbourne *Age* and the Sydney *Daily Telegraph*—with which the *Advertiser* had long-standing cooperative arrangements—that they share her articles and their cost. 'She will go to Ladysmith and if possible Pretoria,' he wrote. 'She is a most capable writer.' By sharing among three papers, the cost to each would be a guinea per article. As both declined, her articles were published only in the *Advertiser* under the by-line 'Mrs E.C.M. Dickenson, Special Correspondent' or 'Our Lady Journalist, Mrs Edith C.M. Dickenson'.[2]

At the beginning of 1900, Ladysmith and Pretoria were the main battlefields of the Second Boer War, fought from 1899 to 1902 between Great Britain and the Boer republics of the Transvaal and the Orange Free State. Ladysmith had been under siege by the Boers since the beginning of November 1899. The British did not recapture Ladysmith until the end of February 1900, and Mafeking in Pretoria until May that year. The Second Boer War resulted from the failed Jameson Raid, also known as the First Boer War. The refusal of the Boer leader, Paul Kruger, to give voting rights to Uitlanders—mainly British drawn to the rich goldfields in the Transvaal—and British High Commissioner Alfred Milner's opposing vision for a united South Africa under the British Empire were other contributing causes to the outbreak of the Second Boer War.

During the 15 years she lived in Australia, Edith had led a life of unusual achievement as a journalist, writer, photographer and amateur ornithologist. She was not only a pioneer woman war correspondent but also the author of a book on her travels in colonial India and other Eastern countries, a photographer and a naturalist, who had lived in remote parts of several Australian colonies. Wherever she lived or travelled she had with her a pen, a camera, a gun and an eye for the birds she was intent on collecting for science. Sometimes she had her children with her. By the standards of the day, her life was extremely unconventional.

She arrived in Melbourne from England on 19 February 1886 with her young sons as Mrs Edith Belcher, travelling first class on the *Austral* and leaving her daughter Edith Belcher, aged 15, behind in England. Her lover, Dr Augustus Dickenson, had arrived in Melbourne as the ship's doctor on the *Rodney* on 8 October 1885. He had left his wife, two stepchildren and four Dickenson children behind in England.[3] In the months before Edith's arrival, he established a practice at Swan Hill on the Murray River.[4] Edith was the wife of the Reverend William Belcher, rector of the well-endowed parish of St Margarets, Heveningham, in the English county of Suffolk. She was the eldest daughter of the Countess of Stradbroke.

Early life and background

Edith Charlotte Musgrave Bonham was born on 30 May 1851 to Colonel Henry Frederick Bonham, 10th Royal Hussars of Carlton Hall, Suffolk, and Augusta Sophia, a daughter of baronet Reverend Sir Christopher Musgrave. When she was four, Edith's father died, and the following year her mother married a retired British soldier, John Edward Cornwallis Rous, 2nd Earl of Stradbroke. Edith and her younger brothers accompanied their mother to Henham Park, the Earl's country estate in Suffolk, where her mother had a further six children. The highly capable governess Ellen Chennells educated Edith. Chennells had been a governess in the family of her grandfather, Sir Christopher Musgrave, and was later governess to the daughter of the Khedive of Egypt.[5]

On 21 July 1870, just after she turned 19, Edith married Reverend William W. Belcher, a graduate of Trinity College, Dublin. Their first child, Edith Augusta Anna Bonham Belcher, was born in 1871, twin sons Reginald and Frederick in 1878 and a son, Musgrave, in 1881.[6] A few years later, Dr Augustus Dickenson, a highly qualified medical graduate from Trinity College, Dublin,[7] arrived to practise at Southwold, a seaside town in Suffolk. Edith met Augustus when she enrolled in his ambulance course. The two subsequently became lovers.[8]

Unconventional life in Australia

After about a year practising at Swan Hill, Augustus moved to Deloraine in northern Tasmania. Edith and Augustus' daughter, Augusta Dickenson, was born in Deloraine on 3 April 1888. She would always be known as 'Austral' (the name of the ship on which her mother arrived). On her daughter's birth certificate, Edith's surname was recorded as Bonham.[9] Several sources state that the couple married in Tasmania,[10] but there is no evidence of a marriage. Edith's husband, Reverend Belcher, outlived her by about a decade and a bigamous marriage is unlikely.

News of Austral's birth appears to have been the trigger for Augustus' wife to begin divorce proceedings in England on the grounds of desertion and his adultery with Edith. He was prosecuted and found guilty of deserting his infant daughter, aged nine months. When news of the costs awarded against him reached Augustus, he disappeared.[11]

Everything points to this being a deliberate disappearance and the start of a pattern for the next ten years. The English Divorce Court tried to track him down through a notice dated 4 March 1890 in the *Sydney Morning Herald*.[12] From then until he left Australia in 1901, Augustus practised in many small country localities in several colonies but, until the mid-1890s, not for long in the same place. Despite the façade of disappearance, Edith and her children were with him wherever he went.

In 1891, Augustus, Edith, her Belcher sons, and three-year-old daughter Austral were living at Warrina, about 1,000 kilometres north-west of Adelaide, a train stop on the old Ghan railway. Because of its extreme remoteness, Edith enrolled her twins and Musgrave at the prestigious Anglican school, St Peter's College, in Adelaide.[13] During the next few years, Augustus and Edith moved briefly to several towns, always getting closer to Adelaide, until they eventually reached Booleroo, a wheat-growing district in the southern Flinders Ranges, where Augustus established a practice.[14] The couple appeared next in Victoria, where on 14 September 1894 their second child, George, was born at Drouin in West Gippsland. On the birth certificate, Edith and Augustus claimed to have married on 20 October 1883.[15] They were in Victoria less than a year before returning to South Australia to settle at Maitland on Yorke Peninsula, west of Adelaide.

Photographer and ornithologist

Life in these small, isolated towns was challenging for Edith. Robert Caldwell, MP, Chairman of the South Australian Pastoral Lands Commission, described her as 'more accomplished' than any other woman he had met, with 'natural ability of the highest order' and a superior education.[16] Caldwell, a consistent supporter of voting rights for women in the South Australian Parliament, was responsible for arranging for Edith's collection of ornithological and plant and animal specimens to be donated to the South Australian Museum.[17]

In April 1891, Edith photographed members of the Elder Scientific Exploring Expedition as it left Warrina to explore the desert country west to the West Australian coast. She is recorded as Mrs Dickenson, photographer, in the expedition's report tabled in the South Australian Parliament.[18] Women had begun to break into photography, particularly studio photography, a few decades earlier, but travelling women photographers were rare because of the weight and cumbersome nature of equipment.[19]

Edith's first-known appearance in newspapers in South Australia was the publication of a graphic account of the wreck of the British sailing ship *Phasis* on Lady Charlotte Reef near Labuan. This was based on an account she received from her 16-year-old son Musgrave, who was an apprentice on the ship.[20] The following year, Musgrave joined the Royal Navy, and during the Boer War he served on several ships before being discharged on 29 October 1901.[21]

Travelling to India and the East

In 1898, Edith seized an opportunity to visit India and the Eastern countries,[22] and soon her informative and engagingly written articles describing her adventurous travels—in what were exotic places to most readers—began appearing in the Adelaide *Advertiser*. From her first article, readers knew Edith as an intrepid traveller with remarkable stamina, who carried a gun she had managed to get through Indian customs. She told stories of hunting wild boar on elephant-back in Bihar, shooting geese and plover from a small boat on the Gandak River, and attempting to shoot a crocodile, which she only wounded and made more dangerous before it was finally killed by a Gurkha. Readers also caught glimpses of her life in Australia when she compared it to the luxury of camping out in India at the Sonapur Cattle Fair, a great Hindu festival held at the junction of the Ganges and Gandak rivers. The fair was also an important social gathering for British planters and managers, senior civil servants and army officers. In India, she had a carpeted tent, her own bathroom and numerous servants. In the Australian bush, sheep drank dry the waterhole on which they depended, possums ate their sugar, and a dingo attacked their dog and destroyed their tent. Her articles from India gave the sense that she moved among higher British Army and planter circles, an indication that she was back in the aristocratic fold as the eldest daughter of the Countess of Stradbroke.[23]

Edith's articles from India, Burma (Myanmar), Singapore and Java (Indonesia) were so popular when they appeared in the Adelaide *Advertiser* as a series of 12 between September 1899 and March 1900 that they were published in book form later that year under the title *What I Saw in India and the East*. By then she was in South Africa to cover the Boer War for the Adelaide *Advertiser*.[24]

Australia's first woman war correspondent

The *Advertiser* made the most of its innovative engagement of a female correspondent. She was one of five correspondents employed by the paper and its associates. The death of one of the *Advertiser*'s shared correspondents, William Lambie, during a battle, and the wounding of another Australian journalist, A.G. 'Smiler' Hayes, who was reporting for the London *Daily News*, emphasised the dangers ahead.[25] Edith arrived in Durban in March 1900, soon after British forces regained the besieged town of Ladysmith from the Boers. Her first article from Durban had the features of all her reporting from South Africa— graphic scene-setting, interviews with survivors, and an even-handed approach to both sides.[26] As soon as she got her correspondent's pass, she began sending articles on the devastating effects of war. She travelled over country ravaged first by the Boers as they advanced to the strategic town of Ladysmith and then by British forces as they fought to relieve the besieged town.

Near Tugela Falls on the road to Ladysmith, she saw the graves of fallen British soldiers marked with names, regiments, crosses and the words '*Dulce et decorum est*'. Close by, among several bodies hastily covered with rocks from which the feet and parts of the arms protruded, she saw the decomposing body of a Boer woman who had fought beside her husband:

> A human head almost fleshless, but with the long black hair streaming over the jacket behind, and the coarsely made skirt showing plainly the sex of the dead. It was a woman's body. Near it lay a broken umbrella and a portion of a straw hat ... The body was not a skeleton, but in such an advanced state of decomposition as to be most unpleasant to approach.[27]

As she passed scenes of recent battles, she wrote of 'the debris of war—saddles, harness, biscuit tins, haversacks, mess tins, clothing' and 'the sickening smell of decaying flesh'.[28] She illustrated the effects of civil war through stories of families in which—through intermarriage between British and Boers—close family members were fighting in opposing armies.[29] Outside Frere, she saw the wreck of the British armoured train that a Boer raiding party had attacked on 15 November 1899. During this attack, the young war reporter Winston Churchill was captured.[30]

Censorship affects news

The culmination of this section of Edith's assignment came when, despite all civilians being excluded from Ladysmith because of the high mortality from dysentery and enteric fever, she succeeded in getting to the town where one of her Belcher sons had fought with the British forces during the siege. The hotel room she stayed in had an enormous hole in the ceiling and another in the wall where shells had passed through, killing a previous occupant. She interviewed survivors, inspected the riverside caves where women and children had lived during the siege, and heard cannon fire from Boer heavy artillery in the distance.[31]

Before setting out from Pietermaritzburg over the battlefields to Ladysmith, Edith warned her readers: 'The censorship of press and post office is very strict, so that much may be written which never appears'.[32] In October 1899, the British Government imposed censorship in Natal and appointed censors at Pietermaritzburg and Durban, in addition to the censorship imposed at regimental level.[33] Military historian Stephen Badsey believed that 'the power of the British military censorship and control over war reporters could be virtually limitless, and that most reporters preferred collaboration to confrontation'. In his opinion, the impact of censorship and 'a growing deference to authority, and the cult of the personalised word-picture rather than the investigative account' meant that reporting of the Boer War represented a falling-off in standards.[34]

It is impossible to know what was cut from Edith's dispatches from Frere, Colenso and Ladysmith but it may have been substantial. The following year, she complained to Emily Hobhouse that censors had cut 'a great deal' out of one of her letters before it reached the *Advertiser*.[35] 'The hand of the "Censor",' Edith wrote, struck again when General Botha's forces attempted to overrun a small British outpost at Mount Itala on the border of Natal during a resurgence of the war on 25 and 26 September 1901. She noted that 'even the leading newspaper the *Natal Mercury*', could not get a correspondent up to the front. News of the Itala battle was of vital importance to her; one of her twin sons fought with the British forces, which, although outnumbered five to one, held the fort. She was anxious until she received a wire from him at Cape Town on 12 October 1901.[36] Censorship did not operate officially in the Cape Colony until January 1902.

Cable news undermines sea mail dispatches

Unlike the British correspondents who reported battles in which Australian colonial troops were involved and whose dispatches were cabled, Edith had to post hers by ship mail, causing a delay of about six weeks before their publication. Although cable transmission was available, the cost was prohibitive when cable news was readily available from London through Reuters, a situation that had widespread consequences. The exceptional circumstances of public interest in the Boer War and the identification of the Australian colonies (and later federated Australia) with British imperial interests created the demand for immediate cable news. At a time of emergent Australian nationalism, culminating in Federation in 1901, British reporters wrote these dispatches from a British standpoint. These dispatches also emerged when 'the sense of the British Empire as an entity' was being fostered and was growing strongly.[37] The effect was to relegate Federation to second-rank status as it was approaching culmination. Federation had always been envisaged taking place within the Empire but, in the decades that it took for Federation to be achieved, enthusiasm for the Empire strengthened, as historian John Hirst argued:

> The distinctiveness of Australia's mode of nation-building could not compete with the psychic satisfactions that Empire offered. The enthusiasm for the South African war was highly indicative, prefiguring the huge satisfaction Australians were going to draw from the exploits of their soldiers at Gallipoli in 1915 when, it is claimed, 'the nation was born'.[38]

The Boer War has been described as the first media war. It was the first major British war with mass readership for a popular press that thrived on the daily drama of the war. It is now regarded as the start of 'the age of the war reporter'. The Siege of Mafeking, a small town 258 kilometres west of Pretoria, became a thrilling drama as journalists kept their readers informed by using African carriers to slip dispatches through Boer lines. The siege ended after 217 days, which was greeted with great joy and celebrations, not only in England but also in Australia. A public holiday was declared, and in Melbourne decorations and a military parade were interpreted as 'the heartiness and spontaneity of the loyalty displayed towards the throne and country'.[39]

By the middle of 1900, the British had taken the Boer capitals of Pretoria and Bloemfontein. With the major fighting over, many journalists left South Africa. The only Australian war correspondents left at the front were listed as Banjo Paterson, Frank Wilkinson and Mrs Edith Dickenson as 'death and disease has incapacitated all the others'.[40] Edith's survival is a tribute to her physical and mental fitness and her ability to cope with difficult and dangerous situations. Most Australian staff journalists were withdrawn because they were too expensive to maintain once the initial interest in the war receded. By October 1900, almost all journalists had returned to Australia, leaving readers to depend on agency reports.[41] Edith went to England where her Dickenson children joined her.[42]

During the next six months, Edith was extraordinarily productive in consolidating her value as a correspondent. She published articles on a wide range of subjects, from the 1900 Paris Exhibition published in the *Advertiser*[43] to one aimed at rehabilitating the character of Australian shearers as cultivated citizens, which was published in the English journal, *Climate*. Over the next six months, this article was republished in many Australian papers from Rockhampton to suburban Melbourne.[44] When Edith became aware of a campaign by William Burdett-Coutts, British Member of Parliament for Westminster, to improve the standard of military hospitals in South Africa, she gave him firsthand information about the terrible situation at the Modder River hospital near the border of Cape Colony and the Orange River Colony. It had only one nurse for 84 patients. Edith's brother, Major Henry Bonham, a former patient at Bloemfontein, reported that an average of 40 men died from enteric fever every day that he was there.[45]

Opening of first federal parliament

Before she left England, Edith had commissions from several British newspapers to cover the Duke and Duchess of Cornwall's tour to Australia, during which the Duke opened the first federal parliament.[46] This founding event of Australian Federation, held at the Melbourne Exhibition Building (now the Royal Exhibition Building) on 9 May 1901, followed the proclamation of the Commonwealth of Australia on 1 January. The following month, Edith travelled around South Australia drawing crowds to her lectures, not on the Federation events in Melbourne but on the Boer War.[47] At several of these lectures her six-year-old son, George, sang patriotic songs dressed in khaki and holding a miniature rifle. Sadly, there is no record in Australian collecting institutions of the lantern slides she used to illustrate her lectures, and it is extremely unlikely that they still exist.

British concentration camps

Later that year Edith returned to South Africa to report on the concentration camps set up by the British to house women and children who were forced from their homes by the scorched-earth policy that was designed to smash Boer guerrilla warfare.[48] Augustus went with her, and their children Austral and George were put in the care of a family near Cape Town. Augustus began work as a doctor at the Bethulie concentration camp, which had a terrible reputation for disease and deaths. During the next six months, Edith's *Advertiser* articles were a savage indictment of conditions in British camps in Natal, Pretoria and the Orange River Colony. Everywhere she reported overcrowded tents, some located nearly two kilometres from a source of water, others set up on marshy ground. Food was inadequate, unsuitable and contaminated. Malnutrition and epidemic diseases were rife, and mothers were separated from their children. The British welfare reformer Emily Hobhouse—who first reported the abuse and who was barred by the British Government from returning to South Africa—quoted liberally from Edith's *Advertiser* articles in her 1902 book, *The Brunt of the War and Where It Fell*.[49] Over 26,000 Boer women and children died in the concentration camps.[50]

'They are really prisons'

When Edith saw Merebank Camp, which was set up on marshy ground about 14 kilometres south of Durban, she wrote:

'Refugee Camps' is a misnomer; they are really prisons … Barelegged children paddled through the mud and pools of water, some carrying a loaf of bread, others a bag of potatoes or a bundle of firewood.

She saw four boys carrying the body of a young child and heard that the child was the second the mother had lost in a fortnight. She saw another woman, with two children lying ill on an oil cloth, who had already lost two children in two weeks. 'The great want in the camp is blankets, boots, and underclothes for those who have no money,' Edith wrote. Some occupants from upper-class backgrounds who had financial resources were able to make their lives a little more comfortable, but Edith believed they too suffered from 'the degradation of camp life'. She wrote that they were obliged to carry their rations and firewood long distances under the gaze of 'a lot of lazy blacks, who hugely enjoy seeing white people made to work while they idle'. Clearly, Edith's compassion extended to Boers who were enemies of the British but not to the Africans.

To get to another section of the camp Edith had to walk through a brickfield and then flounder for half a mile, 'ankle deep in black slush', losing a shoe, 'so thick and sticky was the mud'. There she interviewed a

Boer woman, Mrs Kruger, who described her house being burnt down, her piano and other cherished possessions smashed to pieces and her jewellery stolen as she was forced off her land. All this was done even though she had told her British attackers that her doctor husband was not fighting but attending the wounded: 'your men as well as ours'.[51]

At Pietermaritzburg camp, Edith heard several harrowing stories of women separated from their children who had been unable to trace them, and of a young woman moved to the camp a week before her confinement who died in childbirth, unknown to her Boer commando husband. He also did not know that his child had been adopted by a woman who had lost her two children. Edith reported that enteric fever was prevalent but refuted reports that the death rate in the camps was due to lack of cleanliness among Boers.[52]

When she tried to get to Pretoria, she encountered great obstacles because Lord Kitchener had ordered that no more passes were to be issued to correspondents. Fortunately, a well-placed influential relative, Assistant Provost-General, Captain Walter Floyd Bonham, DSO (Distinguished Service Order), managed to get a pass for Edith provided she undertook not to 'interview, photograph, or otherwise molest Lord Kitchener'. In her report on conditions at Irene Camp, 25 kilometres south of Pretoria, she described 'terrible instances of emaciation among children'. She photographed a child of five whose skin hardly covered its bones and was asked to photograph another child because the mother feared it would soon die. By the time Edith reached the tent the child was dead.[53]

Visits to Bethulie Camp were also difficult to arrange, but after a long train journey in searing heat, she managed to get to Bethulie junction on the Orange River. After a seven-kilometre walk, she reached the camp where her husband was working, which was notorious for its 'terrible mortality'. She wrote:

> *The overworked doctors either fell ill, and sometimes died themselves,*
> *or resigned their hopeless task. The camp had every fault possible ...*
> *overcrowding, tents too near together, and never moved for months;*
> *bad sanitary arrangements; insufficient water supply, and a poor*
> *and scanty diet ... Epidemics of measles and whooping-cough are*
> *responsible for many deaths, but at present debility and atrophy*
> *among the mothers, and a sort of marasmus among the children, are*
> *what the doctors have to contend with. Some of the people are really*
> *mere skeletons.*

An outbreak of enteric fever, formerly unknown at Bethulie, was attributed to contamination of the water supply through the concentration of troops, prisoners and the bodies of slaughtered horses in the Orange River. Edith ended her article: 'The first question I am asked by the women in the concentration camps is—"When will this terrible war be over, and we be able to return to our homes?"'[54]

Tragedy at Bethulie

At her next stop, Bloemfontein, she was unable to get permission to visit the concentration camp. It was the first time she had been refused. 'I drew my own conclusions about the state of it,' she wrote, 'I heard that one of the doctors who had recently left Bethulie to go to it was laid up in the hospital very ill with enteric, and the death rate averaged 14 a day.' Much of this dispatch was cut before it reached the *Advertiser*.[55] Edith's reports on the terrible conditions at Bethulie were prophetic. Augustus died at Bethulie and was buried there between the time she wrote these two articles and their publication in the *Advertiser* in April. His sudden death at the age of 50 on 1 March 1902 was attributed to a heart attack.[56]

Later that year, Edith made a third trip to South Africa. After great effort to maintain her status as a correspondent by continuing to send articles to the *Advertiser*,[57] she left her children in Cape Town. Although unwell, she returned to Bethulie to supervise the erection of a tombstone over her husband's grave. After arranging for the stone to be carved at Bloemfontein and seeing it erected, she became seriously ill. A Dutch family cared for her until she was called urgently to Cape Town because her children were sick. After a harrowing journey, she arrived to find that they had recovered. Edith's health continued to deteriorate despite a sea voyage to Durban arranged by an Army contact. She died on 17 February 1903, aged 52, from bronchitis and pneumonia, the culmination of 'heart strain'. Her death left the Dickenson children— Austral, 14, and George, 8, orphans. In a note announcing her death, the Adelaide *Chronicle*, wrote:

> She had a facility for obtaining accurate and up-to-date information, and most capable critics spoke of her letters as being among the very best published in respect of the war. She dealt not only with the actual fighting but gave interesting and most valuable side-lights concerning the condition of the country and the people.[58]

Temporary fame

After remaining an obscure figure for well over a hundred years, Edith's achievements as a journalist have only begun to be recognised. Apart from the widespread obliteration of women from the historical record, the special circumstances of her death in another country resulted in no trace of her or her children remaining in Australia. She left no personal memorabilia apart from her ornithological collection.[59] Recognition began with Jeannine Baker's book on Australian women war reporters. However, pride of place in that book went to the other

Australian woman who reported the Boer War, a senior nursing sister, Agnes Macready, who had a commission from the *Catholic Press*, a Sydney weekly, to write on the war. [60] Unlike Edith's articles, which were published only in Adelaide, the close association of the Catholic and Irish expatriate press ensured that Macready's articles were 'extensively republished in England and the United States', according to the *Catholic Press* editor. He wrote that her articles were earning 'for the young paper a world-wide reputation'.[61]

An unconventional woman in her private life, Edith Dickenson was an outstanding and tenacious reporter. She remained unequalled for many years, including during the two world wars, when the movements of Australian women journalists were tightly controlled.

Alice Henry

Australian pioneer journalist and feminist

Alice Henry, a pioneer Australian journalist, feminist and social activist, arrived in the United States at the beginning of 1906, aged 48. She was a tall, arresting figure with a reputation as a fighter for the rights of women and for female equality in all fields. She had asserted her independence as Australia's first trained woman journalist by resigning her hard-won position at the Australasian *when she was confined to society reporting. Through the influence of pioneer feminist Catherine Helen Spence, she widened her reformist aims to the fight for women's suffrage, with the goal of bringing gender equality in all fields within the grasp of women. She left Australia, which was a leader in achieving women's suffrage and labour laws, for the United States where women still had to win the right to vote and where many women worked in appalling conditions in unregulated industries. She was employed by the National Women's Trade Union League of America, Chicago, and she edited its new, ambitious, national monthly journal,* Life and Labor. *Throughout Alice's work, the fight for female suffrage and gender equality was paramount.*

During her first five years in the United States—before being chosen to start *Life and Labor*—Alice Henry established her credentials as a fighter for women workers, particularly during the prolonged and bruising strike of garment workers in Chicago and New York. She organised strike relief, joined barricades and, most importantly, publicised the plight of the strikers, gaining wide publicity and mobilising sympathy and support. The article 'Why 50,000 Refuse to Sew' was written with internationally published author Miles Franklin.[1] Alice described the publicity gained as 'immense', something that could not have been achieved except for a 'struggle on a stupendous scale'.[2] She exposed the reduction in piece rates and the long hours and unsafe and unhealthy working conditions. She also exposed the power wielded by foremen in imposing penalties and demanding sexual favours in an industry in which the overwhelming majority of workers were non-English-speaking migrant women. The unsafe conditions they worked under were horrifyingly illustrated by the death of 146 workers in a fire in the Triangle Shirtwaist Factory in New York, where employers had blocked exits and stairwells to prevent workers taking breaks.[3]

As the garment workers strike dragged on, the strikers and their families endured hunger, evictions and cold. They besieged the Chicago league headquarters for basic strike relief of food rations and help with rent and coal. Alice joined picket lines and distributed relief to the workers while publicity raised awareness of the conditions in the industry and the desperate plight of the strikers. The strikers were forced back to work by desperation early in 1911, in what *Life and Labor* referred to as 'the hunger bargain'. Their sole gain was an agreement with a major employer to establish a board of arbitration with employee representation.[4]

The epic fight contributed to a decision by the National Women's Trade Union League to expand the women's section of the *Union Labor Advocate*, which Alice had edited, into an ambitious national monthly journal, *Life and Labor*. The aim was to enlist the interest of a much wider public in the struggle for workers' rights.[5] The new publication had a double function, which Alice described as:

> an organ of the League activities, and the expression of members' views; and as a running diary of what was happening in the world of working women, for the information of students and of all interested in sociological matters.[6]

The beginning of the journal signalled a new era in the league's work.

In the first editorial in *Life and Labor*, published in January 1911, Alice recognised the potential for revolutionary action by workers in situations such as the prolonged struggle of the garment workers and its bitter end:

If the whole burden of remedying unfair industrial inequalities is left to the oppressed social group we have the crude and primitive method of revolution. To this the only alternative is for the whole community through co-operative action to undertake the removal of industrial wrongs and the placing of industry upon a basis just and fair to the worker ... Destructive action peculiarly affects women and as we know that woman's industrial life is inseparable from her civic and social development the purpose of Life and Labor *will be to express the forces both latent and active in the woman movement of this country and thus bring the working girl into fuller and larger relationship with life on all sides.[7]*

Early life and background

Alice Henry's writing and editorial skills stemmed from 20 years' experience in Australian journalism, and her social conscience from an upbringing that made her a feminist and a radical. She was born in the inner Melbourne suburb of Richmond on 21 March 1857 to Scottish immigrants, Charles Henry, an accountant, and his wife, Margaret, a seamstress. Alice wrote of her upbringing in autobiographical notes:

No sex division, still less sex inferiority, obtruded itself on my mental picture ... the distinctions between qualities and standing between boys and girls were literally unknown to me, though it was in my hearing that my mother remarked upon it, when a visitor offered a ride upon his pony to my little brother and not to me. This was perhaps my first lesson in feminism.[8]

First taught at home by her mother, who had a Scottish regard for education, Alice completed her education at Richard Hale Budd's Educational Institute for Girls, one of the first girls' schools in Australia to follow the traditional classical teaching that was usual in boys' school. Barred from further formal education—the University of Melbourne had only recently allowed women to take matriculation examinations but they could not yet enrol as students—she worked as a teacher and private tutor.

Pioneer journalist

Alice's first success in journalism came in 1884 when, at the age of 27, she had an article published in the *Australasian*. When she secured a position on the *Australasian*, she was assigned to reporting social functions and supplying cookery recipes, a 'humble position', as she described it, 'at the bottom of the ladder'.[9] Unsatisfactory as her work may have been, Alice was almost certainly the first woman journalist in Australia to be taken on to the staff of a newspaper and trained on the job. Her account of her training under David Watterston, a strict and conservative editor, is a rare record of this aspect of journalism in Australia before the cadet training system was introduced. She wrote:

> *I owe him much for the training he gave me. But progressive in his opinions he was not. He felt that both the labor movement and the feminist movement should either be ignored or actively opposed.*[10]

Watterston tried to confine Alice to the women's pages, but she was an enterprising reporter who sometimes succeeded in getting articles on suffrage and social problems published under pseudonyms. In the mid-1890s, when Watterston proposed to further restrict her 'to the women's columns of fashions, frills and frivolities', she rebelled and resigned.[11]

For some years Alice supported herself through an enterprising business that she began in Melbourne, offering a range of services for women including as a 'town shopper' for country residents and an employment agency.[12] Free to write on topics that she chose, she was published in many Australian and overseas papers on women's suffrage, recognition and regulation of women's paid work, social issues, and sexual freedom. Her article on the moral training of girls was published in the *International Journal of Ethics* in October 1903,[13] and another on the establishment of children's courts in South Australia was first published in the Melbourne *Argus* and Adelaide *Evening Journal*. It was then reproduced in the London *Times* in support of the establishment of a similar court for juvenile offenders in Britain.[14] In March 1898, her eyewitness accounts of the extensive bushfires raging through Gippsland appeared in London in the *British Australasian*.[15] She also tackled some often-ignored social problems, such as the education of intellectually challenged children and the treatment of people with epilepsy, who were then regarded as having a mental illness.[16]

In 1893, Alice met Catherine Helen Spence—the great social reformer, feminist and Australia's first female political candidate—when she passed through Melbourne on her way to represent Australia at the International Conference of Charities in Chicago. They shared similar views on women's rights and women's suffrage. During the next decade, they publicised each other's speeches and articles while campaigning on suffrage, social problems, voting and labour reform, access to education and better conditions for women workers.[17] Through Spence's influence, Alice became aware of opportunities overseas for women with reforming views. In 1905, Alice left Australia as a delegate from the Melbourne Charity Organisation Society and a representative of the Women's Progressive League.[18]

After about six months in England and Europe, she travelled to the United States where she was surprised by the warm welcome she received as an Australian journalist who had campaigned for women's suffrage. In Chicago she met Margaret Dreier Robins—a women's rights leader, social activist and philanthropist—who had founded the National Women's Trade Union League only a few years before. Robins offered her the job of national secretary, which included editing the women's section of the *Union Labor Advocate*, the journal of the Chicago Federation of Labor. As organiser, Alice was able to grasp opportunities. In 1906, at an event at the White House she took the opportunity to pass on 'Australia's impromptu greetings' to President Theodore Roosevelt.[19] In her first year in the United States, she established her intellectual standing as a social historian with an article published in a New York weekly, *The Outlook,* on the Australian labour movement.[20]

Editor of *Life and Labor*

Alice brought to the editor's role of *Life and Labor* her experience in Australia of the two issues of most concern to the American feminist and labour movements. Following the passing of the Franchise Act by the Australian Parliament in 1902 she had exercised the right to vote alongside men. She had been active in the women's suffrage campaigns in the Australian colonies and during Federation. She had seen the Commonwealth Conciliation and Arbitration Court set a minimum basic wage in a country where there was already an eight-hour day. She was aware that glaring gaps still remained. Some Australian states prevented women from standing as parliamentary candidates, female wages were set at a percentage of male rates and many women slaved for long hours on piecework rates. Nevertheless, white Australian women—Indigenous Australians had no voting rights and rarely received wages—were far in advance of their American counterparts in achieving equality.

Alice came to *Life and Labor* with 30 years of experience in exploiting the print media—the only method of mass communication then available to 'educate, inspire, attract and influence readers'.[21] She had developed her ability to present the underlying need for women's suffrage to effect feminist goals. She had also emphasised to society the defects in an economic system that allowed such an imbalance between employers and the right of their workers to a living wage and just conditions. She had a stimulating mind, enthusiasm and zeal. She also had the skills of acclaimed Australian writer and feminist Miles Franklin to draw on. She described Franklin's talents as 'her ready pen, her fresh interest in everything, her initiative and her easy adaptability' that made her 'an easy addition to the staff'.[22] Alice was educative and earnest; Franklin brought lightness, a human touch and her literary talent that gave 'vitality and verve' to the journal while 'her sense of irony of women's place' added to its 'distinctive feminist flavour'.[23] *Life and Labor* appealed to middle-class professional women, feminists, activists, social workers and community leaders. Many of the unionists it represented, even if they were literate in English, had neither the money to subscribe nor time to read the journal. Alice saw harnessing the power of activist women to gain the vote as a first step in giving women power to influence legislation. Until the passing of the 19th Amendment to the American Constitution in 1920, American women had no right to vote in national elections and could vote in only a minority of states.

With their joint talents, Alice and Franklin produced an attractive, professional publication. They brought together writing by prominent Americans, interviews with political leaders, biographical articles on women workers, articles on the exploitation of women workers, reports of strikes and suffrage conventions, international suffrage and labour news, short stories and poems. Stories on the lives of women who had become union leaders, or those who worked in oppressed industries, were mixed with educative articles on the aims of the league. There were practical series on 'How to Organize' and instructions on letter writing aimed at aspiring union leaders. Alice also introduced a section of book reviews called 'When We have Time to Read'.

The journal nurtured the strong ties between the feminist movements in the United States and Australia. These ties arose from Catherine Helen Spence's first visit in 1893, later reinforced by Vida Goldstein's visit in 1902. During Goldstein's visit, she became a celebrity with huge crowds flocking to her lectures on 'Votes for Women'. She was invited to the White House to discuss suffrage with the president, Theodore Roosevelt, and she gave evidence to a United States Congressional Committee on the operation of women's suffrage in Australia.[24]

Miles Franklin did most of the office work and production, ensuring the 32-page journal got out on time. Alice was often away speaking at events, attending conferences in other cities, and publicising the journal to potential subscribers and supporters. Franklin brought order to the office and in 1913 was the sole editor for about four months while Alice recuperated from illness in Canada. At the same time Franklin ran the America-wide Women's Trade Union League while Margaret Dreier Robins was in Europe. In a letter to her aunt at Brindabella, she wrote in characteristic style:

I have been doing all the editing for months ... I have been crew of the captain's gig and chief bottle washer in all sorts of things. I have even given my opinion on settling strikes and sent organisers and investigators hither and yon. I will have to take in the size of my hat when Mrs Robins comes back ... We have an office suite of four rooms in one of the big skyscrapers and one of them is my private office. I have an assistant to help me. I have my own telephone switch and all sorts of conveniences. Quite a change from the life of an Australian bush girl. We have a mail chute just outside our door in which we drop our letters and when we want a telegraph messenger to take things we press a button in the wall. The building has a barber shop and a restaurant and all sorts of things. There are some thousands of people quartered here. It is a great sight when the buildings light up at night. [25]

Her description of the working conditions at *Life and Labor* would have been a revelation to women journalists back in Australia, most of whom were confined to the crowded back rooms allocated to women's pages staff.

First World War

The beginning of the First World War presented a dilemma for Alice and Franklin in neutral America. In September 1914, they published a joint article blaming the tragedy of the war on the build-up of weapons. 'The fallacy of the argument that armaments preserve peace has been exposed in a way that beggars the descriptive powers of the wildest journalism and leaves sober people aghast,' they wrote.[26] Alice followed this in the December 1914 issue with 'War and Its Fruits' in which she advocated sending a 'Peace Ship' to Europe. She hoped the American peace advocates aboard would bring 'such pressure that at least an armistice must be declared'. If not, she wrote, European civilisation was 'doomed to destruction'.[27]

Alice's frequent absences reporting conferences and strikes and giving speeches made the appearance of the journal each month a remarkable achievement. She wrote and published many articles on industrial problems, particularly campaigns for a minimum wage, sometimes drawing on Australian experience of wages boards and other reforms,[28] and the conditions in which women worked in individual industries.[29] Alice wrote two articles in which she advocated 'a single standard of morality' between the sexes, a living wage for all and votes for women to give them the power to influence legislation.[30] She opened the pages to discussion of some intractable social problems, such as prostitution.

Life and Labor in crisis

Life and Labor maintained its high standard for four years but by February 1915 it was in financial trouble after the major financial backer, Margaret Dreier Robins, decided to limit her support. Alice appealed for new financial supporters and made greater efforts to enrol new subscribers. There were drastic economies, including a reduction from 32 to 16 pages and a move to cheaper premises.[31] None of these measures led to improvement in the underlying problem—its dependence on outside financial support.

Whether voluntarily, through pressure or just by reading the situation, Alice resigned. She stated that she wanted to take less harassing and fatiguing work as the national lecturer and educator for the league, a position that had fallen vacant. This was not unlike the work she had done addressing meetings, conferences and groups when she was publicising *Life and Labor*. At 58, she was a woman who had worked hard all her adult life, so the resignation may have appeared reasonable. It also allowed her the time to finish a book she had been working on for some years, *The Trade Union Woman*, which was published later that year.

Journalistic career ends

Nevertheless, the devastation of losing her journalistic career in such circumstances must have been a bitter blow to Alice. She had maintained her career in difficult circumstances in Australia as a pioneer woman employed in an overwhelmingly male industry. She had resigned her journalist's job rather than being shackled to writing 'trivia' and had maintained herself for years as a freelance journalist in Australia. Then in the United States she had undertaken an extremely demanding and multi-faceted position.

Alice's departure left Franklin an unhappy survivor. As editor with a staff of two, she had to bring out a drastically reduced publication with a problematic future, while maintaining the quality of previous issues. At this stage, Margaret Dreier Robins wrote to say that despite Franklin's 'excellent qualities both as a writer and editor', she did not have Alice's 'knowledge of the labor movement or her fine vision'.[32] In October 1915, Franklin left for England on three months leave from which she did not return. In her roles at the National Women's Trade Union League and *Life and Labor*, Franklin had carried a heavy workload with a great deal of responsibility. It was two years before she began to overcome her resentment at the treatment she had received from Robins.[33] *Life and Labor* continued in truncated form until 1921 when it was reduced to a four-page union paper.

Alice attributed the financial failure of *Life and Labor* to the periodical having to fulfil two different and inconsistent functions 'as an organ of the movement' on one hand and 'a magazine for general reading' on the other.[34] From an Australian perspective, it is surprising that a journal of such quality did not attract enough subscribers and advertisers to make it self-supporting in a country as industrialised and populous as the United States. In 1888, Louisa Lawson started a crusading, radical, feminist paper, *The Dawn: A Magazine for Australian Women*, in Sydney, employing women in all roles. With Australia's population at less than four million, her paper remained a viable, commercial publication for 17 years. Subscriptions and a healthy amount of advertising entirely supported this publication, from its first issue and through the 1890s depression. Some of its success can be attributed to Lawson's pragmatic approach in including enough practical articles of general appeal (even supplying dress patterns) to engage women who were initially only peripherally interested in its reforming agenda.[35]

Australian writer and journalist Dame Mary Gilmore was equally pragmatic in her long-running column for women in the *Australian Worker*. She wrote powerful articles on important women's issues, but she also included a popular section in which she replied to women who wrote for advice, dispensing her own brand of down-to-earth wisdom.[36] While *Life and Labor* maintained a bright, appealing style, its content was almost entirely directed at the lives of women as activists and workers, barely touching their domestic lives and aspirations for their children.

Alice continued similar work to her editorship of the journal in her new role as head of the league's education department. In her book, *The Trade Union Woman*, she covered the campaign for voting rights and reform of labour laws in the United States. After American women won the right to vote and stand for political office, she concentrated on her second book, *Women and the Labor Movement* (1923), promoting labour reform, a shorter working day, a minimum wage, the establishment of competence—not sex—as the basis for promotion and wages, and neither compulsion nor prohibition against wage-earning after marriage. She was described as a 'spokeswoman for the millions of her sex' employed in industry in the United States.[37]

In 1924, Alice visited Italy, Switzerland, Austria and Germany to report on the Workers' Education Movement and to attend an International Workers' Education conference at Oxford. At the end of the year, she visited Australia where she was welcomed home as a distinguished ambassador for her homeland. Her greatest disappointment was the state of Australian trade unions, which, once so flourishing and effective, had in her view become backward and lacking in thoroughness and persistence. In the late 1920s, Alice retired from the league. After suffering a severe bronchial illness lasting 18 months, she moved to the milder climate of Santa Barbara, California, where she was involved in promoting Australian interests following the appointment in 1929 of Herbert Brookes as Australian Commissioner-General.

The unexpected friendship between the radical feminist Alice and the deeply conservative Brookes is revealed in Alice's neat typewritten letters in the voluminous correspondence of Herbert and Ivy Brookes in the National Library of Australia.[38] Alice alerted Brookes to developments in music, art and literature, particularly American reactions to new books by Australian female writers, including reviews of Henry Handel Richardson's *Australia Felix* and *Ultima Thule*, M. Barnard Eldershaw's *A House Is Built*, Mary Fullerton's *A Juno of the Bush* and the first of Franklin's Brent of Bin Bin series. In 1930, Alice had an article published in the *Bookman* (New York) on Henry Handel Richardson. She often sent paragraphs to Australian newspapers about the reception of Australian books in the United States. She also arranged a venue in San Francisco for the 'First Contemporary All-Australian Art Exhibition'. Expatriate artist Mary Cecil Allen curated the exhibition which had been shown successfully at the Roerich Museum in New York.[39]

Return to Australia

In the crisis of the Great Depression, Alice's league pension was reduced, and then ceased. In 1933, she returned to live in Australia where she attempted to re-establish herself as a speaker, broadcaster and writer, promoting the achievements of women. She gave lectures for the Young Women's Christian Association and wrote a chapter on the history of Australian women gaining the vote for the *Centenary Gift Book*, published for the centenary of Victoria in 1934.[40] She became a prominent member of the Press, Letters and Art Committee of the National Council of Women for whom she wrote a 'Bibliography of Australian Women Writers' in response to a request from the International Council of Women, but was disillusioned by its neglect. At the 150th celebration of the arrival of Europeans in New South Wales in 1938, she complained that copies should have been given to international delegates, but it was not available even in libraries and was 'practically lost'.[41]

In 1936, she received a bitter blow to her self-esteem when a broadcast she was scheduled to make on the ABC on Jane Addams—the famous American social activist—was cancelled. The excuse given was that her voice 'did not carry well over the air', but the blow was compounded when she heard studio gossip describing her as 'a back number and an old hen'.[42] In 1937, she had another blow when she was forced to accept that she would have to go through the humiliating process of applying for naturalisation in the country where she was born and to prove that she was literate in English. Ironically, the biography of Alice by Diane Kirkby is titled *The Power of Pen and Voice*.

In 1937, at the age of 80, Alice moved from living independently to a boarding house in Richmond, where Miles Franklin visited her from Sydney, celebrating with a party. 'You know how she adored being given a party,' Miles wrote to a friend in America.[43] In 1940, with her health failing, Alice moved to a rest home where Australian poet, essayist and literary critic Nettie Palmer,[44] her literary executor, encouraged her to continue writing her memoirs. After Alice's death on 14 February 1943, Palmer edited her memoirs, added a postscript, and published it in typescript form the following year.[45] Her significance was not recognised in her lifetime, and she died in obscurity.[46] It was not until long after her death that she was honoured in the Media Hall of Fame.[47]

Jennie Scott Griffiths

Radical socialist and feminist

Jennie Scott Griffiths arrived in Sydney in 1912 with a wealth of journalistic experience but a background that left her without skills in analysing and judging broader Australian society. For the first time in her life, she had gained a job independently of her father or her husband, and she learned quickly that women could exercise rights over their own lives and that there were alternative ways of organising society. Her downfall came when she expressed her radical ideas too enthusiastically in a paper aimed at a middle-of-the-road audience, and gained notoriety evangelising on street corners.

When Jennie Scott Griffiths arrived from Fiji with her husband and nine children (a tenth was born in Sydney), there was little evidence of the radical 'red-ragger' she was to become.[1] After the collapse of her husband's investments, she became the family's breadwinner. But her enthusiastic adoption of radical feminist politics and the openness of her soapbox expression of them, led to her losing her hard-won job as the first female editor of a recently launched weekly women's paper. She would never have a permanent journalistic job again. Growing up in a patriarchal and socially conservative, evangelical section of Texan society, and living in an insular European community in colonial Fiji, influenced her attitudes to society and political ideas, preparing her for rebellion.

Early life and background

Jennie Scott Wilson was born on 30 October 1875 at Wolf Creek, Tyler County, Texas, in a 'double log cabin'. Her father, Randolph Wilson, had built the cabin when he married Laura Cowart, who had several children from her first marriage. The first influence on Jennie's childhood was the immediacy of the defeat of the Confederate side in the American Civil War just a decade before she was born. Her mother had lost all her brothers in the conflict and her father had fought on the Confederate side. Continual reminders of the loss of so many on the Confederate side appear to have conditioned her towards sympathy for the lower-ranked survivors in white society (she makes no mention of slaves) and resistance to authority.[2]

Her father also influenced her childhood when, at the age of two, he launched her into the role of 'Child Wonder'. Newspaper cuttings kept in scrapbooks and loose folders—now in the National Library of Australia—show her prominence as a child prodigy.[3] Her speeches, which her father wrote, were reported under headlines describing her as the 'Baby Elocutionist of Texas',[4] and when she was older as 'The Child Wonder' or 'A Tiny Prodigy'. The words 'tiny' or 'little' were often included: Jennie was an extremely small child and even as an adult was only about 145 centimetres tall. She spoke in many small towns in south-eastern Texas, often to veterans' gatherings and the American Farmers' Alliance, in which her father held office, on subjects like temperance, the importance of attending Sunday school and exhortations to reform. Her father took her to visit prisoners and often took released men home to outfit them and try to get them employment.[5] These causes, particularly temperance, were dominating influences.[6]

Jennie attended school for the first time at the age of 12 and was soon top of the class. At the age of 16, she enrolled at the University of Texas, Austin, to study law. She stayed only a short time because women graduates were not able to practise law. After training at a business college, she was employed in secretarial and court reporting work in San Antonio. At the same time she wrote for and edited the 'Young People's Corner' in the *Texas Farmer*, becoming proficient in some aspects of journalism and the ability to turn out a prolific stream of stories, articles and poems.[7] This ability to produce a huge number of words quickly continued until her death. The content of both her writing and her speeches in Texas conveys the strong impression that she was a typical product of the socially conservative, evangelical Protestantism of Bible-belt America and, in her case, held particular compassion for white social outcasts. She lived her youth largely in her father's shadow, which did not equip her with social skills or worldly judgement.[8]

World tour for Hagey Institute

The Hagey Institute offered a program 'guaranteed' to cure alcohol and drug addiction. Within 3 years of launching in 1889, 75 'Hagey Bi-Chloride of Gold' institutes had been established in the United States.[9] Jennie's support of the institutes shows her lack of judgement given the obvious signs of it being fake. She was part of the publicity machine travelling with Hagey groups through Texas, Colorado, California and Mexico.[10] In 1896, when she was 21, she joined a group with her half-brother, Tom Cowart, and his family, to establish Hagey Institutes throughout the world. After visiting Honolulu and Auckland, they landed at Suva where Jennie met Arthur George Griffiths, the eldest son of the owner and editor of the *Fiji Times*. Her acceptance of his proposal of marriage the day after they met, can be interpreted as overwhelming physical and emotional attraction, but it also raises questions. Did she grasp an opportunity to reinvent herself in a new location? And was Arthur acutely aware of the limited number of eligible women among the small European population in Suva? Fiji was a frontier economy of 1,500 to 2,000 white settlers and traders living on the coastal fringes, and a population of about 140,000 Fijians.[11] Jennie's rebellious and adventurous spirit meant that she was able to launch herself into a new life in the remote Pacific, far from the close-knit communities she had known.

Jennie and Arthur were married on 9 November 1897 at Holy Trinity Anglican Church, Suva.[12] Jennie held the mistaken and probably naïve belief that she was unable to bear children as a result of a childhood accident. She was ignorant of even old wives' tales on birth control and quickly became the mother of a family of ten. The first son, Randolph, was born on 24 July 1898, followed by Tom in 1900, and Don in Scotland in 1901 while Jennie and her husband were visiting her brother and the touring Hagey group. Back in Suva, more children were born. The ninth arrived in 1911 and was named Ciwa, a Fijian word for nine. The final child, Hazel, was born in Sydney in 1913.[13]

Fijian society

A relative wrote that Jennie 'fitted very well' into Fijian society,[14] but her own memoir indicates that she was a misfit in the elite society of Europeans who followed rigid social customs. She wrote:

Dressing and giving elaborate dinners and dances, and keeping up the calling routine, were the rules of life as it should be lived in Fiji. I wore no corsets, had my hair cut short, dressed nearly always in lime ... never gave a formal affair—not even a dinner party—and refused most of the invitations to such affairs when others gave them at first— later I was not invited, of course. Arthur always wanted me to accept invitations to Government House—his mother said such invitations were in the form of a command from the King ... But I went to very few. It wasn't comfortable feeling that you were different and that the women avoided you because you were not properly dressed—besides, there really was not the least thing interesting about the affairs.[15]

Just before they left Suva, Arthur wanted Jennie to attend an afternoon reception, a dinner and a dance at Government House, urging her to buy some clothes whatever the expense. At dinner, she sat next to the Governor who told her what she described as an 'inside story' about the British takeover of Ocean Island. She was as direct and unconventional as ever to a Mr Marsh who sat on her other side. Believing he was watching her to see 'what implement I was using to shovel the peas with', she remarked: 'No use looking at me, Mr Marsh, I don't know which to use'.[16]

Unacknowledged editor of *Fiji Times*

The Griffiths family's apparent lack of money and refinement may have been because the *Fiji Times* was far from a money-spinner. Jennie believed it was only profitable because of her unpaid work as editor and reporter, and because Arthur fixed the machinery when necessary.[17] Jennie's work on the paper began when her father-in-law, George Littleton Griffiths, who had founded the paper, recognised her ability and arranged for her to contribute. After she engaged a governess and family help, Nana Bailey, Jennie worked full-time, including through the birth of babies.

Following George's death in March 1908,[18] formal control of the paper and associated businesses passed to Arthur who, although he had been trained by his father in the 'same tradition of responsible journalism and public service', had concentrated on the business side of the paper and had done little or no writing and editing. Once her husband took over, Jennie became, by her own account, the 'unacknowledged, unpaid editor'.[19] A history of the paper describes her efforts as 'helping' her husband by writing the editorials. However, there is plenty of evidence indicating that since early in the decade she had been writing feature articles and a column, 'Passing Notes'. She published this column under her pen name of Ola.[20]

Jennie described herself as 'a one-man paper'.[21] She took over reporting the Legislative Council, the courts and town council meetings, wrote the foreign news from cables, and edited and proofed the paper. Her later career in Australia is evidence of her skill in many aspects of writing and in single-handedly editing a weekly periodical. Arthur was proud that the newspaper had 'never missed an issue',[22] but he had neither his father's business acumen and drive nor his skills as a journalist. Instead, he invested in some new technological ventures, including importing the first dictaphone to Fiji in 1910 and becoming an agent for the Colombia Phonograph Company. His subsequent life in Australia indicates his inability to consistently make or earn money.[23]

In 1912, at Jennie's urging, Arthur sold the *Fiji Times* and associated businesses and the family moved to Sydney so that the children could have access to a better education. They arrived feeling optimistic for the future. They splurged on the best-quality furniture, linen and clothes, and put down payment on a large house on Darling Point Road that they named 'Hope'. But hopes came crashing down when the firm Arthur had invested in, B & R Motor Company, became bankrupt. The move from Fiji proved a disaster for Arthur who 'never acclimatised to being less than the boss, which made working for others an impossible affair'.[24] The family was shattered further when two of their young daughters became ill with diphtheria and four-year-old Leonie died.[25] Lack of money forced them to change residence several times, even moving to a block of land on the outskirts of Sydney where Arthur attempted to grow vegetables to feed his large family.

As each of the boys reached 14, they had to leave school to get work and Jennie also decided to seek full-time work. In Joy Damousi's *Women*

Come Rally, she is coupled with 'women from a privileged middle-class upbringing' who had the advantage of rearing children 'with the assistance of servants', leaving them free to become activists.[26] This did not fit Jennie's background in Texas, Fiji or Sydney (there is every indication that Nana Bailey was unpaid). Her experience of life was in the lower rungs of the conservative American south, and in Fiji she had not been part of the European elite, despite her husband's position.

Editor of the *Australian Woman's Weekly*

In Sydney, Jennie was exposed to a ferment of ideas in feminist and radical organisations, including the recently formed Feminist Club. She had no previous exposure to such ideas—she had been unpaid at work, and at home she'd had no control over her successive pregnancies. Determined to express her views using her skills as a journalist, she applied to Mary Gilmore, the esteemed women's page editor of the union paper, the *Australian Worker*, for a job. She was initially unsuccessful.[27]

In June 1913, Jennie was appointed the first female editor of the *Australian Woman's Weekly*, a periodical for women that Sydney publishers and printers Deaton and Spencer had started six months earlier as a 36-page magazine aimed at housewives. (There is no connection with the *Australian Women's Weekly*, which started in 1933 and is still appearing as a monthly.) The *Woman's Weekly* relied for its content on syndicated material on fashions, handcrafts, household hints, a children's page, cooking recipes, short stories and serials, and it was supported financially by advertising. Until she was well-established, Jennie continued this format. In publicity, she always stressed these features, including the requirement that a woman edit the content. Initially, women were not necessarily employed to edit early women's magazines and the women's pages of newspapers. However, women began to work in these editorial roles when proprietors saw the appeal of a female editor for their female readers. Jennie made this point in a full-page promotion of *Woman's Weekly*:

> *Do you like a woman's paper? A woman's paper edited by a woman? With women's views of men and things, and men's views of women and life? Do you like kitchen recipes and household hints? Do you like knitting, needlework, and crochet suggestions? Do you like to see what Paris, London and New York fashions are like before they are worn in Australia? Do you like short vivid stories and good serial yarns? And do you think A.W.W. succeeds in giving you all this in an attractive get-up at a ridiculously small cost?[28]*

She explained her rationale to a reader, M.E.P., who deplored the number of pages devoted to fashion and argued against the inclusion of paper patterns, which almost universally appeared in women's papers of the era. Even Louisa Lawson, who had begun the revolutionary *The Dawn: A Magazine for Australian Women* as a voice for suffrage and women's rights, was pragmatic about including features of wide appeal, offering patterns at a moderate price while urging women to dress sensibly and attractively.[29] Jennie told M.E.P that the wartime shortage of paper allowed her to avoid the 'calamity' of including paper patterns until 'that extremely problematic date after the war'.[30]

She gradually made her own mark on *Woman's Weekly*. In her first year as editor, she wrote a series on women prominent in social and political movements, and in some of the professions that had a bias towards progressive women. Her subjects included activist Annie Golding, a worker for children and president of the New South Wales Women's Progressive Association; Mrs Francis Anderson, who, as

Maybanke Wolstenholme, promoted women's suffrage and other feminist causes in her periodical *Woman's Voice*, and who later led the kindergarten movement; social reformers Margaret Hodge and Harriet Newcomb, who were on a speaking tour of Australia; and Ada Partridge, principal of Fort Street Girls High. Another series on women journalists included an article on Mary Gilmore.[31]

Jennie's name did not appear as editor of the *Australian Woman's Weekly* until she had been in charge for nearly two years. Simultaneously she introduced a front-page 'Editorial Chat' in which she expressed her views on controversial social and employment issues affecting women, criticised the conservative views of others, and publicised the activities of socially radical organisations. A column in which she replied to correspondents provided another outlet for comments on social trends and attitudes. In it she noted the wartime demise of the 'at home' day, a custom that she wrote was previously 'sacred to suburbia' in wealthy districts. She used the column to publicise some ideas that were highly radical in a publication aimed at suburban housewives. She advocated for the establishment of co-operative kitchens with paid staff, which groups of families could share, allowing the mothers to work, and a government endowment scheme for mothers that would also meet the most pressing needs of the 'ringless brides'.[32]

Vividly written personal stories were Jennie's forté. She took up the cause of destitute English girls and women aged 14 to 26 who had worked mostly as tailoresses, typists and factory hands. These girls and women were out of work because of the war and had been sent to Australia under the auspices of Queen Mary, provided they agreed to work as domestic servants. Jennie wrote about one of the 129 women, a penniless widow aged 25, with two girls aged 5 and 7. Unable to get work in Sydney because 'neither Mrs Chatswood nor

Mrs Potts Point cared to give her a trial as "domestic servant" and Mrs Less Aristocratic could not take on the additional expense of two children', the widow was referred to a position as a housekeeper in a country town at the meagre rate of ten shillings per week. She was given £1 and told the time the train left Sydney. Jennie foreshadowed what she believed was ahead:

> Her ticket cost her 17/6, so she and the two little girls will arrive at that country wine-seller's place with 2/6 worth of choice as to whether they will stay there or not. There are some things which no polite woman's paper can write about—and I should probably think this case, for which prominent people are responsible, is likely to be catalogued under that heading.[33]

Early in 1915 she devoted well over a page to the first annual report of the Feminist Club, whose aims included working for equality of status, opportunity and payment between men and women, child welfare, reform of the divorce laws and encouragement of women's influence in politics.[34] In September 1915, she included an interview with the secretary of the Tailoresses' Union on the need for a home in Sydney for working girls. This was a subject that she had already written on at length in the *Sunday Times* and *Woman's Weekly*.[35] She also described a clothing depot for the poor run by the Women's Progressive Association and a workroom for unemployed women and girls run by the Women's Organising Committee of the Political Labour League, which hoped to get army contracts.[36]

A few months later, in a single issue, she included an article by American writer Upton Sinclair on the 'social evil', the need for a Family Maintenance Act and for education on sex hygiene and another on the social reasons for the decline of the birthrate.[37] In April 1916, she published an article by Margaret Sanger on birth control and speculated on socialism: 'Suddenly "socialist" has become popular', she wrote. She believed, however, that most who advocated socialism supported only a fraction of its tenets. She defined socialism as 'an absolutely healthy social structure without the diseases of wealth, property and crime!' She then contrasted socialists with liberals who preached ownership of property, Christians who were content with conditions as they were and snobs who regarded themselves as 'porcelain and the rest of the world mere mud'. She again argued for communal homes and the employment of household staff to allow wives to work.[38] While the paper continued to publish the staples of women's periodicals, Jennie's contributions were far to the left of what could be expected in a weekly paper set up as a money-making venture aimed at suburban readers.

Fill-in at the *Australian Worker*

Remarkably, as well as editing the *Australian Woman's Weekly* each week, writing a sizeable part of the contents, and being involved in the care of her family, Jennie also filled in as editor of the women's section of the *Australian Worker* on several occasions. When this first occurred she announced her arrival at the top of the page: 'Our good friend Mrs Mary Gilmore is having a holiday and I am to fill her place for the time being'.[39] These opportunities did not occur as often as she would have liked. Towards the end of 1915 she wrote plaintively to Gilmore that she was waiting 'for you to whistle me up—you haven't'.[40] Her contributions, however, appeared frequently, giving her an outlet to write for a paper that was anti-war and anti-conscription. It also gave her more scope to express her views on women's rights. 'Women have a right to be individuals—neither sex slaves nor pampered poodles,' she wrote.

We have a right to demand to say whether we will do this or that work;
and where we prove ourselves capable of equal work with man, that we
shall be paid an equal wage for that work ... We have a right to demand
that home life be taken off the list of non-productive works and put
upon an economic basis as one of the paying concerns of the nation.[41]

She also wrote for other papers where her socialist and anti-war
views were welcome. In the *International Socialist*, she urged women
donating to war charities not to forget that 'any united effort on the
part of society could within a twelve month [period] sweep away the
reproach of helpless poverty from this fair land of ours'.[42] In a series
on 'The State & the Woman', published in the Sydney *Sunday Times*, she
wrote on the disadvantages of married working women who also had
to do the household domestic work and care for their children.

In answer to letter writers who criticised her articles, she replied
under the heading 'The Sweated Trade of Motherhood' that she
wanted complete recognition that women were, and always had been,
as important as men. She argued that women are indispensable to the
world, that women should be recognised as human beings first and
sex creatures afterwards, that wage slavery be abolished, and that the
State should give recognition to the monetary value of motherhood.
Mothers were 'absolutely the least organised and the most sweated
class of workers in the world,' she wrote.[43]

Conscription debates

The conscription campaigns in 1916 and 1917 transformed women's
organisations. Most supported conscription. The National Council
of Women believed conscription was 'just and democratic' and
the Australian Women's National League 'tolerated no opposing
views'. Women clashed violently at rallies and 'both sides reacted as

women who had lost their sons responded angrily and bitterly'. Pro-conscription supporters appeared to have overwhelming support. A women-only gathering at the Sydney Town Hall, at which the Prime Minister, W.M. Hughes, spoke drew a crowd so great the seating capacity 'was exceeded by nearly one thousand persons'. [44]

Both sides appealed to women as mothers, the anti-conscriptionists famously with Cecilia John's song, 'I Didn't Raise My Son to Be a Soldier', and a pamphlet, *The Blood Vote*. Those against conscription sometimes tied their case to maintaining the widely accepted White Australia policy, arguing that conscription would strip Australia of white men who would be replaced by 'coloured' labour.[45] Jennie used both the appeal to mothers and the eugenics argument in her articles and speeches. She urged women 'to challenge the political, social and economic conditions created by male dominance which had led to a nation that sanctioned the slaughtering of the sons, lovers and husbands'. Adela Pankhurst and Vida Goldstein, campaigners against conscription, also used the theme of women's maternal responsibilities as peacemakers in their anti-conscription campaigns.[46]

Sacked as *Woman's Weekly* editor

During 1916, Jennie's public activities against war and conscription began to take over her life. While much of her writing on radical and feminist issues was published in other papers, the publishers of the *Woman's Weekly* objected to her public appearances at meetings run by the Women's Anti-Conscription Committee, the Women's Peace Army, the Social Democratic League, and the Labor Party. After the defeat of the first conscription referendum, held on 28 October 1916, the *Woman's Weekly* sacked her because, according to Jennie, they 'could not afford to contribute to the support of a woman like me!'[47] Multiple sources reported that she was sacked for opposing conscription. Her son, Don, believed the owners objected to her 'public utterances against the war'.[48] However, the drastic wartime rationing of newsprint, which required the paper to be reduced to 16 pages, may have also had something to do with it.

Jennie made her views clear in her prominent position in the Women's Peace Army, established in July 1915 to mobilise women who opposed war. The Peace Army campaigned under the motto 'We war against war' and flew a flag in the suffrage colours of purple, green and white. Jennie was president of the Sydney branch under Vida Goldstein, the national president, and Adela Pankhurst, national secretary. The organisation's socialist, anti-war ideology gained it a reputation as radical and militant, attracting large numbers to its controversial public meetings. Members took part in peace demonstrations and organised petitions to parliament. As Sydney president, Jennie cooperated with activist Labor women, including Kate Dwyer, Belle Golding and Muriel Heagney. She, Goldstein and Pankhurst often joined them in speaking on street corners and in the Domain.[49]

Jennie's daughter, Civa, painted an overwrought description of her diminutive mother on a soapbox enticing passers-by with her clear, carrying voice. She argued that those who profited most—the manufacturers of bullets and weapons, and the power-hungry who wanted more territory and greater control of government and riches—instigated war. Ciwa wrote:

> The audience could feel the tearing of flesh, the screams of the wounded, the frigid fear of the foot soldiers in the trenches. She painted a graphic picture of those who fought the battles and those who from safe haven[s] profited from the suffering. She dwelt on the deprivation of mothers who lost their sons as she could lose hers.[50]

After she lost her editing job, Jennie may have hoped that a full-time position would be available on the *Worker*, but this did not eventuate. After leaving *Woman's Weekly* she had to rely on poorly paid casual contributions and other journalistic assignments to make any money. She reported a conference on 'The Teaching of Sex Hygiene' for the Workers' Educational Association.[51] She also had articles published in the Sydney *Sunday Times*, the Brisbane Labor paper the *Daily Standard*, the British *Social Democrat*, the Sydney-based *International Socialist* and the *Industrial Worker* in Chicago.

The *Worker* continued to publish her articles, many of them on 'Women and Conscription'.[52] Just before the New South Wales state election in May 1917, she wrote:

> *Will you be true to the best traditions of your race, and stand solidly for free speech, a free press, individual freedom for the workers, and a limitation of sweating and profit-making out of humanity's woes by the capitalists? Or will you, wives, sweethearts, and mothers of Australians, give the freedom of your country—her control over her own affairs—and the very lives of your husbands, lovers and sons into the keeping of a group of politicians who for nearly two years have never ceased to do all in their power to obtain control—military and industrial—of the people of this country?[53]*

Disillusioned with Sydney politics

Although she remained an active member of feminist, socialist and anti-war groups, in addition to the Women's Peace Army, Jennie became increasingly disheartened that they were not pursuing policies that were sufficiently radical. In this she was like Pankhurst, who wrote that she was 'getting more and more near Anarchism and the IWW [International Workers of the World] everyday'.[54] Jennie was particularly disturbed by the prosecution in September 1916 of 12 members of the socialist anti-war organisation International Workers of the World for forgery, felony, conspiracy, arson and treason under the recently amended War Precautions Act. All were found guilty on some or all of the charges and jailed, most for 15 years.[55] Further draconian legislation, the *Unlawful Associations Act 1916*, led to the prosecution, jailing and, in some cases, deportation of more members who became 'martyrs of the working class'.[56]

Hard-line government policies against anti-war protesters increased after the formation of what was known as a national or 'Win the War' government led by former Labor Prime Minister W.M. Hughes. In New South Wales the conscription campaign caused a similar situation—the Labor Premier, W.A. Holman, after being expelled from the Labor Party, formed a 'Win the War' government and remained premier. The situation in Queensland was different with the Labor Premier, T.J. Ryan, a leading campaigner against conscription, continuing to lead Labor in government. This, combined with her own uncertain future in journalism, persuaded Jennie that a move to the radical north would be a good idea. She remained in Sydney long enough to campaign against conscription before the second referendum, which was held on 20 December 1917. She spoke at many meetings in the city, suburbs and country districts. On 20 November, she was a speaker at an afternoon meeting at Queanbeyan's Triumph Hall and that night she spoke at a crowded meeting at Hall in the Federal Capital Territory (now the Australian Capital Territory). In the following days she was at anti-conscription meetings at Michelago, Williamsdale and Bungendore, small settlements within reach of Queanbeyan.[57]

Radical Brisbane

By early 1918, Jennie, her husband and eight of their children had moved to Brisbane. Her son, Don, was amazed to find it 'such a lively place for radical activism'.[58] Almost immediately Jennie came under the surveillance of the Commonwealth Censor and undercover Military Intelligence officers, who made copious records of her correspondence, her attendance at meetings, her movements and her speeches. When she spoke at the second anniversary of the jailing of the 'IWW twelve', the crowd stood with red flags on their lapels, as she denounced 'biased courts and police frame-ups'.[59] From Brisbane she sent many poems and some articles to the *Industrial Worker* in Chicago. In 1919, when the paper employed a new female cartoonist, it announced with pride that its graphic art blended so well with 'the poetic art of our long-time Jennie Wilson'.[60]

Red Flag Riots

Jennie's activism reached a peak in 1919 during and in the aftermath of what became known as the Red Flag Riots, a name given to a 'March of Social Progress' and demonstration that began when marchers set off from the Brisbane Trades Hall on 23 March 1919. They were flying red flags in defiance of the War Precautions Act that banned the public display of the flag (the Irish Sinn Fein flag was also banned). Red was the official colour of the Australian labour movement and of the Queensland Labor Party, and banning it was deeply resented. They also resented that even four months after the end of the war the Act was still in operation. Jennie and others distributed 100 handkerchief-sized red pennants. A small police contingent reinforced by mounted troopers failed to stop the marchers reaching the Domain. Jennie and other speakers addressed the crowd, which sang 'The Red Flag'.[61]

The conservative press described the events in lurid headlines—the *Daily Mail* led with 'Bolshevik Outbreak: Police and Soldiers Badly Mauled'—stirring violent responses.

Fifteen men involved in the Red Flag march were charged under Commonwealth law and most were sentenced to six months jail.[62] Jennie campaigned for their release, arguing that carrying red flags was not a demonstration of Bolshevism but a display of the Labor Party colour, and that the procession had been a protest against continuation of the War Precautions Act.[63] Soon after her appeal and those of other organisations, the men began to be released from prison. The Red Flag prisoners showed their appreciation by presenting Jennie with a leather handbag, which is now in the National Library of Australia's collection. It has a metal plaque inscribed with the prisoners' thanks on the front and an embossed plaque on the back featuring a bird and native foliage. The inscription reads: 'Presented to Mrs Scott Griffiths in a token of esteem from Red Flag prisoners, Brisbane, Australia 1919'.[64]

Return to America

The Red Flag march was Jennie's final public effort in Australia. Disillusioned at what she saw as an increasing trend towards conservatism, and able to get only occasional jobs in journalism (she did not write or have any material published on the Red Flag Riots), Jennie, her husband and most of their family returned to live in Texas in 1920. However, finding only a poor, hard future ahead of them, they settled in San Francisco.[65] For the rest of her life Jennie was a contributor to the *Industrial Worker,* where she was known principally as a poet expressing worker views. She also became a contributor to the *San Francisco Examiner* and other local papers on a semi-permanent basis.[66] She continued to be involved in reformist causes, working for an Equal Rights Amendment to the United States Constitution and supporting commemorative events for American pioneer feminist Susan B. Anthony. She was always ready to spring to the defence of those she regarded as wrongly imprisoned, like the American militant socialist Tom Mooney. In 1928, both Jennie, who had lost her United States citizenship when she married, and her husband, were naturalised.[67]

Jennie continued her life of activism and writing until her death on 29 June 1951 in San Francisco. The *Industrial Worker* described her as 'a lifelong fighter and worker for a better world',[68] and her son, Don, as 'an outstanding speaker on behalf of the less fortunate people in society'.[69] Her daughter, Ciwa, who pioneered a new method of teaching deaf children and founded the HEAR Center in California in 1954, dedicated her family memoir, *One of Ten*, to her mother.[70]

Jennie Scott Griffiths and Stella Allan—who we meet in the next chapter—are examples of contrasting reactions to positions taken by their employers—whether to stick with their views, or toe the line and keep their job. This was a conundrum that affected women journalists to a greater extent a century ago when their mere acceptance in the profession was still problematic.

Stella Allan

Women's page editor

Stella Allan's journalistic career began spectacularly in New Zealand when male journalists refused her entry to the parliamentary press gallery in Wellington. She was then a young, committed socialist and feminist. Her story reveals the social, patriarchal and career influences that led to her transformation to a conservative, establishment figure who edited the women's pages for three decades. It shows the stultifying effects of women's page journalism, and the influence of a notably conservative newspaper on Stella's social and political views. She also conformed to the conservative views of her husband, pointing to the social and gender pressures at the beginning of the twentieth century. Yet Stella, known as Vesta, built up the women's pages of the Melbourne Argus *from a column to a major section. She created many opportunities for women journalists and became a feted and revered figure.*

Early life and background

Stella May Henderson was born on 25 October 1871 at Kaiapoi, about 17 kilometres north of Christchurch in the Canterbury region of the South Island of New Zealand. She was the seventh of nine children of Daniel Henderson, from Wick, Caithness, on the north-eastern coast of Scotland, and his wife, Alice (nee Conolly), a native of Adare, County Limerick, in the south-west of Ireland. Her father, a great admirer of Dean Swift's writing, gave her the name of Stella to honour Swift's book, *A Journal to Stella*. Her mother added May for 'a fine bush' of pure white may that was blooming in the garden at the time of her daughter's birth.[1] Her parents had married on 29 August 1859 in Albury, New South Wales,[2] where Daniel was a draper and Alice a clerk. Their first child, Alice Elinor, was born at Albury in 1860 and their second, Christina Kirk, in 1861 at Emerald Hill, Melbourne.

A few years later, the family moved to Auckland, New Zealand. By the late 1860s, they were living at Kaiapoi where Daniel ran a store, then at Ashburton, on the Canterbury Plains, 86 kilometres south of Christchurch.

Stella's education began at Ashburton school, where from 1878 her two eldest sisters, Alice and Christina, were pupil teachers. When she was 11, the family moved to Christchurch to give the younger children better education opportunities. At 12, she gained a scholarship to Christchurch Girls' High School, where her sister Christina taught Latin and English under the principal, Helen Connan, a pioneer in the education of women in New Zealand and one of the first women graduates in the British Empire.[3] In 1888, at the age of 17, Stella won a junior scholarship to Canterbury College, one of the four colleges constituting the University of New Zealand. She completed a Bachelor of Arts in 1892 and was awarded a college exhibition for excellence in political science. The following year she gained a Master of Arts with first class honours in English and Latin. While studying at university she taught cookery at Christchurch Girls' High, and cooking remained a lifelong interest.[4]

The Henderson children grew up in a family with strict Presbyterian beliefs. They lived in frugal circumstances, particularly after the death of Daniel in 1886. Several of seven girls in the family became active feminists and socialists, including Christina, who advocated for equal pay for women.[5] Stella and her younger sister, Elizabeth, joined Christina as members of a Christchurch socialist club, known as the Socialist Church. All three were on the committee of the Progressive Liberal Association, one of whose goals was the removal of political and civil discrimination against women. In 1898, Stella was selected as the association's delegate to the annual conference of the New Zealand

National Council of Women in Wellington where she gave a paper on local government reform. While in Wellington she spoke on 'Municipal Socialism' at a socialist rally held near the wharves. Described as 'the first woman to address an open-air meeting in New Zealand on a social and political subject', she attracted a 'numerous and sympathetic audience', despite showery weather.[6]

Later that month at a meeting of the Christchurch Socialist Church she supported the 'sweeping away of the capitalistic system as it now prevails' and moved a motion urging the immediate appointment of a judge for the Arbitration Court. The meeting finished with the singing of 'some Socialistic battle hymns'.[7] The following month she spoke at the Canterbury Women's Institute on removing civil and political discrimination against women. In various other forums she argued for the removal of restrictions on the education, employment and freedom of women. She campaigned for the extension of universal suffrage to local government elections, for all women and men to be eligible to stand for election, and for public ownership of community services.[8]

Parliamentary reporter

After graduating with a Master of Arts in 1893, Stella Henderson worked in a Christchurch law firm, Izard and Loughnan, and studied law. However, at the time, women were not eligible to practise. Her employer, William Izard, lobbied for a private member's bill to be introduced into the New Zealand Parliament to allow women to be admitted as barristers and solicitors. In 1896, the Female Law Practitioners Act was passed. Stella finished her law degree soon after, but before she was admitted to the bar, Samuel Saunders, the editor of the liberal Christchurch daily, the *Lyttelton Times*, offered her the position of parliamentary correspondent and political leader writer to report on the national parliament in Wellington. First published in 1851 soon after the arrival of European settlers, the *Lyttelton Times* moved to Christchurch in 1863 but retained the name of the port of Lyttelton until it was renamed the *Christchurch Times* in 1929. It was one of the principal papers in the Canterbury region until it ceased publication in 1935.

Stella described Saunders' approach as 'the most wonderful offer ever made to an untrained journalist'. It meant a seat in the press gallery in the New Zealand Parliament, 'one of the prizes of the profession'. Many journalist members of the all-male press gallery 'were furiously angry that a woman should try to invade this "holy of holies"'.[9] When Saunders wrote to the president of the press gallery asking that the *Lyttelton Times'* seat be allotted to Stella, the members voted 11 to 4 against her admission,[10] claiming that a female would need separate working accommodation and a special 'retiring room'. However, a press report at the time clearly shows that the real objection was the fear that women entering a previously all-male section of the profession would lead to lower wage rates, as had already occurred in several other occupations.[11] There was similar opposition in Australia to Louisa Lawson's employment of female typesetters when she began her pioneering periodical in 1888. This ostensible opposition was on the grounds that the women's health would suffer.[12]

New Zealand newspaper editors joined Saunders in a letter to the Speaker of the House stating that they would not be dictated to on their choice of journalist and must be free to appoint the ablest person. The Speaker referred the dispute to the Reporting Debates and Printing Committee of the House. In the meantime, Stella took notes of parliamentary proceedings from a seat in the ladies gallery, balancing a notebook on her knees. She wired her dispatches and leaders from the ladies tea room as other women chatted around her. The dispute was 'resolved' by the erection of a partition, providing a special cubicle for her use.[13] As a result she became 'well-known throughout the colony' for her fight for gender equality,[14] and the Christchurch *Star* reported that her battle on behalf of female reporters had 'furnished the London papers with quite a nice supply of copy'.[15] For the next two years Stella continued in this groundbreaking job as the first female parliamentary reporter in either New Zealand or Australia. She also continued her involvement with the National Council of Women and many other organisations, speaking on diverse subjects, including neglected children, temperance, and federation with the Australian colonies.

During her second year as parliamentary reporter Stella became engaged to Edwin Frank Allan, a leader writer on the Wellington *Evening Post*, at that time the leading New Zealand newspaper. Unlike the liberal *Lyttelton Times*, the *Post* supported conservative policies and this created problems in their relationship. Stella wrote that after announcing their engagement, Edwin 'made a point of ignoring' her, bypassing her in the corridors of parliament without acknowledging her, to reinforce the opposing political agendas of their papers. 'The difference in his attitude was most pronounced,' she wrote. 'So I realised that it "would not work" for husband and wife to support different parties in politics.'[16] Stella resigned from her hard-won position with the *Lyttelton Times*, incurring the fury of Saunders who had fought for her right to break through the gender barrier. Her decision is an indication of the force of psychological and social pressures to conform to the prevailing norm of male dominance in marriage, which was felt even by a woman who until then had forged extraordinary independence in her professional life.

On 6 March 1900, Stella Henderson, aged 28, and Edwin Frank Allan, 32, were married in Christchurch. Edwin was born in Stockwell, London. He was the youngest son of Frank Allan, a tea merchant of Dumford Manor Farm, Sussex. Edwin was an outstanding student at Westminster School and Oxford University. In 1891, he joined the British foreign service and was posted to the British Embassy in Peking (Beijing). Five years later he became ill and, following a breakdown in health, he resigned his position and moved to New Zealand to recuperate. Although he made a partial recovery, he did not regain robust health.[17] In Wellington, his knowledge of international affairs attracted the interest of the editor of the *Evening Post*, Gresley Lukin, a former managing editor of the *Brisbane Courier* and the *Queenslander*,[18] who offered him the position of senior leader writer. Edwin quickly established a reputation as 'one of the best-informed ablest journalists in the colony'.[19] After her marriage Stella Allan continued to be involved in public life, speaking on many subjects. When she spoke on temperance reform, however, a newspaper report described her as a 'women's righter whose identity has been swallowed up in marriage'.[20] Her younger sister, Elizabeth McCombs, under no similar pressure, remained a committed socialist and was elected a Labor member and the first female member of the New Zealand Parliament in 1933.[21]

As the Boxer Rebellion unfolded in China in 1899 and foreign embassies in Peking were besieged, Edwin's Chinese expertise became increasingly valuable. Editors in both Australia and New Zealand inundated him with requests for articles on China. They were eager to tap his intimate knowledge of the country and the identities involved in the crisis. This culminated in the editor of the Melbourne *Argus* visiting Wellington to offer him a position as leader writer on the paper.

The prospect of a move to Melbourne presented another crisis for Stella who, after her marriage, had become the New Zealand correspondent for the *Brisbane Courier* and for an unspecified 'leading London paper'.[22] She had also planned to begin a legal practice with Edwin who was completing legal qualifications in Wellington. Several newspaper reports had already named her as the first female lawyer to begin a practice in New Zealand. Nevertheless, the offer from the prestigious Melbourne *Argus*, the Mecca of journalism, was difficult to resist. Stella described her dilemma as 'a cruel one', but she decided to support her husband as she felt she could not stand in the way of 'the ablest man I had ever met'.[23]

Journalist on the *Argus*

The Allans and their first child, Alice, born in December 1902, sailed for Melbourne on the *Monowai* in September 1903. In Melbourne, women involved in intellectual, social and philanthropic organisations welcomed Stella and her journalistic experience and legal qualifications. She became a friend of Pattie Deakin, the Prime Minister's wife, who was a leader in organisations that were concerned with the needs of children. Stella also became a friend of Dr Constance Ellis, a prominent medical practitioner and honorary pathologist at Queen Victoria Hospital for Women, who became godmother to one of the Allan children. Stella followed the novelist Ada Cambridge as the second president of the Victorian Women Writers' Club. Like Pattie Deakin, Stella also served as president of the Lyceum Club, a club for women of achievement with which the Writers' Club merged. When the Australian Journalists' Association was formed in 1910, Stella was a foundation member.

Stella's journalistic career was settled within a week of her arrival in Melbourne when she was asked to write a sub-leader for the *Argus*.

Although she claimed this made her the first woman to contribute to its leader columns, Florence Blair (later Baverstock) had contributed *Argus* leaders in the 1890s.[24] Stella described the subject matter of her first contribution as trifling but, although she wrote many leaders later, none gave her 'quite such a thrill'.[25] Some months later she was asked to contribute a regular weekly book-review column as well as special articles—her first 'Fiction of the Day' column appeared in April 1904.[26]

In 1907, after she had organised the first Australian Exhibition of Women's Work, held at the Melbourne Exhibition Building, with Patti Deakin and other prominent women, the managing director of the *Argus* commissioned Stella to write a series on the exhibits. Her articles began in mid-October in the build-up to the opening on 23 October 1907 and continued almost daily until the exhibition closed at the end of November. Her coverage was so successful that she was engaged to contribute a regular Wednesday women's feature.

In May 1908, by then the mother of four daughters, Stella was appointed to the journalistic staff to write and edit a women's section for the *Argus* and its weekly associate, the *Australasian*. Her regular 'Women to Women' feature, signed 'Vesta' (Roman goddess of hearth and household), was to be a feature of the *Argus* for 30 years.[27] At first her single column appeared only weekly, but within a few years it had expanded to several columns, and later it covered four pages daily. When she had been at the paper for 15 years, Stella's title was Social Editress, and she had a staff of five women journalists, including Molly Trait, Bunty Wheeler and her daughter Patricia Allan.[28] The expansion of Vesta's column to several pages showed that it was attracting large numbers of readers, and this led to its being underwritten by increasing numbers of advertisements. The British press baron Lord Northcliffe noted this causal effect in an address in 1912:

The coming of the woman writer in her hundreds has brought the woman reader in her millions; and the coming of the woman reader has developed the advertiser, upon whom all of us journalists, however lofty we may think ourselves, depend for our existence.[29]

Vesta's columns covered domestic topics and community welfare issues. However, many women readers most valued the knowledgeable, commonsense replies to inquirers seeking information, advice and help. Although the subject of Stella's first column—domestic service—was unexceptional, she included the innovative approach of inviting letters from readers. This tapped into a previously almost silent readership and the result was an avalanche of letters. Her technique of involving readers became standard in women's pages and magazines, but at the time it was unusual. Her correspondence became so vast that the *Argus* provided extra staff to help with replies.[30]

Conservatism of the *Argus*

Apart from strong involvement with her readers, the other feature of Stella's columns was the conservative, confined choice of subjects. They were far removed from Stella's radical youth and her own pioneering career choices. At most she advocated for reforms of a moderately forward-looking nature, such as the provision of creches and kindergartens. The extremely conservative paper for which she wrote influenced her choice of subjects and the opinions she expressed. Until the ownership changed in its last years, the *Argus* maintained a 'conservative and establishment-oriented political and cultural stance'. It was part of 'the establishment' and put forward the views of 'establishment interests, that is, the wealthy'.[31] For nearly 40 years, from 1888, it was controlled by Sir Lauchlan Mackinnon, a key Victorian establishment figure. Stella's husband, as a senior leader writer, was closely allied with the views of the *Argus* hierarchy, and her columns conformed.

The way she handled the conscription issue during the First World War shows her strident support for the paper's strong pro-conscription stance. The defeat of the first conscription referendum, held on 28 October 1916, seemed beyond her comprehension—it was a failure of voters, she believed, 'to face the problem before them in the true spirit of citizenship'. She put this down to a failure of education:

> *A sufficient time has not elapsed, since free compulsory education became the order of the day, to secure what we are pleased to call an educated electorate.*[32]

She was more strident still in the lead-up to the second referendum, held on 20 December 1917, attacking arguments for the 'No' case.[33]

It is more surprising to find that Stella modified her view on such a key feminist goal as women's suffrage. In 1917, commenting on a report of a British commission on electoral reform, which recommended only limited women's suffrage, she wrote:

> *I began by being a keen suffragist, and with high hopes of what women's suffrage might accomplish ... We cannot point to any good that it has accomplished ... I think* [universal women's suffrage] *has proved a mistake in Australia ... a large proportion of our women are incapable of voting intelligently.*

She advised the British that to 'double the number of ignorant voters by granting the suffrage at once to all women would be an irretrievable mistake'. She blamed universal suffrage and the failure of universal education (neither of which was universal enough to extend to Indigenous Australians) for the defeat of the conscription referendums:

> *I have no hesitation in saying that universal suffrage in Australia is responsible for our failure to do our full duty in the war, our*

extravagant way of running the country, [and] the absorption of our politicians in party conflicts and intrigues, when the safety of the Empire is at stake.[34]

Women's page journalism

The stifling effect of women's page journalism also wore down the radical stance of Stella's early years. The earliest women writers on newspapers were employed in all aspects of journalism. Even as late as 1891, an article in the *Illustrated Sydney News* stated that women employed on newspapers, were:

doing widely varied ... arduous, journalistic work with a facility for putting pen to any and every topic under the sun, that may happen to crop up and absorb, for the moment, the attention or curiosity of the news reading public.[35]

When Catherine Helen Spence visited America in 1894, she was proud to be writing on general topics for Australian newspapers, in contrast to American women journalists who, she found, were confined to women's page journalism.[36] By then Spence's experience was not typical of Australian women journalists.

The situation of women employed on newspapers changed in the latter part of the nineteenth century when Australian periodicals and newspapers began to publish articles and items aimed at women readers. At first these columns comprised pieces culled from other sources, such as books of recipes or overseas newspapers, and editors saw no necessity to employ women journalists to cobble them together. However, once newspapers and periodicals began printing local news for and about women, they were employed to write and edit these pages. This opened a larger and more regular avenue of employment for women journalists. Although this was an advance, it was also a backward step for women's involvement in general reporting.[37]

Soon almost all women journalists were confined to the narrow field of what were regarded as women's topics, described graphically in a *Bulletin* note as the 'deadly, dreary ruck of long dress reports and the lists of those who "also ran" at miscellaneous functions'.[38] Women journalists were not the only losers in this situation because what they wrote tended to reinforce complacency in their women readers and shield them from issues of wider significance. Their articles were angled at the supposed interests of the traditional middle-class, stay-at-home housewife, an image that was very different from the journalists' own lives as working women.

Ironically, the expansion of women's pages in the late nineteenth century was partly a result of the publicity attached to suffrage campaigns and other women's issues which made women more newsworthy. Social changes—including the expansion of shops into department stores and the increasing availability of new household equipment and ready-made clothing—ensured an increase in advertising revenue to support these pages. The rise of New Journalism—characterised by large headlines, prominent illustrations, 'lively writing' and display advertisements—also influenced the expansion of women's pages and created a demand for women journalists to write 'human interest' stories.[39]

The contrast between the material published in most women's sections and the reporting of the 'real', often disturbing news on other pages of the same paper—a world that included violence, rape, hunger and domestic abuse—is a feature of this era of journalism. A female reader was meant to be satisfied with household hints and reports of society events. However, on other pages she could read of a man hung for repeated and violent incest, of abandoned babies, of a coroner commenting on the extraordinary amount of child murders, or veiled references to failed backyard abortions. The social problems underlying these reports were ignored in the women's pages.[40] Women journalists by and large supported the dominant view among male journalists that the women's pages were the only journalistic work they were capable of.[41] This view was expressed in many forums, from a review of the publication *Ladies at Work* in 1894[42] to an article in the *Journalist* in 1944.[43] Stella was part of this world. The conservative social message in her columns and her mild attempts to come to terms with fundamental social and feminist issues were part of a pattern that continued long after she left the *Argus*.

Emergence as a public figure

Stella's writing appeared less in the *Argus* during 1921, at a time when her husband was becoming increasingly affected by a progressive disease that restricted his mobility, although he continued to work at the *Argus* until the end of the First World War. He died on 1 February 1922 of locomotor ataxia.[44] Many high-ranking members of the management and literary staff of the *Argus*, and prominent public figures were present at his funeral at Brighton Cemetery, a tribute not only to Edwin but also to his widow, who was left with 4 daughters: Alice, 19, Patricia, 17, Elizabeth, 16, and Helen, 14. Pallbearers included the chairman of the *Argus* and *Australasian*, Sir Lauchlan Mackinnon, the Secretary of the Commonwealth Attorney-General's Department, Sir Robert Garran, and the editor of the *Argus*, Dr E.H. Cunningham.[45]

In the following years, Stella became a public figure while maintaining responsibility for the expanding women's pages. In 1924, the then Prime Minster, S.M. Bruce, appointed her substitute delegate to the League of Nations Conference in Geneva.[46] On her return she warned that the 'starving, homeless millions' in other countries would challenge Australia's right to keep a huge continent for six million people.[47] In 1930, she was a delegate to the Pan-Pacific Women's Conference in Hawaii. In 1938, to mark the end of her third decade on the *Argus*, Victorian women's organisations gathered at Melbourne Town Hall to thank her for her work for the community, and especially for women and children.[48] Her daughter, Patricia, wrote that her mother had:

> *created a new field of newspaper journalism directed especially to meet the needs of women in their personal and domestic lives, and to stimulate and encourage interest and responsibilities outside the home, in matters of public concern.*[49]

The conservative, confined scope of Stella's women's pages continued long after she retired. In the 1950s, a journalist on the *Argus* described 'the bread and butter of female journalists' work' as:

> *The comings and goings of the Victorian aristocracy and upper classes [with] a constant and solid coverage of the society balls and diplomatic parties, the glamorous theatre opening nights when ball gowns and bow ties were the norm, the returning ocean-liners carrying wealthy Victorian passengers and interesting international visitors as well as mandatory racing, hunt and polo meets.*[50]

After she retired as Vesta in 1938, Stella moved to England and continued to write for the *Argus*, contributing articles on the experiences of women and children in the Second World War. In 1947, she returned to Melbourne where she died on 1 March 1962 at the age of 90.[51]

In recent years, her induction into the Media Hall of Fame established her importance as a leader in women's journalism who expanded the employment of women journalists. Some remained women's page journalists all their working lives, others used their exemplary training under Stella Allan to grasp wider opportunities. One of the journalists who features in a later chapter in this book, Patricia Knox, began work on the *Argus* women's pages before moving to general reporting during the Second World War.

Frances Taylor

Independent and adventurous editor

Soon after the end of the First World War, Frances Taylor, founder of women's monthly journal Woman's World, *dressed as a young man to search for stories in Rabaul's Chinatown. Travelling to exotic destinations was one of the innovative approaches she used in her new publication to promote female independence. Frances edited, produced and managed* Woman's World *with no financial backing and no editorial help. Against the odds it flourished, and within four years of launching it had 12,000 readers.[1] Her combination of traditional women's magazine topics, such as homemaking and fashion, with her vision of gender equality suited the new world of freedom that had opened for women in the 1920s. She promoted her vision of feminist independence by publicising women travelling to foreign destinations, taking gender-defying occupations, and motoring and building weekenders. To this she added her own pioneering approach of using radio broadcasts to publicise* Woman's World *and attract readers.*

The 1920s was a liberating era for many young women, including Frances Taylor. She rode a horse on a solo journey of nearly 700 kilometres from the north-west of Victoria to Melbourne, built a weekender in the hills outside Melbourne, drove her small car on a challenging interstate trek, and turned her risky venture editing and managing a new women's magazine into a huge success.

Australia had a noteworthy history of women starting feminist periodicals, beginning with Lawson's *The Dawn*, which was edited and produced by an entirely female workforce. From its first issue in Sydney in 1888, and through the 1890s depression to 1905, *The Dawn* was supported by subscriptions and advertising, allowing it to remain a viable, commercial publication. In 1894, Maybanke Wolstenholme began a fortnightly paper called *The Woman's Voice*, which, like Lawson's paper, employed women compositors and printers. Wolstenholme's major campaign during the publication's 18-month existence was women's suffrage, but in her editorial column and in other articles she raised many other issues concerning women's health, education and employment. They included the need for a women's hospital, reform of marriage laws, employment of female police officers and the advantages of cycling, which was seen as a liberating force giving women independent movement.

A few decades later, Frances followed with ideas suited to the 1920s. She had the sporty look and bobbed haircut of the flapper era that symbolised independence and strength, and equality with men. Her friends knew her as The Midge because, so a fellow journalist wrote, she carried so much journalistic sting to the square inch and she whirred gaily from adventure to adventure.[2] Her confidence and courageous spirit were never more evident than when, only six months after she began her magazine, she set out to bring her readers reports from the little-known outpost of New Guinea. She backed her judgment that 'the intelligent woman' would want to read about little-known places within Australia's sphere, even if journeys such as hers were out of reach for most women. Most of her readers were housewives and mothers, and Frances catered for their day-to-day issues with the regular inclusion of homemaking hints, fashion, health and baby care. However, the emphasis of her journal remained on what women were achieving and what could be within their reach.

Early life and background

Irene Frances Taylor was born on 17 December 1890 at St Kilda, Victoria. She was a daughter of Reverend Edward Taylor and his wife,

Alice (nee Mumford). Her father was a graduate of Chesthunt Non-Conformist Theological College, north-east London. When she was a young child her father moved to the ministry at Port Chalmers, New Zealand, where she attended primary school and later Otago Girls' High School in Dunedin.[3] By 1905, her father was back in Melbourne as minister in the inner suburb of Richmond and Frances completed her education at Presbyterian Ladies College in 1907.[4] Frances' friend, journalist Stella Allan, credited her 'Puritan upbringing' with giving her 'the self-command and strictness of judgment' that allowed her to make use of her great powers of thought and initiative.[5]

After school, Frances left Melbourne to take a job as secretary to the manager and editor of the *Mildura Cultivator*, one of the three local papers that in 1920 formed the *Sunraysia Daily*. She may have been drawn to Mildura because of a family association with Harry Samuel Taylor, a congregational lay preacher who was editor and publisher of the nearby *Renmark Pioneer*, later the *Murray Pioneer*.[6] He had been a young member of William Lane's party that established the utopian socialist settlement New Australia in Paraguay, and was one of those who went with Lane and Mary Gilmore in the breakaway group which founded Cosme colony.[7]

In Mildura, Frances began to establish herself as a freelance journalist and writer of short stories and sketches, which were published in Australia and overseas.[8] She gained valuable experience in layout, editing and advertising, which were vital to her emergence as an editor in Melbourne.[9] She also became a friend of Ruth Hollick, an adventurous young woman who made a living as a travelling photographer in her small car, which she had to hand crank at every start.[10] During the First World War, Hollick moved to Melbourne where she became a leading photographer. When Frances began her periodical, Hollick's study of Dame Nellie Melba was the cover of the first issue, and her photographs featured in many subsequent issues.[11]

Frances left Mildura in 1916 on a solo horseback ride. She covered nearly 700 kilometres to the outskirts of Melbourne in 12 days. In her diary she recorded the name of the town she reached each day, the distance she travelled, the cost of food and accommodation when staying in a hotel, and the names of people she met or stayed with, occasionally adding a note about the journey. In 1979, nearly 50 years after her death, Mrs B. Garrett donated Frances' diary of her trip to the State Library of Victoria, with a letter explaining that Frances had made the ride to 'break or establish' a record.[12] Breaking a record may have been Frances' initial impetus but the main outcome of her ride was her deep understanding of the needs of country women.[13]

Between her return to Melbourne and the start of *Woman's World*, Frances gained further experience in editing, publishing and financing publications through her work as editor of two different periodicals. Her first editorial position was at the *Southern Grocer of Australasia* (later the *Australasian Grocer*), the trade journal of the Grocers' Association of Victoria. This role introduced her to the commercial as well as the professional aspects of magazine production. Then, at the beginning of 1919, she was appointed editor of *The Gum Tree*, which was devoted 'to the conservation, propagation and utilisation of Australian trees', which tapped into a different demographic for articles and advertisements.[14] She continued editing *The Gum Tree* until the late 1920s and was made an honorary member of the League of Tree Lovers.[15]

Planning *Woman's World*

Frances planned her monthly for women during an enforced break following an injury in a tram accident in 1920, which she spent in the rough rural hut that she built at Kangaroo Ground in the Yarra Valley outside Melbourne. Her aim for *Woman's World* was 'to provide the intelligent Australian with an up-to-date paper dealing with the latest developments in the world of women'. Housewives and mothers made up most of the likely readers, but she also aimed at working women like herself and her woman friends: 'a new type of woman, well-educated, ambitious and resolutely middle-class'.[16] Among her friends were some of Melbourne's early women journalists, who met for lunch at what became known as the 'Press Gang' table at the Lyceum Club, a social club for professional women. Regular lunchgoers included Melbourne's influential journalist and editor of the women's section of the *Argus*, Stella Allan. Other lunch-goers were Molly Trait, and Allan's daughter, Patricia, from the *Argus* women's page staff, Kathleen Syme from the *Age*, Barbara Katz from the *Sun*, Edith Allen from the *Herald*, and well-known writer and lawyer Anna Brennan. Even in this high-powered group, Frances was 'at the centre of all lively conversation'.[17] Networking not only led to friendships but also to likely stories and authors, and access to useful connections.[18]

Dressed in a tailor-made suit and a Woodrow-style hat (a soft-peaked, wool-felt hat made for lady motorists),[19] and armed with her dummy magazine with no text but with indications of section headings and spaces available for advertisements, Frances got her monthly off the ground by soliciting business houses in the city. 'Without capital or business influence,' Anna Brennan wrote, 'she inspired sufficient confidence to induce business firms to give advertisements to her "skeleton" magazine.'[20] A later editor, Betty MacMillan, attributed Frances' success to her 'persuasive efforts and her clear conception of what a woman's magazine could achieve'.[21] As she planned the magazine, Frances referred to the books she had acquired on magazine production, colour printing, layout and advertising.[22] After canvassing by day, she prepared the contents at night. She kept costs to a minimum by writing a considerable part of the magazine herself. She used several pseudonyms, most frequently Jane Townsend for articles on practical housekeeping and home furnishing, keeping her own name or her initials 'I.F.T.' for general subjects and interviews with prominent women and visiting celebrities. On the day of publication each month, she worked until 2.30am, then walked with the copy to the printers. She got to know the policeman on the beat so well that he often accompanied her.[23]

The first issue of *Woman's World: An Illustrated Monthly for Australian Women*, published on 1 December 1921, was an impressive, well-illustrated publication of 40 pages. Frances described *Woman's World* as 'neither a fashion journal nor a society paper', non-sectarian and non-political. She promised 'the latest developments in the world of women', interviews with prominent women, coverage of individual women in work and sport, the activities of women's societies, women's work in professions, trades and crafts, and articles on domestic architecture and labour-saving devices. The issue included the start of several series including 'Palette and Pen' on art, craft and books, and another on child and baby care. Within a few issues she had included children's stories by well-known children's author and journalist Mary Grant Bruce, and articles on music and the theatre.

Appeal to country women

From the start, *Woman's World* set out to appeal to country women. In the first issue, Frances described her ride from the north-western boundary of the state to the capital in 1916, which left her with the memory of scores of women pioneers and an insight into their trials.

During one stop she invented a milk cooler from a kerosene tin for a sick mother,[24] and many women entrusted her with requests for goods and services that were not available in the country. One asked her where she could buy a certain type of baby's feeding bottle, another where she could locate a pipe of a 'truly weird and wonderful' design to give to her husband and another asked for information on the quality of a particular material. When she got to Melbourne, she carried out these requests and many others. However, there was one that she could not fulfil from a young country girl who wanted her to check on the whereabouts and faithfulness of her lover who had left the bush for Melbourne and had not been heard from since.[25]

These requests made a big impact on Frances and became part of her plans for her publication. She undertook to provide practical solutions through a 'special buying service' to overcome the inability of country women 'to personally conduct' their shopping.[26] Frances knew 'the mothers in the bush,' a friend wrote, and would take endless pains for 'a woman in a shack in the Mallee with £1 to spend'.[27] She also offered to purchase articles from contributors on women in all fields of work, labour-saving schemes, household management, current issues and 'bright Australian sketches'. She gradually built up a stable of regular contributors and engaged women canvassers to sell subscriptions in country districts. A friend who witnessed the start of *Woman's World* wrote of 'the trials and tribulations, the alarums and excursions and the amazing enthusiasm and bravery of its growing years'.[28]

Exotic destinations

The prominence of travel articles in the early years of *Woman's World* catered to a desire among women for freedom and independence and escape from convention. Just a few months after the monthly launched,

Frances began publishing a series of articles on islands in the Pacific by an intrepid Melbourne woman traveller, Flos Greig, the first woman to graduate in law in Victoria. Greig travelled with her companion, Alys Jones, to Norfolk Island, the New Hebrides and New Caledonia, writing a series of articles about their adventures which were published between April and October 1922.[29] In mid-1922, Frances set off on her own adventure to write articles on New Guinea—a brave step for an editor and manager of a new periodical with an uncertain future. The former German New Guinea was an unknown exotic land to most Australians. Australian naval forces had seized New Guinea at the start of the First World War. Under the postwar Treaty of Versailles, it had become an Australian Mandated Territory.

At the capital Rabaul, Frances dressed as a man by wearing a tropical riding costume and an Australian Army officer's helmet. She set out to explore the 'restlessness, wickedness and mystery' of Chinatown after dark. By day, Chinatown was the chief business centre and an important trading centre in the Pacific. At night, vice was an allure amid the throbbing sounds, lights and scents of its crowded streets and ramshackle buildings. As Frances explored the network of alleyways through wafts of incense and opium pipes, she described Chinatown as 'openly wicked', but nowhere does she mention brothels.[30] Prostitution and sex slavery may not have been the usual fare of women's pages in the 1920s, but it is surprising that she did not raise these subjects such as these given they were a concern to women's groups in Australia and overseas. Perhaps it was a step too far for a fledgling magazine.

Frances also travelled to the Witu Islands, a sparsely populated volcanic group in the Bismarck Sea. She rode through thick jungle tracks on a Macassan pony to explore an island that had a native population still decimated by the effects of a smallpox epidemic and a European population of only five males and no females.[31] Back in Rabaul, she dressed more conventionally to interview newsworthy women, including Mrs Wisdom, wife of the Administrator, Brigadier General Evan Wisdom, and Mrs Kaumann, who ran an extensive coconut plantation near Rabaul. Frances also interviewed an altruistic young woman, Margaret Bechervaise, who had left a teaching career in Geelong to teach in a small isolated village on the coast of Papua.[32] On the way home to Melbourne, Frances travelled in the Northern Territory and across the Nullarbor, writing about people and places that were almost as unknown and inaccessible as New Guinea was to Australian readers in the early 1920s.[33] *Woman's World* continued the travel theme with another series by Flo Greig from Java, Batavia (Jakarta), Sourabaya and Bali, and from Singapore, Penang and Rangoon. When she returned, Greig gave lectures illustrated with lantern slides and talks on radio stations across Australia.

Motoring route to independence

Catering to a similar desire in women to savour independence, Frances included many articles on motoring. In one issue a page of photographs of women in their Austin 7s sat opposite an article on 'Driving the Light Car',[34] and an interview with the first woman to race her own car in a motordrome. Articles on repairing and maintaining a motor car also featured. In 1927, Frances related her own motoring adventure, driving from Melbourne to Canberra with her companion Molly Trait in her Austin 7, to attend the opening on 9 May of federal parliament by the Duke of York. After negotiating 800 kilometres of meandering bush roads, she described her happiness and that of other car travellers from Victoria as they gathered at night around a camp fire in the paddocks near the new building. She wrote:

Like many another Victorian, I first saw the Capital City at night, though, like many another Victorian I had been planned to be there well before sunset; but the long 500-mile trail ended in a natural Australian bush road, which wound a devious way, in that happy, impractical fashion that old bush roads have which began their lives as stock routes ...

With the palest of infant moons above, its light challenged by a myriad stars, our car rose and dipped through the hills that shelter Canberra, until, topping a rise, out of a sudden blackness we saw the light from scores of windows of the great Government buildings, streaming into the night. Stranger, and more beautiful still was the sight of the winding hill road, lit by the brilliant headlights of incoming cars. From our vantage-point, we could see them circling Canberra, coming in for miles; from north, south, east and west. Nothing could have given us a more vital sense of the isolation of this, Australia's brand new city, that was grown up before it was born, and never passed through its growing pains as an adolescent township.

Blazing on the hills facing Federal Parliament House were the long lines of camp fires, where the motorists from far States were pitching their tents. Here was the spirit of the fine Australian comradeship that exists between those who set out on a fine adventure. The greatest discomforts were laughed at, mud and water were wiped from the engine, broken springs were mended with wire, hungry motorists shared their thermoses and their biscuits, everything was worthwhile to that band of enthusiasts, and that was the very spirit of Canberra ...
In the cold frosty morning, men struggled to shave in cold water beside their cars and one woman was shocked to find her false teeth embedded in a glass of water while another wrestled with a Primus stove.
At last, shaved and brushed, powdered and curled, and praying that

the sun would remove the creases from our best clothes, we arrived on the stand. No pen could describe, no brush could paint the beauty of that morning—clear and still, with the sun melting the white frost from the lawns. Out of all the threatened bad weather came the gift of one perfect day for Canberra. The details of that simple, yet magnificently impressive, ceremony have been printed and reprinted in every paper of the Commonwealth. No one who was there will ever forget the solemnity of the scene ...

A touch of poignant humour was leant by the dramatic entrance of an aged Aboriginal [King Billy], with his string of nondescript dogs, his worldly wealth, trailing behind. His feet were bare, his clothes tatters. He walked to the line of gilded potentates, and informed them that he was King of the Territory.

Independent women

Intermittently, Frances shared with her readers her experience of buying a block of land on Melbourne's outskirts. She portrayed herself as part of a movement of single women who were acquiring cheap, one-acre blocks in the Dandenong Ranges, on which to build small shacks. She described 'scores of mountain cottages of quaint artistic design owned by bachelor women', and in one spot alone in the hills she wrote of five cottages in what was known as 'Spinster Crescent'.[35] Each weekend after changing into breeches and riding boots, a soft shirt and slouch hat, she would catch the last train on Friday night or the first train on Saturday morning on the north-east line from the city to Hurstbridge, 30 kilometres away. Leaving the train at Wattle Glen, she would catch and harness her pony, Tommy, and drive in her dog cart up the narrow, winding, tree-lined road to Kangaroo Ground. Later she followed the same routine in her small motor car.[36]

Woman's World's best years

In its first eight years, *Woman's World* was a vibrant magazine reflecting Frances' original vision. Interstate news and features widened its national appeal and even in Sydney it was described as 'the finest women's paper being produced in Australia today'.[37] Attractively designed with good-quality photographic coverage, *Woman's World* made a feature of its modernist covers, including flower woodprints by Margaret Preston,[38] which became collector's items.

Reader interest was maintained by frequent announcements of new features and series by new writers. There were articles on a female cartoonist, the youngest female barrister in Victoria, a female marine engineer, three female pioneers in film production and female naturalists. Australian women delegates to overseas conferences were almost invariably featured, and they often contributed accounts of their experiences.[39]

When commercial radio stations began, Frances grasped the opportunity to widen the appeal of her publication. Just a few months after 3UZ began transmitting on 8 March 1925, she became a pioneer in the use of radio as a means of publicity and contact with readers. Soon her 'Morning Tea Talks', broadcast each weekday at 11am, were a popular regular feature.[40] 'She sensed the value of wireless broadcasting as a means of friendship,' Anna Brennan wrote.[41]

As *Woman's World* reached a peak in performance, Frances' achievement as the founder and editor became better known to the public. This occurred in a striking manner when she came to the notice of delegates at the Third Imperial Press Conference, a major international event held in Australia in 1925 that generated no less than four books.[42] As delegates from many countries in the British Empire listened to a speaker describe British feminist Lady Rhondda, founder of the London weekly *Time and Tide*, as unique, they were surprised when an interjector told them that Melbourne's Frances Taylor was not only the founder but also the editor and business manager of *Woman's World*.

The following year Frances and Kathleen Gilman Jones, headmistress of Melbourne Girls Grammar, were chosen to represent the Victorian Women's Citizens' Movement at two international conferences in Europe. Leaving Mary Grant Bruce to act as editor of *Woman's World*, Frances attended the tenth International Woman Suffrage Alliance Congress in Paris from 30 May to 6 June 1926 and, a few weeks later, the Empire Conference of Women in London.[43] In England, she had the opportunity to follow up the comparison between her publication and *Time and Tide* when she met Lady Rhondda. She described *Time and Tide* as the only independent woman-owned magazine in the world apart from her own. In a world survey of women's magazines, *Time and Tide* concluded that Frances' position as founder, editor and business manager of a women's magazine was unique. Frances worked for a month in Fleet Street then joined a friend from the Lyceum Club, journalist Kathleen Syme, touring England and Wales for a month in a Ford truck.[44]

More competition from women's periodicals

When she began her monthly, Frances' main competition in attracting country readers came from the weekly editions of capital-city dailies in Melbourne. The weekly *Leader* was the daily *Age*'s stablemate, the weekly *Australasian* was associated with the daily *Argus* and the *Weekly Times* was associated with the daily *Herald*. In Sydney, the independent *Town and Country Journal* had ceased in 1919 but the *Sydney Mail*, the weekly associate of the daily *Sydney Morning Herald*, remained. By the early years of the twentieth century, crusading early women's magazines[45] had given way to magazines published by media interests or established publishers that offered the staples of homemaking, mothercraft, short stories and serials. By the 1920s, *Woman's Budget*, a Sydney publication based on this model, was selling about 95,000 copies per issue.[46] Interstate competition quickened when the *Bulletin* started the weekly *Australian Woman's Mirror* in Sydney on 25 November 1924. There was further competition when, in 1928, the publishers of the long-running *Everylady's Journal* added *New Idea*, which is still being published today.

Following the onset of the Great Depression with a collapse in employment and purchasing power, women faced drastic economising with food and household essentials, and this inevitably affected discretionary expenditure, including the buying of a relatively high-priced monthly. Frances used her radio program to foster a sense of unity, inclusion and a shared purpose. She invited her listeners to help each other by passing on economy hints and recipes, which she broadcast and then publicised in *Woman's World* in a column called 'Let's help each other'. Ideas came from all parts of the country and from suburban and country housewives. One reader sent in a recipe for 'mock duck', which resulted in so many recipes for 'mock' foods that Frances wondered on her program whether there were any 'real' meals in her listeners' menus.[47]

In 1929, Frances appointed Betty MacMillan to the role of editorial assistant. MacMillan was born in Childers, Queensland, the daughter of a Colonial Sugar Refining Company official. Educated at Melbourne Church of England Grammar School, MacMillan's first job was in an advertising agency, before freelancing briefly as a journalist in London. When she returned to Melbourne she continued freelancing for London and Australian papers until she began working at *Woman's World*.[48] From about this time the paper began to rely more on fiction and homemaking articles, although some distinguishing features remained, including the editor's reply to queries and the buying service for country women.

In June 1931, MacMillan was formally named Assistant Editor, coinciding with the price of the publication being cut in half. Although no figures are available, this would appear to be a response to a drastic fall in buyers with its consequent effect on advertisements. *Woman's World* began to include more syndicated serials, a relatively cheap method of reducing costs, which also catered for the need among subscribers for escapist reading as diversion from pressing problems. By 1931, fiction had pride of place in the contents list, and *Woman's World* was proud to be known as 'the Married Women's Paper'.

In terms of circulation, *Woman's World* was a minor player in the battle for mass readership. The success of the *Australian Women's Weekly* dwarfed *Woman's World*, as it did other women's papers. The *Women's Weekly* began in 1933. By the end of the 1930s, it had reached a circulation of 400,000.[49] Frances' accomplishment was on a lesser but still significant scale. It was an achievement just getting her paper to the printer for the first issue and then preventing it from folding, as had been the fate of many periodicals begun like hers without major financial backing. Its 'speedy death' had been foretold as Frances remarked when she celebrated one year's publication.[50]

Ill health and early death

Frances' role decreased as ill health took over. She died on 26 December 1933 in a private hospital in Melbourne, from breast cancer. She was buried two days later at Kangaroo Ground Cemetery near her 'hut in the hills' following a service by Reverend Penry Evans, Minister at the Independent Church in Collins Street. Typical of many articles published following her death, the *Australasian* praised her 'unfaltering courage, initiative and understanding' and remarked on her 'personal magnetism'. The *Argus* described her as 'one of the most distinguished figures in journalism in Australia'.[51]

Woman's World announced her death to readers in the February 1934 issue. Stella Allan wrote a major article entitled 'In Memoriam' and Molly Trait wrote about her 'Home in the Hills'. Shortly after her death the club appealed for donations for the Frances Taylor Gift. Money raised was used to improve the equipment and aftercare of patients in the cancer ward of Melbourne Hospital.[52] Betty MacMillan was appointed managing editor of *Woman's World*. The *Argus* later took over *Woman's World* and continued to publish it until 1954 when the *Argus* closed.

Janet Mitchell

Eyewitness in Harbin

In the early 1930s, Janet Mitchell was in a unique position to report the Japanese occupation of Manchuria (Manzhou), now regarded as a forerunner of the Second World War. She watched as Japanese troops marched into the strategic city of Harbin in January 1932, and observed the League of Nations remain impotent as Japan occupied the province. Unable to leave Harbin for about nine months, she could not send reports to Australian outlets. Her only contact was through family letters. When she reached Australia, she made a series of broadcasts for the Australian Broadcasting Commission, which had been established only six months before. Her revelatory firsthand broadcasts from 'the storm centre of Asia' and her press interviews were widely reported and valued for their analytic, not sensational, reporting. Despite her ability, Janet's opportunities in journalism were precarious and she turned to senior roles in education for intermittent financial security. Her life story illustrates the difficulties highly qualified and dedicated women faced pursuing careers in journalism during the interwar period.

In November 1931, while visiting Peiping (Beijing), Melbourne-born journalist Janet Mitchell came across a street named after her relative, the legendary George ('Chinese') Morrison. Morrison was a former correspondent for the London *Times* and renowned as an influential political adviser to the Chinese Government. Janet decided to contact an Australian journalist, William Henry Donald, who had known her cousin. Donald had been in China since early in the twentieth century, originally in Hong Kong with the *South China Morning Post* and later as a correspondent for the *New York Post* and the *Manchester Guardian* and editor of the *Far Eastern Review*. 'Hullo, cousin-of-Morrison,' Donald greeted her. 'So *you're* one of the scribbling tribe too.'[1]

Janet was in China as a member of the Australian delegation to the Fourth Institute of Pacific Relations Conference and had commissions to write for several Australian papers, including the Melbourne *Argus* and the Sydney *Daily Telegraph*. The conference, originally scheduled to be held in October 1931 in Hangzhou, was moved to Shanghai following the 'Mukden incident'. This event began with an explosion on the railway near Mukden (Shenyang) in Manzhou on 18 September 1931 that had far-reaching consequences. Japan had been granted a lease to the South Manchuria Railway, a branch of the Chinese Eastern Railway, giving it administration of the railway zone, but Japanese soldiers often carried out manoeuvres outside the zone. Although Japan attempted to blame the event on Chinese dissidents, it was widely known that radical Japanese army officers engineered the explosion as a pretext for extending their military control over the whole of Manzhou.

Overnight, Japanese forces took control of the arsenal, aerodrome, barracks and the Chinese walled city in Shenyang. This event is now recognised as 'the unquestioned beginning of World War II', being 'one of the first of a series of confrontational acts by militaristic governments that would shatter the fragile peace created after the Great War'. It also changed 'the fate of China under the leadership of Chiang Kai-shek and his Nationalist Party'.[2] The forces of the warlord of Manzhou, Zhang Xueliang, presented little resistance, although fighting with some other Chinese resistance forces was fierce and many were killed and wounded on both sides. Japanese aggression resulted in its military occupation of Manzhou, which was later extended to adjoining provinces.[3]

Janet had been undecided about whether she would risk travelling into the war zone, but meeting Donald strengthened her resolve. She described him as 'a man of remarkable personality' who was on 'the inside of most political happenings in China'.[4] By the time she met him he was political adviser to Manzhou leader, the 'Young Marshal', Zhang Xueliang, and later was adviser to General and Madam Chiang Kai-shek, who regarded him as an influential and close friend. 'You call yourself a journalist and you're talking of returning to Australia,' Donald challenged her:

> Don't you realize you're on the verge of the greatest drama in history— the Japanese bid for the ascendancy of Eastern Asia? ... Of course you're going to Manchuria.[5]

Donald was one of the few journalists who recognised that the staged event at Shenyang, far from being an 'incident', was of extreme significance to the future of China and eventually the world.

Janet was about to become one of the journalists thrown into what appeared to those without long experience of China to be a confusing world of war and chaos. Although much less prepared than seasoned correspondents, she achieved a triumph with a series of broadcasts after she emerged from Manzhou. Janet had not come up through the ranks of trained journalists, but she was used to writing for newspapers. Like many women journalists, she 'worked freelance or on assignment', and like some she was a 'highly educated, activist' woman.[6] She was also far from ignorant about the situation in China. She had been critical of the discussions at the recent Institute of Pacific Relations conference, where delegates had 'talked about everything except the one thing we were all thinking about—war'.[7] She had travelled widely and was an active defender of the League of Nations. She had also been involved in the Institute of Pacific Relations and was the only female Australian delegate at the founding conference at Honolulu in 1925. Through her work with the Young Women's Christian Association she had developed contacts with the organisation's representatives in Japan and China.

Early life and background

Janet Charlotte Mitchell, the youngest of four girls, was born on 3 November 1896 into a talented and influential Melbourne family. Her father, Edward Mitchell, was a leader at the Victorian Bar and held many public offices in religious, sporting and charitable organisations. He was appointed Knight Commander of St Michael and St George in 1918. Her mother, born Eliza Fraser Morrison, was a daughter of Reverend Alexander Morrison, principal of Scotch College from 1857 to his death in 1903. She was also a niece of George Morrison, principal of Geelong College, one of whose children was George ('Chinese') Morrison. Janet's sister, Mary Mitchell, became a renowned novelist following the international success of her first novel, *Warning to Wantons*, and her mother and another sister, Nancy Adams, wrote family histories.[8]

A delicate child, Janet was educated by governesses at the Mitchell homes in East Melbourne and Macedon, but she was able to persuade her father to allow her to study music at the Melbourne Conservatorium of Music and later at the Royal College of Music in London. After deciding she did not have the temperament or talent to become a concert pianist, Janet enrolled at Bedford College, University of London, graduating in 1922 with an honours arts degree.[9] After a decade in London, she returned to Melbourne as a well-educated woman but with a limited range of career possibilities. She wrote music and literary reviews for a Melbourne weekly. She was elected to the Council of the League of Nations Union, for which she organised talks on the league in schools. She also became an active member of the Australian Institute of International Affairs.[10]

Work for YWCA

In 1924, Janet was appointed education secretary for the Victorian Young Womens Christian Association (YWCA). Margaret Dunn, in her history of the organisation, queried whether it adapted well to the needs of the 'new woman and her freedom' who emerged after the First World War. Many leaders, she wrote, 'looked on the shingled hair and short skirts with a very jaundiced eye'.[11] Janet regarded her work organising classes in homemaking and community skills, to which she added lectures on international affairs and music, as futile and unproductive carried out in 'an atmosphere of vague, sloppy religious sentimentality ... and unbusinesslike inefficiency'.[12]

The international aspect of the YWCA's work provided Janet with the new and creative challenge that she longed for. YWCA members were reminded frequently that the organisation was part of a world movement and 'a feeling of responsibility for its sisters in foreign lands' was deeply embedded. From 1920, Australia provided financial support for representatives in several overseas countries.[13] Janet appreciated the value of this goal and through the YWCA's World Fellowship Movement she came into contact with workers in China and Japan. She began to see the YWCA's 'big international possibilities, as a world-wide organization working for peace through developing fellowship between individuals'.[14] This challenge changed her life when, in 1925, the Victorian YWCA chose her to represent the organisation at the founding conference of the Institute of Pacific Relations, in Honolulu. History lecturer Stephen Roberts (later professor of modern history at the University of Sydney and knighted) led the Australian delegation, which included Dr E.J. Stuckey, a medical missionary in China, and male experts in international relations and economics.

Institute of Pacific Relations delegate

Janet was successful in her suggestion to the institute that it seek to attract women involved in industrial reform, citing trade unionist and feminist Muriel Heagney, and Eleanor Hinder, who worked on industrial relations for the YWCA in Shanghai.[15] Janet's outlook widened through her contact at the institute's Honolulu conference with delegates from other countries, particularly Japan and China. She believed that young women were 'fundamentally the same everywhere, irrespective of colour, creed, or class' but, as David Walker pointed out in *Anxious Nation*, this did not affect her opinion when she observed interracial citizens in the melting pot of Honolulu.[16] Racial intermarriages, she wrote, 'seemed to produce the worst features of both races'.[17] As Walker also observed, Janet seemed comforted that 'the feeling of racial superiority was not confined to the white races' after noting that Japan discriminated against mixed marriages.[18]

She returned home more aware of the YWCA's importance in Asia and anxious to find a role in world affairs. Half an hour after landing in Sydney, she gave a radio talk on the conference and that night she addressed a meeting of the Workers' Educational Association in Newcastle. In Melbourne she addressed a crowded meeting on 'The Pacific Today and Tomorrow', recounting conference debates and conclusions, and warning that the 'gravity of the present situation in China' could not be overestimated. She believed that world powers would have to give up their spheres of influence and extra-territorial rights, and predicted that a future educated Chinese nation would be the most potent force for good or evil that the world had ever seen.[19]

Director, Thrift Division, New South Wales Government Bank

Soon after she returned, the commissioners of the Government

Savings Bank of New South Wales offered her the job of director of the bank's newly established Thrift Service Division, making her the first woman in Australia to be appointed to a senior position in a bank. In September 1926, the bank sent her to the United States to study the saving and budgeting schemes adopted by New York, San Francisco and many other cities.[20] She spent Christmas week at Hyde-Park-on-Hudson, the home of Mrs James Roosevelt, with Mrs Roosevelt's son and daughter-in-law, the future president Franklin D. Roosevelt and Eleanor Roosevelt.[21] The invitation came through a letter of introduction from a friend, one of several occasions on which letters of introduction from influential Australians eased Janet's way.

Janet returned a thrift expert, promoting savings schemes covering most sections of society.[22] Her work was successful but left her 'utterly depleted' by night time. Five years later, her work ceased abruptly on 23 April 1931 when the bank closed suddenly, a casualty of the Great Depression.[23] The abolition of the thrift department left Janet without a job and a feeling of guilt over having to abandon her customers.[24]

IPR Conference, Shanghai, October 1931

A week after her bank job ceased, Janet was appointed a delegate to the Institute of Pacific Relations Conference, scheduled to be held in Hangzhou in October 1931.[25] Since the first conference in Honolulu she had accumulated wide experience of life through her work with the factory and domestic workers, clerks and typists, teachers, nurses and recent arrivals from the country or overseas at the YWCA. She had been hardened by the reality of families struggling to survive the Depression, following the collapse of the bank. She was also experienced in the international aspirations and the work of the Institute of Pacific Relations, the Australian Institute of International

Affairs (AIIA) and the League of Nations Union (LNU). The United Associations of Women, an organisation formed in Sydney in 1929, held a luncheon where members farewelled Janet.

The influential feminist and activist Jessie Street had resigned from the Feminist Club to become the first president of the United Associations of Women. The United Association's aims included supporting qualified women to stand for public office, the study of social, political and economic questions, and promotion of international peace and understanding and the League of Nations.[26] Janet was conservative in background and ideas,[27] but agreed with the United Association's promotion of international peace and support for the league. Professor Francis Anderson, a long-time president of the NSW League of Nations Union and a passionate advocate for peace 'grounded securely on justice', supported Street in honouring Janet.[28] Janet indicated how aware she was of developing tensions in Manzhou, and how internationally important this made the forthcoming conference as 'it would deal specially with the Chinese, Russian, and Japanese contacts in Manchuria'.[29] Her prediction proved to be sanguine.

Janet became increasingly critical of the unreality of the Institute of Pacific Relations as delegates discussed economic and cultural relations, diplomacy in the Pacific, and China's economic development and international relations. She was also disturbed by conflicting views of many 'liberal internationalists or moderate intellectuals' among the delegates who defended Japan's actions in Manzhou, leading her to doubt the institute's influence for peace.[30] As war raged to the north, she observed the cohesive and unified Japanese delegation and the Chinese delegation's unwillingness to face unpleasant truths about their country. As news of the Japanese advance into Manzhou 'with its trail of fighting, suffering and chaos' continued, she found the meetings in Shanghai 'a mockery' and her 'early idealism, the open-hearted naïve enthusiasm' with which she viewed the institute as a constructive force, ebbed away. By the end of the conference Janet's belief in the institute and the League of Nations was 'crumbling'. She wondered whether Japan with its 'dangerous fusion of patriotism and religion' would ever relinquish Manzhou, even in the face of 'international pressure or adverse world opinion'.[31]

Sino-Japanese crisis

Janet's disillusion with the conference and what she saw as the unreality of delegates, including her fellow Australians, left her open to Donald's evaluation of her as a working journalist unable to resist a breaking story. After her meeting with him, she left for Tientsin (Tianjin), three hours by rail from Beijing, on the first stage of her journey north to Manzhou. When she arrived, martial law was in force and parts of the Chinese and foreign sections of the city were sandbagged and barricaded with barbed wire. The Japanese section was deserted, 'its shops all barricaded, its windows shuttered, here and there a frightened face peering out from behind blinds'. At night she slept close to the sound of shooting.[32] She avoided being stopped from getting further north by producing a letter from the Australian Prime Minister with an impressive seal requesting her safe conduct. She left Tientsin for Shenyang in time to be there by 16 November, the date when the League of Nations' ultimatum expired for Japan to withdraw its troops to the South Manchurian Railway zone. She was anxious to be present for this climax. She was also on the trail of a story she had heard in Tientsin that Chinese tailors in Shenyang were making green and gold flags ready for a Japanese celebration after they had installed a Chinese puppet leader.

As the train passed Shanhaiguan—the boundary between China and Manzhou where the Great Wall touched the sea—she was the only woman passenger left on the 'unspeakably filthy and very hot' train. Further north, she saw the mutilated bodies of Chinese on a railway platform and soldiers digging 'an enormous common grave' nearby. After the train stopped south of Shenyang, where the line had been destroyed by fighting, she travelled the rest of the way in a rickshaw over a shelled-out road.[33]

'Harbin is the centre of the crater'

In a hotel lobby in Shenyang, Janet joined the throng of foreign press correspondents congregated in the city to watch the withdrawal of troops if Japan complied with the league's demand. But the ultimatum came and went and there was no Japanese withdrawal. Instead, Japanese forces continued to drive further north to Harbin, where the railway from the south met the east-west railway from Soviet Russia to Vladivostok. The editor of a Shanghai paper advised Janet to get to Harbin: 'Manchuria is a volcano, Harbin is the centre of the crater,' he told her.[34] Even before the Japanese advance, Harbin was a city with a constant undercurrent of conflicting Soviet and Chinese interests, in addition to a community of White Russians who had fled from communism. Wedged between Russia, China, Japan and Korea (a Japanese colony from early in the century), Manzhou was described by Janet as a 'seething cauldron of tension, suspicion and fear' and 'a bone of contention', being relatively undeveloped in a continent of over-populated countries.[35] Russia and China owned the Eastern Railway that ran east through Harbin. When Japan took the city, the state of Manchukuo—the name the Japanese imposed on Manzhou—took over China's interests in the Eastern Railway.

Nine months in Harbin

Once in Harbin, Janet was anchored there for the next nine months. On 25 January 1932, she watched as Japanese troops began to attack the city. The following week she saw them march, bedraggled but triumphant, through the city. Donald's biographer described the situation: 'The biggest of Asia's storms had begun. In a prelude to a universal cataclysm, Japan's Army had swept through Manchuria, and stood looking toward the Great Wall'.[36]

Despite being in this 'flash point' of what Donald had told her would be the start of a world war, Janet found no way of sending news flashes from the city. A critic, Jacqui Murray, looking back after many decades, attributed this to Janet's inexperience and inability to analyse a fast-moving situation,[37] but Janet's comments and actions preceding her journey to Harbin demonstrate this was not correct. In her biographical work on Australian women, Heather Radi acknowledged Janet's wide understanding of both sides in the conflict, particularly 'her exceptional understanding of Japan's internal problems in the 1930s'. Radi also acknowledged Janet's informative writing and talks on the situation in Manzhou 'at a time when detailed information about the events was scarce'.[38]

Reporting from Manzhou in 1932 was a challenge. Foreign correspondents were only able to file dispatches from cities occupied by the Japanese after overcoming great difficulties, such as costly and slow transmission of cables, inexplicable delays, and censorship and translation problems. Unfamiliar with these channels, Janet managed to get some informative articles to Australian papers in letters she sent to her mother. In the first, published in the Melbourne *Argus* in mid-February but datelined in December well before the Japanese reached Harbin, she described the simple rural life she observed at a village market outside Harbin.[39] After the Japanese took over she looked for news but there 'did not seem to be anything to report—except rumours and they were endless', in a city where the Japanese controlled news outlets.[40] In an article published in Melbourne in July, datelined 7 May, she wrote about the facts she could rely on from her own observation. She reported the terrible plight of refugees flocking into Harbin from villages and towns that were being burned and looted on the Eastern Line between Harbin and Vladivostok:

> One evening a week or so ago I watched the reflections of burning villages from a high point in Harbin. The more fortunate villagers perish; the less lucky escape to a nomadic life of slow starvation ... many [drift] to Harbin to swell the already appalling number of the destitute here. It would be difficult to imagine more pitiable human wreckage than that which lines the streets of Harbin.

She saw them as 'orphans of the storm', victims of 'inhumanity and lawlessness', although many were 'morphine maniacs and vodka-sodden'.[41] In Harbin she observed the Japanese indoctrination of the population. She described a huge calico banner stretched across the main railway bridge carrying words that translated as 'Manchukuo is the Herald of Peace in the Orient and the Herald of Universal Peace' in lettering two feet high. Nearby another banner inscribed in Chinese and English as 'Manchukuo—the earthly Paradise'.[42]

The arrival of the League of Nations' Lytton Commission of Inquiry in May 1932 raised hopes of definitive news. But although the press bombarded members with questions, they came away without clear answers. Donald, the person who could have enlightened Janet, was not free to talk as he was employed as adviser to Dr Wellington Koo, a Chinese representative on the Commission and a former Nationalist Prime Minister and Foreign Minister. When Janet met Donald, he warned her that it was dangerous to be seen talking to him, telling her that a journalist who had done so in Shenyang had been imprisoned.[43]

The weather, combined with rudimentary communications and transport services, made even sending letters difficult. Janet was in Harbin during extreme winter conditions, when for six months temperatures fell far below zero, ranging from maximums of -1 to -4 degrees with icy blizzards. In summer, shortages of food and other essentials became worse after the rivers flooded, leaving tens of thousands of people without shelter, which led to an outbreak of cholera. Unable to eat meat, fish, and many vegetables for fear of infection, she lived on sweet corn, sterilised bread and beans from the garden.[44] She was not only in financial distress—she taught English to Russians, Chinese, Japanese, Koreans, Czechs and Germans to earn some money—but she was also in acute physical danger in a city riddled with bandits, making it unsafe to walk at night.

Janet had good reason to fear bandits. An Australian woman, Kathleen Buchanan Rouse, whom Janet befriended after she arrived in Harbin on 24 June 1932, was killed by bandits a little over a month later. Rouse undertook a highly dangerous journey in the vain hope that she would be able to obtain an Australian visa for her fiancé, White Russian émigré Andrew Gaylit, who was living on Solnechny Gorodok, then an island in the Sungari (Songhua) River. He usually visited Rouse on the mainland each day. After he failed to appear for several days, she boarded the ferry on 29 July to visit him. On 2 August, a body recovered from the river was identified as Kathleen Rouse. At the inquest Janet gave evidence that Rouse usually wore a gold watch and several diamond rings on each hand. As the body was found without jewellery, the inquest concluded that Rouse had been murdered by bandits.[45]

During the months she spent in Harbin, Janet lived in White Russian households. Three of her Russian acquaintances were murdered and another kidnapped, tortured and killed when a ransom was not paid.[46]

When Janet was able to leave Harbin in September 1932, she was fortunate to travel on the only train that week that was not derailed and attacked by bandits. As the train crossed the Manzhou border with China, she and a Canadian seated near her exchanged congratulations. Once she was away from Manzhou, her opinions were in great demand. But before returning to Australia she visited Korea and Japan to gauge reaction in those countries to events in Manzhou. She left Japan depressed at the prospects for peace. In Tokyo she found only an occasional 'flickering of a liberal spirit', concluding that she 'was looking into a darkening world'.[47]

Triumph of ABC broadcasts

Janet's great triumph from her experiences in Manzhou came when the ABC invited her to make a series of weekly radio broadcasts beginning on 2 January 1933. Remarkably, since very few scripts have survived from the 1930s, the texts of three of her five broadcasts have been preserved in the National Archives of Australia.[48] Her talks are thoughtful and considered, and provide a firsthand, graphic description of a unique experience. In her first broadcast, she described Manzhou as 'the storm centre of Asia':

> *The present conflict raging in Manchuria itself, in China and Japan, and in Geneva, may develop in to a worldwide conflagration ... it is a topic of vital importance to every nation—to Australia much more vitally than to many of those European powers which from the distance of Geneva attempt to settle the destinies of Asia and the Pacific at the League of Nations.*[49]

In this broadcast, which set the scene for those that followed, she described the makeup of the population and how she came to be in Shenyang and Harbin—the two main cities that the Japanese attacked during their conquest of Manzhou.

In her second talk on 9 January 1933, she described her role in her broadcasts as similar to the chorus in a Greek drama, introducing the mighty actors in a tragedy—China, Japan and Russia—in a theatre of conflict situated in 'one of the great frontiers regions of the world'.[50] At the end, she asked listeners to send in questions. She answered these at the beginning of her third broadcast, which covered the lead-up to the 'Mukden incident', and this pattern presumably continued in her fourth and fifth talks. [51]

No transcript of her fourth talk on Manchukuo has been found but it is probable that it was similar to an ABC broadcast she made in 1941 on Japan's colonising methods.[52] The fifth may have been on the League of Nations efforts to find a solution to the crisis in Manzhou. The failure of these efforts influenced world opinion on the futility of the League of Nations and on prospects for peace, disarmament and non-aggression. When Janet was chosen to go to Geneva in 1935 as a 'temporary collaborator' her earlier 'idealistic faith' was momentarily reawakened, but attending meetings and studying the league's organisation left her disillusioned. She saw no prospects for the league while it remained in the hands of men and women actuated by 'national self-interest ... leading inevitably to international distrust', leaving humanity once more 'betrayed by political expediency'.[53]

Australian foreign policy in the 1930s

Before Janet's ABC broadcasts, little analysis had appeared in Australian newspapers about the Mukden incident. One month later, the ABC banned 'expressions of opinion on the Sino-Japanese situation', following an internal censorship dispute. The ban remained in force until The Watchman (E.A. Mann), a controversial ABC commentator, began his news commentaries three years later.[54] In an analysis of the news in the Australian press in the 1930s, William Macmahon Ball, academic and diplomat, noted the absence of informed discussion. Overwhelmingly, Australian readers had to rely on the Associated Press' coverage from London for overseas news. This presented a picture of the world through British eyes and left Australia with an inadequate coverage of Asia, 'the very countries about which Australia needs full information'.[55]

This distortion in the source of news and the lack of regular informed opinion may have contributed to the wide variation that commentators found in attitudes to Japan. In a chapter in *Press, Radio and World Affairs*, A.G. Pearson wrote that apart from the pro-Japanese *Sydney Morning Herald*, the daily press was neutral or opposed to Japan, and gave considerable prominence to the possibility of war between Japan and Britain, or of a Japanese invasion of Australia.[56] Historian W.G. Hudson held the view that the Australian press was 'in varying degrees sympathetic to Japan' while in the wider community, pacifism was in vogue and Japan was not unpopular.[57] Through the 1930s, the Lyons government continued to avoid offending Japan and from 1937 followed British foreign policy, including its policy of appeasement. Donald deeply resented Australia's attitude towards Japan and its lack of assistance to China in the 1930s. After he was liberated in Manila, the Philippines, in 1945 from a Japanese prisoner-of-war camp, he told an interviewer that China's 'cries to the humanity of the world' went unheeded during the time it had been at war with Japan. China had fought under:

the discouragement of international scorn, futilely endeavouring to prevent expanding invasion, and watching the nations busily doing their utmost to appease Japan and supply her with the wherewithal to destroy China. She was overwhelmed by a barbarism which beggared comparison and defied description.[58]

Press coverage of Janet's talks

In addition to her ABC broadcasts, Janet addressed many organisations. Those to the Country Women's Association and the League of Nations Union covered her dramatic journey from Shenyang to Harbin and the nine months under Japanese control.[59] In others, including two to the Royal Empire Society on 'Manchuria: The Riddle of Asia', she spoke of Manzhou's great strategic importance to Japan in the light of Soviet control of Outer Mongolia.[60] Her speech to the Sane Democracy League stressed that a knowledge of the history of Sino-Soviet relations was essential to an understanding of the Sino-Japanese conflict.[61] She also had many articles published in newspapers including a series in the Adelaide *Advertiser*, the first covering the difficulties faced by the Lytton Inquiry, and another series in the Sydney *Sun* beginning on Christmas Day 1932.[62]

Life after Manzhou

In London in 1935, Janet's novel on her experiences in China, *Tempest in Paradise*, was published to good reviews.[63] She had arrived in London early in 1934 after spending the previous year as acting head of Women's College at the University of Sydney. In the next two years she established a precarious existence as a journalist in a city where, as Australian author and literary agent Florence James wrote 'scraping a living was almost a 24 hours a day job' for writers.[64]

Once again Janet had to turn to another field for employment. In 1936, she was appointed Warden of Ashburne Hall for Women at the University of Manchester. The following year her autobiography, *Spoils of Opportunity*, was published. In the last pages of the book, she wrote of the loss of her earlier belief in international movements for peace, with another world war 'no longer an unthinkable nightmare but an actual possibility'.[65] In 1940, she resigned her position at Ashburne Hall and returned to Melbourne. There, she was appointed deputy supervisor of the ABC's Victorian Youth Education Department where her duties included writing scripts, devising and producing programs, and engaging writers and actors.[66]

After 14 years at the ABC, by far her longest period of continuous employment, Janet retired in 1955 due to ill health. She died in Melbourne on 6 September 1957. An article in an ABC staff journal described her as 'a woman of great cultivation, possessed of taste and judgment, widely read and widely travelled, as well as being extremely well informed'. She brought to her position 'very considerable literary talents, her wide reading and her deep knowledge of people gained from an extremely varied career'.[67]

A tall woman with dark hair and a strong, interesting face, Janet was witty, amusing and deeply spiritual. She had become interested in the Oxford High Anglican Church Movement in England in the 1930s, and in Melbourne in 1949, she converted to the Catholic Church. She died unmarried, hinting only in two sentences in her autobiography at a male friendship that did not survive when she left Melbourne to work in Sydney, China and England.[68]

Caroline (Lynka) Isaacson

Editor to Army officer

A charismatic, talented and versatile woman, Caroline Isaacson succeeded in several branches of journalism in an era when there were few opportunities open to women. She was always known by her childhood pet name of Lynka, even enlisting in the Australian Women's Army Service under that name. Lynka progressed from women's page editor to foreign news editor, through Army public relations, to editor of a Jewish periodical and editorial director of a chain of suburban newspapers. In 1961, just before her death, she reported the trial of Adolf Eichmann in Israel for war crimes and crimes against the Jewish people. But it is her involvement in a bold scheme to establish a Jewish homeland in Australia during the Second World War that reveals her surprising private life, which played out in a tragedy in the rugged south-west of Tasmania. It also opened a door to an important job in journalism, previously held only by men.

Early life and background

Lynka was born Caroline Jacobson in London on 14 September 1900, elder daughter of Emile Jacobson, a director the Royal Holland Shipping Line, and his French-born wife, Bettina (nee Lipmann). As she travelled with her parents, Caroline was educated by a governess who gave her the name of Lynka, short for *Lynkushka*, a pet name in Polish. She completed her secondary schooling at Highbury Park, London, and at 18—highly intelligent, speaking seven languages and an author of freelance articles—she enrolled at King's College London to begin a medical course.[1]

Early the following year her life changed dramatically when she met Australian-born Lieutenant Arnold Isaacson, who was on leave from the Australian Imperial Force at the end of the First World War.

He had tales to tell of participating in the landing at Gallipoli and of being an aide-de-camp to the commander of the Anzac Corps, Field Marshal General William Birdwood. Arnold, who had served with the Australian Army Service Corps in Egypt and France, was born in Stawell, Victoria on 29 March 1881. He had been a commercial traveller before the war.[2] Although there was a difference in age of nearly two decades, Caroline Jacobson and Arnold Isaacson were married on 30 March 1919 at Dalston Synagogue, Islington. After a honeymoon trip to Australia in 1919, they returned to London, a city that Lynka always regarded as her home.

In 1926, at Arnold's insistence, he and Lynka and their two children, Peter and Joan, migrated to Melbourne, where Arnold established a business as a manufacturer's agent. After the business failed some two years later, Arnold reverted to his pre-war work as a commercial traveller representing printing manufacturer Lamson Paragon Ltd.

Leader's women's pages

Desperate to help support her young family, and probably bored with life in suburban Melbourne, Lynka began at the top, approaching the managing editor of the *Age*, Geoffrey Syme, for a job on the women's pages. It was work that suited her confident manner, stylish appearance and the contacts she had established in Melbourne society. Working under the women's page editor, Kathleen Syme, one of her first tasks was to organise the *Age* toy fund, which raised money to buy toys for children in hospital.[3]

Before long she was editor of the women's pages of the *Leader*, the rural weekly associated with the *Age*, where she wrote under the name of 'Viola'. Although far from a typical housewife, Lynka embraced the domestic interests of her readers, encouraging them to contribute household hints and stories of their lives which she published in a column named the 'Spare Corner'. She travelled through country areas to address innumerable gatherings, spoke at Country Women's Association meetings and organised picnics for her legion of country followers who flocked to Melbourne to attend.

Editor of *Leader Spare Corner Book*

In 1929, Lynka collected and edited *The Leader Spare Corner Book*,[4] described as 'a unique collection of home and household hints and kitchen recipes: For Australian women'. David Syme & Co., the printing arm of the *Age* and *Leader* newspaper enterprise, published the book. It was such a success and became such a money-spinner that she was called on to bring out a least six editions between then and 1940.[5] Long after Lynka left the paper, and newsprint became freely available again after the Second World War ended, Syme continued to publish many editions in the 1950s and 1960s under the title *Selected Recipes: The Leader Spare Corner Cookery Book*, or some variant. The work that Lynka did was typical of the demands made on women journalists who managed to keep their jobs during the Great Depression of the 1930s. Like Lynka, they were called on to succeed in jobs that were below their intellectual capacity and journalistic capability and, in some cases, demanded considerable organisational skills. As in Lynka's case, they were often enterprises that provided substantial financial returns for their employers, but this was not reflected in their pay.

In the early part of the Second World War, when male journalists began to enlist in the forces, Lynka moved to a demanding job on the foreign desk at the *Age* at a time when war news dominated newspapers. Described as 'one of Melbourne's leading journalists',

Lynka listed the characteristics required of a woman journalist as 'tenacity, determination and [a] strong physique'.[6] She oversaw an increased amount of space allocated to overseas news. In 1942, for the first time, she saw news instead of classified advertisements published on the front page of the *Age*. The paper had maintained this age-old custom of broadsheets long after it had been abandoned by most other dailies.

Homeland for Jewish refugees

During the 1930s, Lynka was active in moves by the Victorian Jewish Board of Deputies to resettle Jewish refugees who had escaped from Nazi Germany and German-occupied countries. She was a committed supporter of the Freeland League for Jewish Territorial Colonization, a body founded in London that attempted to find a homeland for persecuted European Jews. One of the founders, Dr Isaac Nachman Steinberg, had been a minister of justice in Lenin's Russian Government during the Bolsheviks' shortlived coalition with the Socialist Revolutionary Party. Banished from Russia (then the Soviet Union), he lived in Germany until 1933 when he moved to London after Hitler seized power.[7]

In 1939, Steinberg arrived in Australia to promote the Freeland League's plan to buy seven million acres (nearly three million hectares) of land in the East Kimberley. The land began 80 kilometres inland from Wyndham, taking in the Ord River and the huge Argyle Downs cattle station, and east across the Northern Territory border towards Victoria River Downs. The Freeland League undertook to settle 75,000 Jewish refugees on the land where they would develop agricultural and pastoral industries at no cost to Australia. The scheme gained the backing of the Western Australian Government and the Australian

Council of Trade Unions. It also gained support from leading public figures and major newspapers, but it also provoked considerable hostility. It needed the support of the Commonwealth Government for the entry of the refugees into Australia and for the settlement of the five-seventh section of the scheme, which was in the Northern Territory.[8] As late as November 1942, Steinberg continued to advocate the Kimberley scheme. Lynka was a supporting speaker when he gave a lecture on 'Jewish colonisation in the last 100 years' to 'a very large crowd' of Jewish people in Melbourne.[9]

While he continued to lobby the Commonwealth for support for the Kimberley scheme, Steinberg met the Tasmanian Premier, Robert Cosgrove, and through Tasmanian officials became aware of vague plans for a Jewish settlement in south-western Tasmania. Lynka and Critchley Parker Junior, an idealistic young Melbourne man, had promoted this scheme to the Tasmanian Government. Their scheme was based on material from a book Parker's father, Critchley Parker Snr, had written and published for the Tasmanian Government in 1937, extolling the state as the 'Jewel of the Commonwealth'. The book emphasised the state's natural resources, the opportunities it offered and its potential for the establishment of secondary industries using hydroelectric power.[10] Parker was an enthusiastic promoter of the potential of the almost uninhabited and inaccessible south-western part of Tasmania centred on Port Davey and Bathurst Harbour, now in the Tasmanian Wilderness World Heritage Area. Linking his interest in the development of the area with the settlement of Jewish refugees in Australia occurred when he met Lynka socially in a Melbourne bushwalking club. Despite a difference in age of about a decade and their different life experiences, they became intimate friends.

A city in south-western Tasmania?

Soon, Lynka's interest in establishing a Jewish homeland in Australia and Parker's enthusiasm for the unlimited potential of south-western Tasmania coalesced into a grand vision. As revealed in his journal, Parker developed grandiose plans for the settlement of Jewish refugees in the remote and wild south-west, followed by the development of major industries and a new city that would rise in this pristine wilderness.[11] Lynka's son, Peter, believed Parker pursued the idea of a Jewish settlement in Tasmania for his mother.

Early in 1941, the Tasmanian Government arranged for Lynka, Parker and Steinberg to visit the area around Port Davey.[12] Premier Cosgrove wrote to Steinberg on 21 January 1941 undertaking to have the scheme investigated and considered by Cabinet when a concrete plan was developed.[13]

As fears of war with Japan increased during 1941, culminating in the attack on Pearl Harbor on 7 December, and the rapid advance of the Japanese through Asia, Jewish resettlement schemes receded into the background, except in the mind of Parker. Although a frail young man—he was rejected as unfit for military service—he was an accomplished bushwalker who had once trekked across northern Lapland in severe weather.[14] Early in 1942, as Singapore fell and the Japanese posed an imminent threat of invasion, he set out on a lone expedition to search the forests and precipitous mountains of south-western Tasmania. His idealistic plans involved setting up a utopian community based on communist principles. Initially, rich mineral deposits would be mined, with the proceeds used to finance an iron and steel industry, followed by a range of secondary industries. The famous architect Le Corbusier would be invited to plan the city, which would have cultural institutions and a university.[15]

Disaster in the wilderness

Critchley Parker's single-minded pursuit of realising Lynka's desire to help Jewish refugees led him to ignore numerous warnings about the danger of travelling alone, and he set out on a solo expedition. Enlisting the help of a fisherman, Charlie King, he landed late in March 1942 near Mount Mackenzie in a bay off Port Davey, where a channel led to the shallow waters of Bathurst Harbour. From there he intended to follow a track some 100 kilometres through rainforest, across mountain ranges and over wild rivers to the nearest settlement at Fitzgerald, recording his assessment of the country in his journal. In an emergency he was to light a fire, sending smoke signals from Mount Mackenzie to attract King's attention. Parker, who saw many swans in the area, chose Poynduk, a Tasmanian Aboriginal word for swan, as the name for his planned city.

As weeks went by and no word was heard from Parker, Lynka became increasingly fearful as hope faded for his survival. In the diary she had given him, Parker recorded messages to her during the first few days of his journey. On 28 March 1942, he wrote:

> If only you were with me that we could enjoy together the beauty of Port Davey. A sheet of water studded with green islands & beyond hills & massive mountain ranges now blue in the evening light. To the west protecting the camp are the massive ramparts of Mt Berry.

The following day he recorded that the weather was so hot he had to make frequent stops and in the middle of the day he swam in an ice-cold stream, which rose on Mount Berry. Soon the weather turned to wild gales, cold and incessant rain, and hail. Parker was forced to abandon his trek and return to Mount Mackenzie. The story of his fate only emerged four months later when his body was found with his journal in which he chronicled his slow descent to death. It revealed that he was cold and wet and suffering from pleurisy. Parker's food ran out and after a series of misadventures, his remaining matches became soaked and unusable, and he was unable to signal for help. As he realised that he would die from exposure and starvation, he wrote to Lynka on 8 April 1942:

> *I have so much to say to you as this is the last letter I shall write to you ... this is Nemesis for had I carried out our plans then I would not have now been lying in a tent on the shores of Port Davey, but knowing that I mean something to you I would like you to save something from them ...*
>
> *We had planned so much & each had brought something to the life of the other but if this joint existence cannot be in the flesh let it be in the spirit & I would ask you to live on, developing the powers which you possess, spurning the non-essentials of existence to reach that perfection which we had dreamed of for us both.*
>
> *Fare thee well my sweet*
>
> > *Critchley.*[16]

Parker's body was not found until 4 September 1942 at the foot of Mount Mackenzie. His letters and his journal, both addressed to Lynka, were found near his body which was lying in his tattered tent.[17]

While she waited to hear of Parker's fate, Lynka was also never free from worry for her 22-year-old son, Peter, a Royal Australian Air Force bomber pilot serving in Britain, whose survival became more and more unlikely with each bombing mission he made over Germany and occupied Europe. He survived 45 missions in Bomber Command and was awarded the Distinguished Flying Cross (DFC), Airforce Cross (AFC) and Distinguished Flying Medal (DFM), making him one of the most highly decorated airmen in the Second World War.[18]

Rapid rise in Army Public Relations

Lynka resigned from the *Age* in July 1942. On 18 August 1942, she enlisted as a private in the AWAS, putting her age back two years to bring it to just under the enlistment limit.[19] Promoted rapidly through the ranks from private to officer, by the beginning of 1943 she was a lieutenant in the Directorate of Public Relations. She had successive postings to Sydney, Brisbane, Townsville and Cairns, and was assigned at different times to act as Press Relations Officer to generals Blamey and Savage.[20] Her most important assignment was escorting a group of senior women war correspondents early in 1943 to secret military bases from Wagga Wagga and Uranquinty in New South Wales to Townsville, Cairns and Mareeba. In all the bases, members of the three women's services were taking over male jobs so that more servicemen could be sent to fight in New Guinea.

The tour required all of Lynka's journalistic, organisational and interpersonal skills, as well as her knowledge of the diverse roles of women in the services and the three levels of censorship to which the journalists' stories were subject. She needed to an extreme degree the qualities she had listed that a woman journalist required—tenacity, persistence and physical strength. She was also to discover that she needed exceptional mental stamina.

Her daughter, Joan Isaacson, who joined the AWAS in the same month as her mother, was assigned to the tour as a press photographer.[21] In a comment typical of the era, when women were often portrayed by their attractiveness not their intellectual ability or work experience, a male wrote:

The twenty years' difference between mother and daughter of this unique AWAS team counts for confusingly little in appearance. They have identical slim little figures, golden hair matched to the last curl,

repetitious features and the same calm, unruffled temperaments.[22]
This was the first time a woman had escorted a group of correspondents on a tour of forward bases. As described in detail in the following chapter, at the bases the male journalists, consumed by animosity towards a woman whom they saw as invading their space, subjected Lynka to extraordinarily derogatory remarks.

Back to the women's pages

As the Allies won major battles against the Japanese in the South West Pacific theatre and General Macarthur's headquarters moved north from Brisbane, there was less demand on the Directorate of Public Relations and Lynka was placed on AWAS' retired list in October 1943. Her first job in civilian life was as fashion writer for *Vogue*. Before long she was appointed a feature writer and women's page editor on the *Argus*, to which Brigadier General Errol Knox had returned as managing editor from his wartime appointment in charge of Army Public Relations. In the period after the Second World War, when women's page journalism mirrored the most conservative and conformist aspects of postwar society, Lynka found the 'trivia of the Women's pages' less than stimulating and she resigned from the *Argus* in 1948.[23] For a brief period, she was owner, editor and reporter of the outer suburban *Dandenong Ranges News*.[24]

Editor of *Australian Jewish Outlook*

In May 1947, Lynka became honorary editor of a new journal, the *Australian Jewish Outlook*, whose policy was markedly different from her previous wholehearted support for a Jewish settlement in Australia. The *Outlook* opposed the creation of an independent Jewish state in Palestine or elsewhere. Instead, it supported Zionism as a humanitarian and cultural movement designed to facilitate the migration to Palestine of Jews who could not or would not live in the country of their birth or adoption. It demanded that Jews of all countries be given full civil and political rights and freedom of worship, and supported the right of all members of the Jewish faith—conservative, liberal or reform—to worship in the way that appealed to their intellectual or spiritual needs. It was opposed to all forms of religious minority group settlements. Furthermore, it supported an 'open door' policy on migration to Australia with the proviso this was to be 'consistent with the White Australia Policy', making it open only to white people. The former Governor-General Sir Isaac Isaacs wrote the first article for the first edition.[25]

The *Australian Jewish Outlook* survived only until September 1948 when its opposition to the creation of an independent Jewish state became redundant.[26] By then the state of Israel, although still not recognised by all countries, was 'an established fact'. In its last editorial the *Outlook* stated:

> *We who previously had criticised the creation of a Jewish state because we felt that it would complicate the problem it proposed to solve are now ready to hope that our fears will prove groundless.*[27]

Soon afterwards, Lynka began working in her son Peter's rapidly expanding group of suburban newspapers, which he was building into a multi-national, multi-million-dollar publishing empire. Beginning with the *Elsternwick Advertiser* (later the *Southern Cross*) in 1947, he capitalised on the need for local news and the emergence of large-scale suburban shopping centres that enabled targeted advertising. In 1953, Lynka took over as editorial director, bringing a professional eye to the chain's content and establishing valuable connections with local councillors, council officers and local members of parliament.[28]

Reporting Eichmann's trial

After her husband died in 1960, Lynka left on a lengthy visit to Europe, during which she visited places where she had lived as a child and a young woman, particularly London, where she reunited with family members whom she had not seen for 40 years. Commissioned early in 1961 by the Melbourne *Herald* to write a series of articles on Israel, she arrived at an opportune time. Adolf Eichmann—who had been the manager of Hitler's final solution for the elimination of the Jewish people in Europe—had just been captured in Argentina and brought to Israel to face trial on war crimes, crimes against humanity and crimes against the Jewish people. The trial, which ran from April 1961 to the end of August, was widely reported in the world press and was the subject of several books.[29] Lynka described the first day of the trial as 'a stupendous and unforgettable experience, heart-stirring in the extreme'. As she listened, she wrote that her throat constricted and her heart began to pound:

> *If that is how I felt on seeing this arch fiend responsible for the death of millions, I, who had not suffered myself and, as far as I know, had no relatives or close friends who had, what must others in this vast assemblage feel I wondered. He looked an ordinary fellow, so nondescript, he might have been a clerk, some city worker who regularly caught the train home.*[30]

Lynka also interviewed well-known figures including Golda Meir, Foreign Minister in the Israeli Government, who told her how she had defended Israel's position in the kidnapping of Eichmann in Argentina before the United Nations, arguing that it had been carried out by private citizens. As a result of their meeting, Meir asked Lynka to set up an Australian–Israeli association. Just before Eichmann was sentenced to death in December 1961, Lynka interviewed Mrs Eichmann in Linz, Germany. She asked her whether her husband ever spoke of 'work' and whether he discussed his 'activities' during the war. Mrs Eichmann replied: 'In the home politics were never discussed. Dear Adolf could never have killed anyone. My conscience is clear and I'm sure his is too'.[31]

During a leisurely journey back to Melbourne through France, Spain, Switzerland, Germany, Austria, Italy and a return visit to Israel, Lynka interviewed representatives of international organisations, including the League of Red Cross Societies, the United Nations Commissioner for Refugees and the Inter-Governmental Committee for European Migration. In Haifa she progressed plans for an Australian–Israeli Association and the Israeli Foreign Ministry offered her the post of honorary consul in Melbourne. In December, Eichmann was found guilty of 15 charges, 12 carrying the death penalty. He was hanged on 11 May 1962. Lynka did not live to see that day. On 23 January 1962, she died suddenly in a hotel room in Genoa, on the final leg of her journey home, and while Eichmann's appeals were still proceeding. Her death at the age of 62 was due to a heart condition.

Lynka Isaacson combined a refined European outlook with a down-to-earth practicality that made her a unique figure in Australian journalism. Towards the end of her life, the importance of her Jewishness reasserted itself, adding an element of symmetry to her last work as a journalist reporting the trial of Adolf Eichmann, and her last important interview with Golda Meir.

Connie Robertson, Iris Dexter and Patricia Knox

Confined to Australia

Early in 1943, at a critical point in the Pacific campaign in the Second World War, the Australian Government arranged a tour for selected women journalists to operational war bases in eastern Australia. The purpose of the tour was to gain publicity and increase enlistments in the women's services so that servicemen could be released from base jobs and sent to fight in New Guinea, where troops were urgently needed. Women were not integrated into the Australian Army, Navy and Air Force until the late 1970s and early 1980s, and could not serve in combat roles until well into the present century. The tour was a break from the Second World War government policy under which women journalists were only allowed to report war activities that were close to the headquarters of the organisations they worked for. It was a far cry from accrediting women journalists to report from overseas battlefields—a goal Australian women journalists had so far pursued without success during the Second World War. Even on their restricted tour to bases, designated 'Somewhere in Australia' for secrecy purposes, male journalists resented their presence and disparaged them.

Australian women journalists barred from travel

In 1941, in the early part of Australia's Second World War campaign in the Middle East, Constance (Connie) Robertson, editor of the *Sydney Morning Herald*'s women's department, sought permission to go to the Middle East to report on war work being undertaken by women. She gained some support from the Minister for the Army, Percy Spender. He passed on her request to the Minister for Information, Senator Harry Foll, saying that her proposal had 'substance and merit', although he acknowledged that the government had imposed a ban on 'womenfolk engaged on work of this nature proceeding to theatres of war'. The Department of Information supported Spender's request, but Foll was adamant, arguing that 'our official correspondents' could cover all assignments 'including the work of the nurses and the V.A.D.s [Voluntary Aid Detachment]'.[1] Needless to say, all Australia's official correspondents throughout the Second World War were male. Women journalists continued to be banned from reporting, not only from overseas fronts but also from Australia's northern cities and towns. This was the case even in 1942 at the height of the Pacific War when Australian troops were fighting on the Kokoda Track to keep Japanese forces from taking Port Moresby, and while Japanese planes were bombing Darwin, Townsville and Broome. Women journalists were confined to reporting how women were contributing to the war effort on the home front.[2]

Tour to 'Somewhere in Australia'

In October 1942, Prime Minister John Curtin announced that, as part of a comprehensive plan to make the best use of manpower (the universally used term for men and women in this context), the government was preparing for a compulsory call-up of women for national service to release men for combat.[3] When the Australian Women's Army Service (AWAS), Women's Auxiliary Australian Air Force (WAAAF) and Women's Royal Australian Naval Service (WRANS) were formed in 1941, women had begun to enlist. However, both the AWAS and WAAAF needed more recruits.[4] Brigadier Errol Knox, the Director-General of Army Public Relations—a wartime position which he held concurrently with his role as Managing Director of the Melbourne newspaper group the Argus & Australasian Ltd—saw the opportunity to use the skills of women journalists to help in this objective. He proposed a conducted tour by accredited women correspondents from

8 February to 11 March 1943, covering operational bases in New South Wales and Queensland, where servicewomen were replacing men in specialist occupations that had previously been seen as men's work.

The eight women nominated for the tour came from the major daily newspapers and magazines in Sydney and Melbourne, the serious broadsheets, popular tabloids, and women's magazines. They were Connie, who represented the *Sydney Morning Herald*, Melbourne *Age* and the ABC; Alice Jackson, *Australian Women's Weekly*; Rita Dunstan, Sydney *Daily Telegraph*; Patricia Knox, Melbourne *Argus*, Adelaide *Advertiser* and *Examiner*; Kathleen (Kay) Paine, Sydney *Sun* and Melbourne *Herald*; Chrissie (Mrs Laurie) Seaman, Sydney *Daily Mirror*; and Helen (Nell) McMahon, Melbourne *Sun-News Pictorial*. Alice Jackson withdrew from the tour and Iris Dexter, representing *Woman*, took her place. Lieutenant Lynka Isaacson was put in charge.

The choice of correspondents reflects the fact that in 1943, print was the major method of mass communication. Daily newspapers and weekly periodicals and, to a lesser extent, radio bulletins and newsreels that ran in cinemas, were the main sources of news. During wartime, access to news was important for the functioning of daily life. Both morning and evening papers were widely read in cities and those who did not buy papers could not avoid the pervasiveness of news posters, the cries of newsboys and displays at newspaper kiosks. News reached country people through the weekly editions of the major dailies. Radio stations ran frequent news broadcasts, compiled from news agencies, official bulletins and press reports.[5] Even the ABC did not have a completely independent news service until 1 June 1947.

The government used newspapers and magazines for 'their ability to raise funds and disseminate wartime propaganda',[6] and they carried much government advertising to encourage recruitment and raise money through war bonds and other means. The *Australian Women's Weekly* was credited with playing a key role in maintaining morale on the home front, adopting slogans like 'Make do and mend' and 'Keep the home fires burning'.[7] Its value to the government lay in its circulation, which rose from about 250,000 copies in 1935 to 500,000 in the early war years. By the end of the war in a population of about seven million, it sold 650,000 copies a week and was believed to be read by many times that number.[8] Newsprint was rationed for all publications, a cause of constant complaints of unfair allocations, and all news outlets were subject to censorship.

Accredited war correspondents

The women journalists chosen for the tour of the operational bases were no doubt flattered by their designation as war correspondents, even though they were aware it was a propaganda trip. They were issued with shoulder flashes in green and gold, reading 'War Correspondent', to wear on their Army-issue uniforms.

Iris Dexter decided that the tour was a good subject for gentle satire. Each week in addition to her reporting work on *Woman*, she wrote a column under the pseudonym Margot Parker, in which she took a humorous look at the foibles of personal relationships and at the public's rather bemused adaptation to war regulations. She introduced an invented friend, Frenzia Frisby, to her range of characters and made her a recently accredited war correspondent. Frenzia was puffed up with importance, as she prepared to leave for 'Somewhere in Australia':

> For a long while I have put up with Frenzia, The Girl Reporter. This indicates my devotion and tolerance. But I feel now, with this Frightening New Turn the war has taken, that I can no longer cope with Frenzia, The War Correspondent.

> *My eyes have assumed a blazing green incandescence because I am not*
> *the one to be dashing around in khaki officers' uniforms, hobnobbing*
> *with Squadron Leaders, looking important in Staff Cars and setting*
> *the jaw interminably.*

As she travelled around the city with Frenzia, she noted that she was immediately cast in the role of batman as Frenzia became sterner and more military:

> *She began calling trams Transport immediately, and got into them very*
> *gravely, twitching her jaw muscles at people and looking as though*
> *She Knew Something They Didn't Know.* [9]

From Wagga to Mareeba

The group's crowded itinerary ranged from night flying training operations at a wartime airfield at Uranquinty near Wagga Wagga in inland New South Wales, the Balmoral naval base and Concord Military Hospital in Sydney, and observation and defence installations along the New South Wales coast. In Queensland they visited United States General Douglas MacArthur's headquarters in Brisbane, war industries in Toowoomba, the garrison city of Townsville, the leave centre on Magnetic Island, Mareeba on the Atherton Tableland, and coastal defences around Cairns. In the first week of March 1943, the group was inspecting a far-northern coastal defence outpost in the first week of March 1943 while the battle of the Bismarck Sea was underway. They watched in the control room as WAAAF personnel plotted the course of the battle. It was a pivotal naval engagement of the Pacific War, ending Japanese hopes of regaining the initiative in New Guinea and eliminating any possibility of an invasion of Australia. At another secret base they saw the work of members of the AWAS who had taken over jobs previously done by servicemen. They watched as the women compiled 'the complete story at a glance of the war in the South West Pacific' on situation maps and blackboards around the room.[10]

The tour began when the women journalists converged by train from Sydney and Melbourne at Wagga Wagga, where Lieutenant Lynka Isaacson met them together with WAAAF Section Officer Hunter and Isaacson's daughter, Private Joan Isaacson, who was assigned as a photographer.[11] A highly controlled and packed itinerary and layers of censorship circumscribed the tour, making it almost impossible for one correspondent's story to differ markedly from that of another. Most stories featured newsworthy young women in the AWAS, WAAAF and WRANS who were being trained to work in specialised technical positions, some highly secret, rather than the bulk of servicewomen who worked as clerks, nursing orderlies, telegraphists, signallers, drivers and in mess rooms and stores. The stories of the more challenging jobs were popular because they were more likely to appeal to young women who were considering enlisting as a welcome change from their unexciting lives and civilian jobs. Those already in these jobs were portrayed as adaptable, happy and cheerful women even in the most adverse circumstances.

Gendered roles and language

At this distance the content of the touring journalists' articles is unimportant except for historical research, but it is interesting to note that they reflected the era in their use of gendered language and their sharp delineation of male and female roles. Young servicewomen 'manned' searchlights and ack-ack guns, and worldly-wise journalists appeared to accept that a man was always in charge. Near Uranquinty, the women journalists noted without comment (or perhaps any comment was censored) that the male sergeant in charge 'padlocked' highly qualified WAAAF personnel inside the operational structure in a secret bush location because their work was so 'hush hush'.[12] In one journalist's report there was also no comment on gender discrimination when she noted that it was part of the duties of the WAAAF timekeepers (who checked pilots and planes on night-flying training in and out from the airfield) and the WAAAF signals clerks and transport drivers (who drove the fire and ambulance vehicles) to make tea and toast for the exclusively male trainee pilots.[13] At a base north of Cairns, the ack-ack women told the journalists they hoped it was only a matter of time before 'the Number One Man (the gun-position officer)' would be a woman.[14]

The journalists also noted that servicewomen retained their femininity, for example, the flowers in jam jars and the improvised curtains in isolated camps and makeshift quarters. And they reassured parents that male and female personnel were housed in separate compounds, at a time when rumours were spreading of the rate of pregnancy among servicewomen.[15]

Early lives and backgrounds

Each of the journalists' life stories is unique, collectively they are part of the social history of Australia. A more detailed study of the lives of a representative few reveals a great deal about family backgrounds and social positions, different routes into journalism and career trajectories. Connie was a senior, experienced journalist, and Patricia had the advantage of being the daughter of the managing director of the Argus. Both represented the leading daily papers in their respective capitals, as well as multiple outlets in other states. Iris represented a weekly national women's magazine and was a well-known columnist. She and Connie began work in their early to mid-teens; Patricia was still at school until her later teens. Connie, whose father was a well-known journalist, kept a job during the 1930s Depression, whereas Iris had to survive with a succession of jobs. She was denied a divorce even though the judge accepted that she had been subject to repeated violent attacks by her husband.

These random facts plucked from three life stories raise questions about the education system, the varied paths into journalism, employment standards and pay, and the divorce laws. A study of their working lives points to the lower status of women reporters in the hierarchy of journalists and the historic reasons for the gender-based discrimination against women journalists. It also points to the efforts women made to be accepted on an equal basis with male colleagues and the disparaging attitude to which male journalists subjected their female colleagues. In addition, it reveals the different histories, characteristics and policies of the publications these women wrote for, whether this influenced what and how they wrote, and the different skills required to write for dailies and weeklies.

Connie Robertson: An institution

Connie suited both the standing and the conservative mould of the *Sydney Morning Herald*. She was a highly competent and experienced journalist who kept ahead of trends in society, but always within boundaries acceptable to her mainly middle-class readers and the paper's management. At 48, with a wealth of experience behind her and holding a prize job as head of the women's department of a major newspaper, Connie became the unofficial leader of the group. She was born in Sydney on 16 October 1895, the eldest child of Constance and Alfred Stephens. Her father, a former editor of country newspapers in Queensland, had just taken over editing the *Bulletin*'s Red Page, which he transformed into the country's most influential and widely read literary outlet. After he left the *Bulletin* in 1906, he began a literary monthly journal, the *Bookfellow*, where Connie began work at the age of 13, running errands, typing and filing. She also observed her father's work in managing contributors and editing and producing the publication. She met many of Sydney's literary figures, including poet and journalist Mary Gilmore, who partly financed the *Bookfellow* and who was editor of the Woman's Page in *The Australian Worker*. Gilmore became Connie's model.[16]

Newspaper career

After the *Bookfellow* ceased, Connie's first job was proofreading on the afternoon Sydney tabloid the *Sun*, but soon she was 'social editress' of the popular *Sunday Sun*, and not long after that she was in charge of the *Sun*'s women's pages and supplements. By 1927, her reputation was so well established that she was chosen to represent the women's sections of all Australian evening papers. She was one of only two women journalists to report the historic opening of federal parliament in Canberra.[17]

At age 32, she married sports journalist Bill Robertson, but even on their honeymoon in Hawaii, she covered the first Pan Pacific Women's Conference, and her articles made the front page of the *Sun*. Six months after the birth of her only child, Margot, on 5 June 1929, Connie was back at work in a new job as editor of the weekly *Woman's Budget*, taking her baby with her in a basket, which she placed in a filing cabinet drawer while she worked.[18] When *Woman's Budget* was incorporated in a new magazine called *Woman*, established by Associated Newspapers Limited in 1934 to compete with the *Australian Women's Weekly* begun just the year before, Connie became editor.

Two years later she moved to the prized position of women's editor of the *Sydney Morning Herald*, where she remained for 26 years, becoming an institution in Sydney journalism. She established a formidable reputation, presiding over a staff of eight who worked under constant pressure to meet her exacting standards. Her staff wrote about society balls and weddings. They even climbed up rope ladders in their high heels to get stories from celebrities who had arrived by ship. But Connie was a versatile journalist who 'prided herself on getting hard news as well as "social" news into the women's section'. She also had a flair for recognising and passing on new trends in fashion, home design and cooking.[19]

Connie's measured approach suited the *Sydney Morning Herald*, where the conservative tradition associated with the paper since it began in 1838 continued to flourish under the Fairfax family. It was still alive during the reign of Warwick Fairfax Snr (later knighted), which covered the period when Connie was head of the women's department.[20] It could be relied on as the upholder of conservative views on politics, society and economics. The paper was also conservative in design, maintaining classified advertisements on its front page until wartime newsprint rationing forced a redesign. News was placed on the front page for the first time on 15 April 1944.[21]

Patricia Knox: The *Argus*

Patricia, aged 22, was probably the youngest of the group of women journalists chosen to go on the tour. Whether or not she was favoured over more senior colleagues on the *Argus* because of her father's dual roles as managing director of the paper and head of Army Public Relations, she would have felt under pressure to prove her value. The *Argus* demanded high standards from its journalists. The founder of the paper, Sir Lauchlan Mackinnon, set out to make it an elite newspaper modelled on *The Times* in London, distinguishing it from its competition, the *Age*, which was regarded as 'the workingman's paper'. Until the last few years of its existence when it was acquired by the London *Daily Mirror* group, the *Argus* was regarded as the epitome of conservative thinking. But even readers who detested its conservative opinions praised the impeccable quality of its reporting standards.[22]

Patricia Monica Knox was born on 28 September 1920 in Sydney. She was the eldest child of Errol Galbraith Knox and his English wife, Gertrude Mary Coore, whom he met during his service in the First World War.[23] Patricia grew up in Sydney where her father moved rapidly up the journalistic ladder. In 1922, he was appointed managing editor of the Sydney *Evening News* and, in 1929, he became a director of the newly formed Associated Newspapers Limited, resigning two years later when the *Evening News* closed.

Patricia finished school at Loreto Kirribilli, a Catholic school for girls, in 1937, coinciding with her father's appointment as managing editor and, later, managing director of the newspaper group Argus & Australasian Limited, and the family's move to Melbourne.[24] Patricia soon had a job as a young journalist on the women's section of the *Argus*. Between 1941 and 1942, as male reporters were called up for war service, she was one of the younger women reporters who moved to general reporting duties,[25] a move that would have been unlikely for women in peacetime.[26] The most productive of the touring journalists, Patricia had 22 articles, each of 500 to 1,000 words, published in the *Argus*. The *Australasian* published a much longer, illustrated, wrap-up article. Most of her articles were also republished in one or more New South Wales regional papers.

Iris Dexter doubles as Margot Parker

Iris, 36, the senior reporter on the weekly magazine *Woman*, looked the part of a stylish, sophisticated journalist. Her private life—married to one man, living with another—reinforced the slightly bohemian aura the public tended to attach to women journalists. She was born Iris Chapman Norton in the Sydney suburb of Haberfield, in July 1907, to engineer Wykes Strange Chapman Norton and his wife, Grace. When she was 15, Iris began work editing comics for the *Sunday Times* children's section and the following year she moved to editing work on a new weekly film magazine, *Photoplayer*, and filled in as editor of *Theatre Magazine*. A few years later, she was appointed publicity manager for Hoyts Theatres Limited, telling an interviewer that she believed women were especially suited to publicity work. Iris understood publicity from a newspaper angle and was attuned to its newness.[27]

In 1928, at age 21, Iris married Harry Norman Dexter, a sports journalist on the *Sun* and a member of a well-known family of horse racing writers. The marriage was short-lived, Iris alleging her husband was often drunk, had assaulted her on many occasions and had driven her out of their home in December 1930. In 1935, when she applied for a divorce on the grounds of constructive desertion, *Truth* newspaper reported the case in salacious detail, delighting in having a 'pretty' young journalist and a racing writer as protagonists. It devoted headlines to Iris' evidence of her husband's violent physical attacks and her disclosure that soon after she left him, she met cartoonist and commercial artist George Aubrey Jack Dolphin (Aubrey) Aria,[28] with whom she had lived from March 1931. George gave evidence that he and Iris wished to marry. The judge found that constructive desertion was proved, but refused to use his discretion to grant a divorce, citing the need to maintain morality.[29] Iris and George were not able to marry until 1951 when Harry, who wished to remarry, gained a divorce from Iris on the grounds of desertion, stating that she would not give up journalism for a domestic life.[30]

From 1929 to 1932, Iris had a regular film review column, 'At the Pictures: Latest Talkies Reviewed', in the *Sydney Mail*. During the Great Depression of the 1930s, when journalism jobs dried up, she worked in the advertising section of a department store,[31] supplementing her income with freelance articles contributed to *Smith's Weekly*, the *Sunday Telegraph*, the *ABC Weekly*, the *Sun* and the *Guardian*.[32] Proud of her profession, she continued to list her occupation as 'journalist' on electoral rolls from the time she enrolled at 21 to her death. In October 1940, Iris got a job on *Woman*, and by 1943 she was described as the paper's ace reporter.

Woman was a down-to-earth magazine designed to appeal to housewives and working girls coping with the problems of day-to-day life who were looking for escapist entertainment, succinctly written news stories and practical help. The fashion section often featured ways to enhance or remake an existing garment, and cookery recipes made the most of limited supplies of rationed meat, butter and sugar. Slightly more daring than similar women's papers in its approach to social subjects, from 1941 *Woman* included a regular sex education page by Dr Norman Haire, a medical practitioner and sexologist, who wrote under the name of Dr Wykeham Terriss. It also included a column on relationships by a popular left-wing writer, Alan Marshall, who offered advice well in advance of conservative opinion.[33] Haire's series on venereal diseases (VD) backed up the wartime anti-VD propaganda campaigns by the federal and state governments. Nevertheless, these columns provoked strong criticism from some readers, as did Marshall's column. The paper made the most of a flood of supportive letters to the editor, publishing representative ones backed by comments from the editor. A supportive comment from the Anglican Bishop of Goulburn, Dr E.H. Burgmann was published in a prominent position in a box.[34]

Iris' reports of the 1943 tour needed to differ from those in the dailies. By the time her articles were published, their news value had disappeared. Instead of competing she employed her more arresting writing style and often centred her articles on a striking character. In the tropics, she wrote, the sun brought out 'the choking reek of furry weeds and the undergrowth steams like vegetables in a pot'.[35] At a North Queensland air base, she found a suitable person to feature—a WAAAF squadron leader in charge of the largest concentration of servicewomen in Australia who rode around her scattered outposts on her bicycle. Iris described her striking personality in an article titled 'Starkie of the Waaaferies'.[36] She also wrote a feature story on Lynka Isaacson when her son, Peter, was awarded the Distinguished Flying Cross (DFC).[37]

In her 'Margot Parker' column, Iris used her invented character Frenzia Frisby to picture the journalists' adjustment to communal living in accommodation ranging from makeshift barracks, tents and airport hangars to officers' quarters. Contemporaries could have identified the quirks and idiosyncrasies of Iris' fellow travellers as Frenzia shared her conclusions 'on all this Girls Together stuff in the Quarters':

> The idea is not to borrow the shoe polish, talcum powder, astringent lotion, soap flakes, pills, bobby-pins, cigarettes and cottonwool of others. At first. This powerful scrupulousness lasts for several days, after which everyone relaxes and becomes totally irresponsible and unselfish. It is all this comradeliness, this one for all and all for one

spirit, which will, Frenzia thinks, be The Making of many a girl who is now effortlessly sleeping in her own bedroom, undisturbed by sleep-talkers, girls who've lost tooth-paste caps, and those who hum "Elmer's Tune" over and over and over again.[38]

Frenzia concluded that 'dormitory life fosters a spirit of Communism unguessed at by Those Accustomed to Privacy and Seclusion'.

Denigration of women journalists

The women on tour would remember an event that occurred on their two-day train journey from Brisbane to Townsville on Queensland's narrow-gauge railway. However, any account would not have passed the censors—it could have alerted the enemy, not only to the poor state of Queensland railway tracks but also the effect of the weather in delaying a trainload of troops destined to fight in New Guinea. Major flooding stopped the train as it approached Townsville, forcing it to return to Bowen, 170 kilometres to the south. Isaacson needed to arrange emergency accommodation while ensuring they could resume their tight itinerary—no mean feat. Journalist Major Frederick Howard, Public Relations Liaison Officer in the Directorate of Public Relations,[39] described the women's situation in terms that convey the prejudice and contempt many male journalists harboured towards their female counterparts. In a letter to a fellow journalist, he wrote:

First of all—the Women ... they had to return to Bowen, where they spent two or three days of idleness with the Air Force. I only hope they behaved themselves in that Eveless Eden.[40]

He described the Air Force station where the women journalists were billeted as 'the most desolate' he had seen, with its general air of 'misery and decrepitude'.[41] In a letter to the Assistant Director of the Public Relations Officer, Major R.J. (Reg) Denison, Howard expressed his derision: 'Three days there for Les Femmes must have meant hell for little Lt Isaacson'.[42]

As the tone of Howard's correspondence indicates, it was a view of women journalists that permeated the attitudes of male members of the profession as they saw women invading roles previously sacrosanct to men. The appearance of this sizeable group of women reporters, led by the formidable Isaacson, stirred their fears. Howard, who had been an official war correspondent in the Middle East, was aware that, less than two years before, even a lone woman journalist, Connie Robertson, had been barred from that theatre of war.[43]

After the war

Captain Henry Steel, a British Army liaison officer, rescued the women stuck in Bowen. He arranged for several small planes to fly the group from Bowen to Cairns, where they resumed their tour in reverse. The rescue turned out to be the start of a romance for Henry and one of the rescued journalists. In February 1944, at St Patrick's Cathedral, Melbourne, Patricia married her rescuer, Henry Alfred Steel, by then a major. After the Japanese surrender, he was the first newspaperman to return to Singapore, parachuting in on 4 September 1945.[44]

Iris finally achieved the aim of Australian women reporters in getting overseas but not until shortly after the war ended.[45] During an interview in Perth on her way to Asia to interview newly released civilian evacuees and Australian prisoners of war in Java and Singapore, she contrasted the wartime ban on Australian women reporters with the numbers of American women correspondents who reported the war overseas—127 American women reporters were accredited just to the war in the Pacific.[46] Iris continued to work for *Woman* until it ceased in 1951, then for its successor, *Woman's Day*, and as a feature writer for the Sydney *Sun* and the *Sunday Sun*. After her death in Sydney on 24 March 1974, it was her work as the 'wry, wise, sometimes astringent, always affectionate Margot Parker' that was remembered.[47]

Connie continued her long reign at the *Sydney Morning Herald* in the postwar era. As women returned to more traditional roles, the women's pages reverted to an emphasis on homemaking skills and the social circuit. Connie maintained a leading position among women journalists in being the first to introduce her readers to some overseas influences, including Dior fashions, new homemaking ideas and exotic foods.[48] When she died on 3 March 1964, at the age of 69, the influence of the women's liberation movement was beginning to reverberate around the world and was reflected in the demise of the old-style women's pages that she edited up until her retirement in 1962.[49]

Doors open, others close

The tour by women journalists in 1943 led to a slight but temporary break in restrictions on female reporters. In October 1943, Australian journalist Lorraine Stumm grabbed an opportunity to go with a group of journalists to New Guinea to witness some of the first Allied air attacks on Rabaul. She was an unusual case, accredited by a British newspaper to General MacArthur's headquarters in Brisbane, placing Australian Army Public Relations in an invidious position of not wanting to overrule MacArthur. But she never witnessed the raids on Rabaul as, once she reached Port Moresby, Australian authorities re-established control, ensuring that she got no further than watching Liberator bombers take off at daybreak on their bombing mission. Following publicity arising from Stumm's trip to New Guinea, *Australian Women's Weekly* editor Alice Jackson was also allowed to visit New Guinea briefly. Although she was away only seven days, she wrote many articles about Australian and United States hospitals and units.[50] Other women had to wait until the end of the war to get overseas. Many seized the opportunity, and soon their stories from war-ravaged countries began appearing in the papers.

The lives of Patricia, Iris and Connie after the Second World War typify the lives of Australian women in the same period. Many became housewives and mothers. The adventurous grabbed any opportunity to travel overseas as shipping became available, and many reverted to their pre-war roles. For women journalists, the war had opened opportunities in general reporting as male journalists left to join the armed services. Some retained these jobs but many tentative gains towards gender equality slipped away in the postwar wave of domesticity. By 1948, the ratio of female to male journalists on the *Sydney Morning Herald*'s editorial staff had fallen to 1 in 13, significantly lower than before the war.

In the 1950s, women were not only a small percentage of the journalistic workforce but most were still employed on the women's pages. A few women's page editors ventured cautiously into controversial subjects like equal opportunity in employment, and a few women secured jobs reporting parliament and the courts. Changes in the role of women in the media and the material they wrote for women began to occur in the 1960s under the influence of the women's liberation movement. Gradually, the old staples of women's reportage disappeared as the women's pages changed to more sexually neutral lifestyle sections with a wider agenda on social issues. Despite resistance by more conservative publications, by the end of the 1970s old-style women's pages had virtually disappeared, although many of the limiting factors on the equal employment of women journalists remained.[51]

Epilogue

I became a journalist in the first half of the 1950s, less than a decade after the last chapter of this book. Much of the discrimination described in it was still rampant. Gender inequality was simply a part of the era, and sexual harassment was so common that it was dealt with as part of life. The boast of women journalists of getting equal pay, when women in other industries were paid only a proportion of male wages, was made rather hollow by the pervading male culture that dominated all aspects of press and radio work.

It was the days of crowded newsrooms, clattering typewriters, overflowing cigarette trays, fixed round-faced dial telephones with earpieces, and long lunches at nearby pubs. It wasn't until the 1970s that women were allowed into hotels to drink at bars, but there was no ban on having counter lunches. Newspapers and radio—widely referred to as the wireless—were the main sources of news. Black-and-white television transmission did not begin until towards the end of 1956, and only then in Sydney and Melbourne, in time to broadcast live from the 1956 Melbourne Olympic Games, which began on 22 November. Crowds gathered outside television shops and in public viewing places to watch the events. For years after, television was primarily a source of entertainment, not the major news outlet it would become.

My route to journalism began in 1951 when I was employed at the Australian News and Information Bureau (ANIB) in another capacity. I soon discovered that I had joined an organisation with a traumatic past and an uncertain future. The Australian News and Information Bureau was what remained of the Department of Information. The Menzies United Australia Party/Country Party coalition government had established this department in 1939 at the beginning of the Second World War as an 'auxiliary to governments engaged in war'. The department was responsible for wartime censorship, publicising the reason for the war, and keeping the public 'as enlightened as possible and their spirit firm', more commonly referred to as propaganda and morale building. The Act establishing the department stated that it was to be dissolved at the return of peace. In June 1940, when Sir Keith Murdoch, Managing Director of the *Herald* and *Weekly Times*, became Director-General, the brief was widened to include 'the informative and psychological side of the war and Australia's war effort'.

After the Menzies/Fadden government lost office in 1941 and was succeeded by the Curtin Labor government, the Menzies Opposition became increasingly critical of the department. At the 1946 federal election, the first held following the end of the Second World War, it campaigned for the department's abolition, seeing it as 'primarily a propaganda medium for the Labor Government'. The return of the Chifley Labor government in 1946 ensured that the department would continue. During the following three years, its focus changed from being directed mainly towards the Australian public to overseas campaigns, particularly towards attracting European migrants, and trade and investment, and attempts at mitigating the adverse publicity in Asia stemming from the White Australia policy. Nevertheless, at the 1949 election, one of the election promises of the Liberal–Country Party Coalition was to abolish the Department of Information. This occurred on 8 March 1950 following a decision by the newly elected Menzies government.

Some functions of the Department of Information disappeared. The short-wave division (later Radio Australia) was transferred to the ABC. The Australian News and Information Bureau was established to absorb what remained, principally the much-reduced Editorial Division and the Film Division, later renamed the Commonwealth Film Unit, and its work redirected. Staff of the Editorial Division was halved from 65 to 32, with those stationed overseas reduced from 17 to 8. In a move that could not have sent a more denigrating message, the bureau was made an agency in the Department of the Interior, the most unlikely department to find an organisation whose main role was overseas publicity.

I joined the organisation while the break-up of the old Department of Information was still underway, and put in charge of the 'morgue', the name by which libraries in news organisations were known. When I began work at the Olderfleet building in Collins Street, Melbourne, in mid-1951, the morgue shared the huge room at the back of the ground floor, overlooking the warehouses on Flinders Lane, with the Radio Australia newsroom, which had not yet moved to an ABC building in Lonsdale Street. The morgue served the editorial and film divisions of the Australian News and Information Bureau and Radio Australia journalists until the newsroom moved. The library contained rows of filing cabinets packed with newspaper clippings, hanging shelves to which newspapers were added each day, files of Australian and overseas periodicals, a shelf of dictionaries, encyclopedias, atlases, biographical references, and other standard reference works, plus files of articles written by the organisation's journalists and stringers (local part-time reporters).

As I was soon to discover, the Australian News and Information Bureau was an organisation still finding its way. The Department of Information had been saved from complete abolition following the 1949 election because of representations from the ministers for External Affairs and Immigration who praised the effectiveness of its overseas publicity. The Australian News and Information Bureau redoubled efforts in these areas, seconding several journalists to the Department of Immigration and, in consultation with the Department of External Affairs, increasing its flow of material designed to counteract the effects in Asia of the White Australia policy. Private students had begun to arrive in Australia from Asia soon after the war, and the flow increased when the Colombo Plan for Cooperative Economic and Social Development in Asia and the Pacific got underway. Following its launch in 1951, more students began arriving in Australia. Both these Colombo Plan students and those who came privately provided opportunities for favourable publicity in Asia, but keeping up with this work stretched the capacity of the small number of journalists left in the bureau.

This shortage of journalists enabled me to grasp an opportunity to research and write articles based on interviews with Asian students in Melbourne. These articles focused primarily on their field of study. They also explored their experiences of living in an Australian city, boarding in family homes, negotiating public transport, earning money during vacations picking fruit or serving in department stores during the Christmas rush, and joining university and technical classes in a population that was overwhelmingly Anglo-Celtic. I submitted these articles as a freelance contributor, in the same way as many women had done since the nineteenth century when they bombarded newspaper offices with articles that, if published, sometimes led to the writers being taken on as staff. When my articles were successful in gaining widespread publicity in Asian newspapers, a vacancy arose in the very reduced Melbourne newsroom. I was offered a journalist's job on D grade, the lowest grading and the usual starting point above cadet status. I was the only female on the Melbourne staff, and I joined two others, one in the Sydney office and one at head office in Canberra, each on a low grading. Regardless of ability or value to the organisation, we appeared to be token women. No woman had ever been sent on an overseas posting.

I joined the Australian Journalists Association once my articles began to be published. Initially, I was proud to be a member of the organisation that had been the trade union for Australian journalists from 1910 until 1992, when the association amalgamated with other groups to form the Media, Entertainment and Arts Alliance. Under the association's federal award, women journalists were entitled to equal pay for equal work, signalling an achievement at a time when women employed in other industries received only a percentage of male pay, some as little as half. It was some time before I realised that equal pay was largely negated by women being employed on the lower rungs of the profession with no easy route to promotion. Most women journalists were employed on the women's pages where, in the 1920s and 1930s, proprietors made several attempts to designate them social writers, not journalists, and pay them below the award rate. While these moves did not succeed, a four-year cadetship followed by a grading that rarely rose above the lowest level amounted to inequality based on gender.

Once I was on the staff, I continued the human-interest stories about individual students that had won me the job, but I was also assigned to cover many other subjects. Successive assignments included writing about an Indonesian group at Altona oil refinery; Indian engineers meeting with the Minister for External Affairs and former governor of Bengal, R.G. Casey; Burmese nurses at the Children's Hospital; a mosque at Shepparton; Thai social workers; army officers from Pakistan, India, Thailand and the Philippines; trade and friendship missions; and visits by government officials and many individual technicians, managers and experts in manufacturing, agriculture and medical fields. Many of these people were visiting Australia under the Colombo Plan. I had the advantage over most women colleagues working for newspapers who were confined to work on the women's pages. I was employed to cover general stories, although I soon discovered that, rather unsurprisingly given the almost universal view of sex stereotypes, I was assigned disproportionately to cover social events.

I covered many displays of national dances and customs, always good for photographs by accompanying bureau photographers. When the British Prime Minister, Sir Harold Macmillan, and his wife, Lady Dorothy Macmillan, visited Australia, I was assigned to write about her carefully orchestrated search for lyrebirds in the Dandenong Ranges. Then when the Queen Mother visited, I went to a garden party at Government House to report the reaction of a group of Asian students who were invited to the event. But I was still very fortunate to spend most of my time covering general subjects, such as a visit by a group of engineers to the General Motors Holden plant at Fishermans Bend where Holden cars—a success story of Australian postwar manufacturing—were being produced. And I still have a small, embossed metal tray that members of a high-level Indonesian goodwill mission, led by a former Minister for Foreign Affairs, presented to me. The inscription reads: 'Tanda Mata dari Misi Goodwill Republic Indonesia October 1955', which translates roughly as token or mark of the Indonesian Goodwill Mission 1955.

The approach of the Olympic Games in Melbourne led to an extra couple of journalists moving temporarily to the Melbourne office to take advantage of the world focus on the city and to publicise unique aspects of Australian life, its economic and social achievements and advances in agriculture and manufacturing. It also added a new dimension to my articles aimed at Asian countries. In the lead-up to the Games, Melbourne people were asked to offer accommodation in their homes to overseas and interstate visitors to augment the very limited hotel accommodation, which quickly booked out. I got good exposure in the Asian press with an article on the Rajah of Perlis' experiences as a guest in a pleasant, well-equipped Melbourne suburban home. Once the Games began, I spent most of my time at the Olympic Village writing stories about how contestants from Asian countries coped with living in houses destined to become public housing after the Games. I also wrote about their experiences of eating food that, while attempting to cater for their tastes, retained an inevitable Australian flavour in what was still a long way from being a multicultural society.

The bureau continued on this trajectory during the rest of the 1950s and 1960s, buoyed by monthly files of newspaper cuttings sent back from overseas posts and circulated among staff, together with tables of statistics on placements such as total column inches, width of columns and number of illustrations. The statistics are the only evidence of the bureau's success; the files of clippings were destroyed under a National Archives policy that it was unnecessary to keep them because the originals could be accessed in newspapers, an unrealistic expectation for historic Asian publications.

After the Games I was promoted to C grade, the highest level reached by females in the organisation at that time. I moved to Canberra where my work changed to sub-editing and assignments further afield. Later, I wrote a weekly digest of government and political news, and monthly newsletters on specific subjects such as agriculture and education. I did several stories centred on the work of Asian experts and students at the University of New England in Armidale. I also accompanied a group of Burmese mining engineers down a mine in the Hunter region of New South Wales in connection with a booklet I was assigned to write in a series aimed at individual Asian countries.

By far my most interesting experience was an assignment to travel with the flying doctors who covered outback Queensland from their bases at Charleville, Cloncurry and Charters Towers. This assignment stemmed from an article I wrote about two final-year medical students at the University of Melbourne, Rajaratnam Sundarason, who was studying under the Colombo Plan, and Kandiah Thevarajah, a privately financed student. I interviewed these students about their newsworthy posting, gaining experience with the flying doctor service based at Cloncurry. The story demonstrated several aims of bureau reporting for Asia. It conveyed a great deal of information about Australian life, character and customs, the acceptance of Asian students in Australia, information on the Royal Flying Doctor Service (a unique aspect of Australian life), the huge expanse of the inland and the sparse population living in an inhospitable country. It also conveyed the inventiveness and expertise of the technicians who made the service possible through radio transmission of messages, and the adaptability and can-do attitude of doctors and pilots. The story implied the students' acceptance into Australian life, and the accompanying photos showing them with patients and nurses illustrated this. As a result, the Royal Flying Doctor Service arranged that I spend several weeks flying out with the doctors from each of their Queensland bases to gather information for detailed articles. Flying doctors held clinics at tiny towns, airstrips, station homesteads and nurse-run medical facilities. They carried out medical evacuations from the Channel country in western Queensland, remote cattle stations on the route to the Gulf, medical centres at the northern towns of Normanton and Croydon, Mornington Island, and the Aboriginal missions.

I resigned from the Australian News and Information Bureau towards the end of 1961, shortly before the birth of my first child early in 1962. All journalists except those who held managerial positions were employed as temporary public servants, and even discussion of maternity leave was far in the future. For the next couple of years, I did some freelance work until I was employed as a casual journalist in the ABC newsroom in the press gallery in federal parliament. When a B-grade position was advertised, I was invited to apply, but I preferred to remain in casual employment at a time when the conditions of employment were more important to me than advancing my career. Being casual gave me the freedom to accept only the 2pm to 11pm shift, which suited my family obligations better than the 10am to 7pm shift. I could also choose to take holidays when it suited my family and take a six-month break when I had our second child. These breaks were unpaid, but casual pay at the B-grade rate included a loading for holidays and sick leave.

The downside of this employment relates to the theme of this book. Work on the 2pm to 11pm shift involved doing the regional news, which was a career backwater when it wasn't interspersed with the daytime shift. During the four or five years that I worked at the ABC there was Prime Minister Menzies' resignation, the sensational disappearance of his successor Harold Holt in the surf at Portsea, the turbulence during the brief tenure of Country Party leader John McEwen, and the choice of John Gorton to succeed him. Of greater national significance, Australia sent military advisors to support the United States in Vietnam in 1962, a commitment that escalated into a decade of war with conscripted troops following the passing of the National Service Act in 1964. All these events occurred during the daytime shift or when parliament was sitting.

The ABC regional news, unlike the ACT radio and television news, which was recorded in the ABC studio building on Northbourne Avenue, was prepared in the press gallery so it could cover parliamentary debates and proposed legislation of relevance to the region for the 6pm and 6am radio news bulletins. During non-sitting weeks, as the journalist assigned to the 2pm to 11pm shift, I was the only ABC journalist on duty in the press gallery after the day shift finished at 7pm. I was responsible for covering any national news that occurred. In the days long before the 24-hour news cycle was on the horizon, the bell often rang signalling that another press release had been put in the press boxes at the end of the press gallery corridor. Sometimes these could lead to a national story, but important national news could be slow on a non-sitting night, so choosing to do only this shift, rather than being available for both shifts, limited covering important stories. During sitting days, a couple of journalists were sent from Sydney to augment the reporting staff and they took over cover of national stories. I remember one of the young journalists arrived just after he had taken part in a Sydney demonstration against conscription for service in Vietnam.

The regional news involved driving to the ABC building and handing over the 6pm news bulletin to the newsreader just before the deadline, and repeating the drive at 11pm. I slid the 11pm bulletin under the door of the deserted building, ready to be read the following morning. Sometimes, on the way to the ABC building, I stopped at the police station if there was a developing story, perhaps a major flood or a search for missing skiers.

These conditions of my employment in the press gallery of what is now Old Parliament House seem part of a time warp, and there were other aspects that reinforced this view. There was the much-publicised lack of female toilets in the press gallery, and the legendary meetings between journalists and members in the non-members' bar or in the back bar of the Hotel Canberra (now the Hyatt Hotel), which was the source of many leaks. I characterised our working conditions in an oral history interview: 'We had a basic desk, a basic typewriter and a telephone'. I could have added that we looked out of the windows on to the lead roof of the parliament building, which made the heat just about unbearable on a hot day. Although I never witnessed it, I believe journalists could step out the window and make a quick dash over the roof from the Representatives side to the Senate side to follow a developing story in that chamber.

There was only the most basic security, consisting of doormen who knew everyone who entered regularly and only checked strangers. I remember one day walking in the front door and up the stairs to start my 2pm shift, making my way through the huge crowds in Kings Hall and turning left along the ministerial corridor to the steps on the right that led to the press gallery, quite unimpeded by any security. In the middle of the throng of people in Kings Hall was the towering figure of the United States President, Lyndon B. Johnson, during his visit to Australia in October 1966 when, under Prime Minister Holt, Australia was America's strongest ally in the Vietnam War and Australia was officially 'All the way with LBJ'.

I left the ABC in 1968 just before the birth of our third child, happy to move to what I regarded as an ideal job, writing and editing in my own home.

I could not say that I experienced gender inequality at the ABC. I did the same work under the same conditions as a male journalist on the same shift. Society imposed the gender inequality I operated under. In the 1960s, there was no government-supported childcare, no maternity leave, no time off when children were ill, and no expectation that men would help with housework or childcare. These absences prevented most women from working. Those who did were disadvantaged within the workforce. But the 1960s was also the decade that saw the beginning of a new era for women, which was very slowly reflected in employment conditions. Social changes, including the adoption of the birth control pill, which began a challenge to male domination of society, were reflected in the Australian media. A few women's page editors ventured cautiously into controversial subjects such as equal opportunity in employment, while Charmian Clift's popular weekly columns in the *Sydney Morning Herald* and Melbourne *Herald* indicated just how much women readers craved a meatier brand of social commentary. But there was still much more to be done. Into the 1970s the union paper, *The Journalist*, still consistently portrayed journalists as male—'The Newspaperman in the Changing World' was a typical headline—and the executive of the Australian Journalists Association remained an all-male body.

When I left the ABC, I was employed by economist and finance journalist Maxwell Newton Publications to write and edit tariff, trade and political newsletters. After a stint as editor of the *Australian Financial Review*, Newton became the first editor of *The Australian*, begun by Rupert Murdoch in Canberra in 1964. After a falling out with Murdoch, Newton started a series of insider-style newsletters, which were printed and distributed from his own home in the Canberra suburb of Deakin and the house next-door occupied by journalist associate Richard Farmer. Apart from one or two daily trips to pick up material or drop off copy, I worked in my home only a few streets away. Later Maxwell Newton Publications aspired to become a newspaper empire. In its later years, I was the Canberra representative of its daily and weekly publications covering economics, trade and mining as an A-grade journalist. In the 1970s I moved to a position as Editor of Publications for the National Capital Commission where I was graded A-plus—the peak level for graded journalists.

The 1970s was a turning point for participation of women in the media, or it seemed so at the time. Continuing widespread social changes and the influence of the women's liberation movement as it reverberated around the world led to a revolution in both the material presented to women and the role of women in the media. The old staples of women's pages disappeared over the decade, as the pages changed to more sexually neutral lifestyle sections with a wider agenda on social issues. Not all change came without resistance. The *Sydney Morning Herald*'s women's editor, Suzanne Baker, was disparaged as a campaigner when she introduced enthusiasm for the 'revolution' women were experiencing. Management described her publicising of controversial subjects as 'not the purpose of the women's pages'. But by the end of the 1970s, old-style women's pages with their reports of society events and the latest fashions had virtually disappeared from the Australian media.

Women journalists no longer tolerated their confined status in the industry and moved to previously out-of-bounds areas. Feminist Anne Summers joined the *National Times* and wrote on topics formerly avoided, or underreported, such as rape and prison reform. Others were employed for the first time as financial journalists on the *Australian Financial Review*, where its enlightened editor, Vic Carroll, believed women journalists had been underutilised in the past.

During the next decades, women became commonplace over the spectrum of reporting and presenting, some achieving senior gradings. There were some high-profile appointments to editorial positions, although most of these were shortlived. Many media industry structures, however, remained fundamentally unequal and patriarchal. Most women were still employed in the lower grades, pigeonholed in traditionally female areas, such as women's issues and fashion, and to a lesser extent in health, the arts, entertainment and education, which were perceived to be less important in comparison with highly valued areas such as politics and sport. Childcare responsibilities affected opportunities for promotion. Sexual harassment remained a major issue, and discrimination in promotion remained widespread.

After I left full-time journalism I pursued the dream of many Australian journalists—including Alan Moorehead, George Johnston and Charmian Clift—to write books. I found the pangs of journalism hard to shake off, but after some searching I discovered subjects that I wanted to write about. By the time I had a manuscript ready, I was fortunate in knowing many publishers. My husband, Hugh V. Clarke, was a well-known author of many books, principally about his experiences as a prisoner of war of the Japanese in the Second World War at the notorious Hellfire Pass on the Burma–Thailand railway, and at Nagasaki in Japan. Consequently, commissioning editors were frequent visitors to our home. After a glitch or two, in 1985 my first book, *The Governesses*, was published by Century Hutchinson in Melbourne and London. It was widely reviewed and sold well. Shortly after, Allen & Unwin acquired the rights and published a paperback edition. As many authors have remarked, having your first book published is the most difficult achievement. A string of books followed, with some based, like *The Governesses*, on the role of letters and diaries in the lives of women—*A Colonial Woman* (1986), *Life Lines* with Dale Spender (1992), *Tasma's Diaries* (1995) and *Eilean Giblin* (2013). Others were biographies of women writers—*Pioneer Writer* (1990), *Tasma*

(1994) and *Rosa! Rosa!* (1999). There was also a group biography, *Pen Portraits: Women Writers and Journalists in Nineteenth Century Australia* (1988), which was a forerunner of this book, my fourteenth.

When I was asked to write a major entry on women in the Australian media for *A Companion to the Australian Media,* published in 2014, I did extensive research on the subject to augment my own experience and historical knowledge. I discovered that in the twenty-first century the presence of women anchors of prestigious current affairs programs on radio and television, and as writers on the opinion pages of newspapers, is an enormous advance on their small, almost insignificant, presence in the newsrooms of the middle of the last century. Many women have made a mark reporting politics, war and public affairs in spite of sometimes being a token presence on pages otherwise dominated by male writers, and sometimes being assigned to 'softer' areas. The public profile of notable women disguises the fact that women journalists struggle to attain real influence in decision-making roles. Few reach leadership positions with power over recruitment and promotion, and content is still determined predominantly by men, resulting in sexual bias. From the 1980s, females have greatly outnumbered males in tertiary journalism courses, yet women employed in the media are still disproportionately found in low- and middle-range positions. In 2012, the work culture was described by a media academic as 'blokey', a description ABC presenter Leigh Sales repeated in 2021.

Bold Types tells the stories of the courageous women who began the journey towards equality, and who achieved so much.

We still have a long way to go.

Acknowledgements

I wish to record my deep appreciation to journalist Amy Remeikis for her generosity and friendship in writing the introduction to *Bold Types*. It is a great piece of persuasive writing expressed with clarity and verve, as she jolts the reader from the struggles of the past to the challenges women journalists continue to face in the fight for female equality.

My warm thanks to Lauren Smith, Assistant Director of Publishing, National Library of Australia, who was enthusiastic about my manuscript from the start and has overseen its development with speed and with an inspired eye for marketing. My warm thanks also to Amelia Hartney, Program Manager of Publishing, National Library of Australia, for her acumen and wisdom in seeing the manuscript through to book publication. I thank editor Irma Gold, designers Nada Backovic and David Potter, and indexer Rebecca Cotton for their dedicated work, often to tight deadlines. Nada's cover of *Bold Types* is an inspired example.

At a more basic level, I record my thanks to Australian collecting institutions, particularly the National Library of Australia, for their acquisition of manuscript and pictorial material about the women journalists who feature in *Bold Types*. This is particularly valuable as, in the past, journalists rarely wrote about themselves or their careers.

Initially I was very reluctant to break out of this mould. I record my deepest thanks to writer, editor and publisher Susan Hall, who persuaded me to write about my own experiences as a journalist from the 1950s in the Epilogue in this book.

I wish to acknowledge with thanks the media, historical and cultural journals that published versions of articles about the subjects that feature in this book.

My deepest thanks to my children, John, Justin and Brigid, and other family members who are ever ready to help and sustain me. I would never have reached my advanced age and my continuing research and writing without their encouragement and interest in my work. My daughter Brigid Veale has made a special contribution with her expertise as a journalist and her practised editorial eye.

Over the years I have been researching and writing this book, I have relied on the help of many librarians, archivists and friends and I thank them all. In particular, I thank the National Library's Special Collections Coordinator, Andrew Sergeant, and friends and colleagues in the Petherick Room, particularly Kay Walsh. I also record my grateful thanks to my long-standing friend Kerrie Glennie and my relative Catherine Ryan for their constant support.

Endnotes

Anna Blackwell

1   'Franco-German War', Encyclopaedia Britannica, britannica.com/event/Franco-German-War.

2   *Sydney Morning Herald*, 29 September 1870, p.4.

3   Alistair Horne, *The Fall of Paris: The Siege and the Commune 1870-1*, London: Macmillan, 1965, p.88.

4   Michael Howard, *The Franco-Prussian War: The German Invasion of France 1870-1871*, London: Rupert Hart-Davis, 1962, p.1.

5   Howard, *The Franco-Prussian War*, p.247.

6   *Sydney Morning Herald*, 31 October 1870, p.3.

7   ibid., 31 October 1870, pp.2-3.

8   *Sydney Mail*, 31 December 1870, p.8.

9   See Elinor Rice Hays, *Those Extraordinary Blackwells: The Story of a Journey to a Better World*, New York: Harcourt, Brace & World, 1967; Patricia Clarke, *Pen Portraits: Women Writers and Journalists in Nineteenth Century Australia*, Sydney: Allen & Unwin, 1988, pp.108-12.

10 'Brook Farm', Encyclopaedia Britannica, britannica.com/topic/Brook-Farm.

11 'Sixty Years of Newspaper History', *Sydney Morning Herald*, 19 June 1897, p.10.

12 Papers of the Blackwell family 1831-1981, Schlesinger Library, Radcliffe Institute, Harvard University, hollisarchives.lib.harvard.edu/repositories/8/resources/4858; Women of the Blackwell Family exhibition, radcliffe.harvard.edu/event/2016-women-of-the-blackwell-family-exhibition; George Sand, *Jacques*, 1831, translated by Anna Blackwell 1847, reprinted 2016.

13 *Sydney Morning Herald*, 18 December 1860, p.3.

14 Fairfax Archives, James Reading Fairfax to John Fairfax, 31 January 1865. (I thank Peter Putnis for copies of these letters.)

15 Gavin Souter, *Heralds and Angels: The House of Fairfax 1841-1992*, Ringwood (Vic.): Penguin Books, 1992, p.34.

16 Fairfax Archives, James Reading Fairfax to John Fairfax, 29 August 1865.

17 Hays, *Those Extraordinary Blackwells*, p.172.

18 Souter, *Heralds and Angels*, p.36.

19 Fairfax Archives, James Reading Fairfax to Anna Blackwell, 4 June 1881.

20 Papers of the Blackwell family 1831-1981, Schlesinger Library.

21 Hays, *Those Extraordinary Blackwells*, p.263.

22 ibid., p.287.

23 *Sydney Morning Herald*, 4 June 1910, p.12.

Jessie (Tasma) Couvreur

1 Patricia Clarke, *Tasma: The Life of Jessie Couvreur*, Sydney: Allen & Unwin, 1994, ch.1.

2 ibid., ch.2, pp.63–4.

3 ibid., ch.3.

4 Patricia Clarke (ed.), *Tasma's Diaries with Another by Her Young Sister Edith Huybers*, Canberra: Mulini Press, 1995, p.2, Windward diary.

5 Windward diary, 17 June 1873.

6 Clarke, *Tasma*, pp.42–4.

7 Fraser v. Fraser divorce evidence, *Argus*, 14 December 1883.

8 'A Hint to the Paris Commissioners', The Lady's Column, *Australasian*, 24 November 1877, p.7.

9 See Clarke, *Tasma*, p.191, for list of articles by Tasma.

10 'How a Claim was Nearly Jumped in Gum-Tree Gully', *Australasian*, 19 January 1878; 'Concerning the Forthcoming Melbourne Cup', *The Australian Ladies' Annual*, 1878; Malus Oculus', *The "Vagabond"* Annual: Christmas 1877, Sydney: Turner and Henderson, 1877. See Clarke, *Tasma*, pp.189–90 for list of published short stories.

11 Phillip Mennell, *In Australian Wilds, and Other Colonial Tales and Sketches*, London: Hutchison, 1889, p.9; Tasma, 'Monsieur Caloche', *Australasian*, 27 April, 4 May 1878.

12 Edward Alfred Huybers diary, Fryer Library, FL MSS F373, 18 May 1879.

13 Tasma, 'The Familistères of Guise', *Australasian*, 21 August 1880, pp.230–1.

14 Tasma, 'Autumn in Paris', *Australasian*, 14 January 1882, p.7.

15 Tasma, 'Professor Nordenskiöld's North-East Passage', *Australasian*, 12 June 1880, p.8.

16 Tasma, 'A Trip through Central Europe. Hamburg', *Australasian*, 2 December S870, p.3; 'A Trip through Central Europe. Berlin', 16 December 1882, S872, pp.2–3.

17 Tasma, *A Knight of the White Feather*, London: William Heinemann, 1892, p.12.

18 '"Tasma", Mme Jessie Couvreur', *Queen*, 13 January 1894 (states article published in *Nouvelle Revue*).

19 Papers of Patricia Clarke, MS8363, series 5, box 25, folder 4, has text of lectures in French.

20 Tasma, 'Bordeaux, in its Relation with Australia', *Australasian*, 14 June 1881, p.743; 18 June 1881, p.275; *Queen*, 13 January 1894.

21 Edward Huybers, FL MSS F372, 'Arts, Science and Literature, Cercle artistique et littéraire. Madame Tasma', Anvers, nos 3, 9, 10.

22 Tasma, Brussels diary, 18 February 1889; Compte-Rendu des actes de la société royale géograhie, vol.13, no.1, January–February 1889, pp.12–13; *l'Indépendance belge*, 17 February 1889.

23 Tasma, 'An Interview with the King of the Belgians', The Traveller, *Australasian*, 16 July 1881, p.71.

24 Edward Huybers diary, FJ MSS 373, 5 February 1882.

25 Tasma, 'Bordeaux', *Australasian*, 14 June 1881, p.743; 18 June 1881, p.275.

26 Letter to author from J. Gencourt, Le Secrétaire Général Association des Membres de l'Ordre des Académiques, 8 January 1992.

27 Margaret James, 'Marriage and Marital Breakdown in Victoria 1860–1960', PhD thesis, La Trobe University, Melbourne, 1984, Appendix D; *Age*, *Argus*, 14 December 1883. The Fraser v Fraser divorce file is not in the Divorce Case Files 1861–1917, Victorian State Records Office, to which it was supposedly transferred from the Archives Division, State Library of Victoria, in 1968.

28 Clarke, *Tasma*, pp.89–91.

29 Edward Huybers diary, 17 February 1884.

30 UK Middlesex Marriage index, 144/1885.

31 Home Notes, 16 November 1896; *Queen*, 13 January 1894; *l'Indépendance belge*, 13 January 1889.

32 *Queen*, 13 January 1894; London *Times*, 2 May 1890.

33 Gail Cunningham, *The New Woman and the Victorian Novel*, London: Macmillan, 1978, p.1.

34 Clarke (ed.), *Tasma's Diaries with Another by Her Young Sister Edith Huybers*, Canberra: Mulini Press, 1995; Jessie Couvreur's Brussels diary 1889–1989, 3 December 1889.

35 *Times* (London), archives Wapping, Manager's Letter Book (MLB) 9/534, 27 April 1894.

36 MLB, 9/649, 25 May 1894.

37 Clarke, *Tasma*, p.131. The text of the letters is in the Manager's Letter Book (MLB) and the Foreign Manager's Letter Book (FMLB).

38 FMLB, 2/606, 8 August 1894; FMLB 3/178, 14 October 1895.

39 FMLB, 2/567, 5 July 1894.

40 MLB, 10/342, 29 October 1894.

41 FMLB, 2/786, 20 December 1894.

42   MLB 10/655, 3 January 1895.

43   *The History of The Times: The Twentieth Century Test 1884–1912*, London: The Times, 1935–1952, vol.3, p.176.

44   MLB, 12/199, 14 May 1895.

45   *The History of The Times*, vol.3, pp.223–4.

46   FMLB, 3/636, 11 November; 3/643, 15 November 1896.

47   Clarke, *Tasma*, pp.152–3, letter Jessie to Willie, 16 September 1897. Copy in MS8363, box 28, folder 22.

Flora Shaw

1   E. Moberly Bell, *Flora Shaw (Lady Lugard, DBE)*, London: Constable, 1947, p.167.

2   Helen Callaway and Dorothy O. Helly, 'Crusader for Empire: Flora Shaw/ Lady Lugard', in Nupur Chaudhuri and Margaret Strobel (eds), *Western Women and Imperialism*, Bloomington (USA): Indiana University Press, 1992, p.85.

3   *Worker*, Brisbane, 14 January 1893, p.1.

4   C. Kegan Paul, *Castle Blair: A Story of Youthful Days*, London: 1877. Four more children's novels followed.

5   *Pall Mall Gazette*, 28 June 1887.

6   Moberly Bell, *Flora Shaw (Lady Lugard, DBE)*, pp.50–5, 59.

7   ibid., p.76.

8   *The History of the Times: The Twentieth Century Test 1884–1912*, London: The Times, 1947, vol.3, p.139. Her first column was published on 29 May 1890.

9   ibid., pp.139–40.

10   Moberly Bell, p.120.

11   Bodleian Library, Papers of Flora Shaw (Lady Lugard), diary Bodleian, Library MSS Brit. Emp. s590, box 6/7. Extracts published Patricia Clarke, 'Flora Shaw: A "Lady from London" in 1890s Queensland', in *Celebrating Independent Thought. ISAA Twenty Years On: 2015 Conference Proceedings*, Independent Scholars Association of Australia, 2016, pp.33–50.

12   Shaw papers, letter to Lulu, Townsville, 9 October 1892, p.7.

13   ibid., p.8.

14   Shaw papers, letter, 9 October 1892.

15   Shaw papers, diary, 8 November 1892.

16   Dorothy O. Hely and Helen Callaway, 'Journalism as Active Politics: Flora Shaw, *The Times* and South Africa', in Donal Lowry, *The South African War Reappraised*, Manchester (UK): Manchester University Press, 2000, p.50.

17 K.H. Kennedy, 'Chataway, James Vincent (1852–1901)', *Australian Dictionary of Biography*, vol.7, 1979, pp.621–2.

18 Shaw papers, letter, on board SS *Peregrine*, Mackay, 15 October [1892].

19 ibid.

20 David Carment, 'D'Arcy, William Knox (1849–1917)', *ADB*, vol.8, 1981.

21 Shaw papers, diary, 20 October 1892.

22 'The Lady from London', *Worker*, 14 January 1893, p.1.

23 Shaw papers, diary, 20 October 1892.

24 ibid., 25 October 1892.

25 *Times*, 2 February 1893, p.6.

26 *Times*, 31 January 1893, p.3.

27 Shaw papers, letter, Blue Mountain Hotel, Toowoomba, 18 November 1892; *Times*, 31 January 1893, p.3.

28 Shaw papers, diary, 23 October 1892.

29 *Times*, 2 February 1893, p.6.

30 *Worker*, Brisbane, 14 January 1893, p.1.

31 Shaw papers, letter, 18 November 1892.

32 ibid.; *Times*, 2 February 1893, p.6.

33 *Times*, 2 February 1893, p.6.

34 Shaw papers, diary, 5 November 1892.

35 Shaw papers, letter, 18 November 1892.

36 The Times *Special Correspondent: Letters from Queensland*, London, Macmillan, 1893. The letters first appeared in *The Times*: 'Queensland', Brisbane, 27 December 1892, p.10; 'The Sugar Industry in Queensland', 7 January 1893, p.12; 'The Mineral Wealth of Queensland', Rockhampton, 12 January 1893, p.12; 'Pastoral Queensland', Blackall, Western Queensland, 31 January 1893, p.3; 'Pastoral Queensland' (cont.), 2 February 1893, p.6; 'The Queensland Separation Question', Brisbane, 9 February 1893, p.3.

37 Shaw papers, letter, 18 November 1892.

38 *Times*, 'New South Wales—Finance and Government', Sydney, 4 March 1893, p.5; 'The Labour Question', Sydney, 18 July 1893, p.3; 'New Unionism', Sydney, 26 July 1893, 13; 'Federation', Sydney, 2 August 1893, p.3; *Queenslander*, 14 January 1893.

39 *Times*, 'Victorian Finance', Melbourne, 30 March 1893, p.13: 'Victoria: The Mallee Country', Hopetoun, 5 April 1893, p.13; 'Intense Culture in Victoria', Mooroopna, Vic., 8 April 1893, p.15.

40 *Times*, 30 March 1893, p.13.

41 *Times*, 'The Wine Industry', Adelaide, South Australia, 24 May 1893, p.3;

'Broken Hill', 14 July 1893, p.3.

42   'Queensland', *Times*, Brisbane, 27 December 1892, p.10.

43   Callaway and Helly, 'Crusader for Empire: Flora Shaw/Lady Lugard', p.85; Moberly Bell, *Flora Shaw (Lady Lugard, DBE)*, p.167.

44   Callaway and Helly, p.79.

45   *The History of the Times*, p.182.

46   ibid., p.187.

47   ibid., pp.186, 192.

48   *Times*, 4 March 1893, p.5.

49   *The History of the Times*, p.192.

50   ibid., p.206.

51   Moberly Bell, p.188.

52   Callaway and Helly, p.88; Jos Sharrer, *The Journalist: The Jameson Raid, the Klondike Gold Rush, the Anglo Boer War, the Founding of Nigeria, Flora Shaw Was There*, North Charleston (USA): CreateSpace Publishing Platform, 2014, ch.20. (Jos Sharrer is a descendant of Flora Shaw's youngest brother.)

Edith Dickenson

1   Sir John Langdon Bonython Letterbooks (1845–1939), State Library of South Australia, BRG 10/18/12. (I am indebted to Peter Putnis for a copy of these records.)

2   ibid.

3   General Register Office, Dublin, Marriages, 2 April 1877.

4   Ludwig Bruch (ed.), *Australasian Medical Directory and Handbook*, 1886, doctor at Swan Hill; *Ballarat Star*, 27 January 1887, p.4.

5   Robert Caldwell, 'Mrs E.C. Dickenson', Adelaide *Advertiser*, 25 March 1903, p.6; Ellen Chennells, *Recollections of an Egyptian Princess by her English Governess*, Edinburgh: W. Blackwood and Sons, 1893.

6   Civil Registration Birth Index England Wales, Reginald G. Belcher, twin Frederick H. 04/1878, Blything, Sussex; Musgrave V. 7/1881; UK Incoming Passenger Lists 1978–1960, Reginald George Belcher born 22/4/178; South African Death Index Frederick Henry Belcher born 22/4/1978, death Natal 3/8/1945; Birth Musgrave Belcher 30/7/1881.

7   Licentiate Royal College of Physicians, Royal College of Surgeons, Midwifery Rotunda Lying-in Hospital Dublin; lecturer Anatomy, Carmichael School of Medicine.

8   'A Doctor's Desertion', p.4; *East Anglia Weekly News*, 8–9 December 1884.

9   Australian Birth Index, 1788–1922, 1125.

10   These sources include Steve Lipscombe, Edith's great grandson, a descendent of her eldest daughter, Edith Augusta Belcher, who remained in England. Lipscombe wrote a short biography of Edith for the Boer War Memorial in Anzac Avenue, Canberra.

11   UK High Court of Justice, Dickenson v. Dickenson, 15 November 1888; decree nisi 31 October 1889.

12   *The Sydney Morning Herald*, 4 May 1891, p.1.

13   St Peter's College enrolment records. Correspondence Andrea McKinnon-Matthews, archivist, with author, 14, 18, 19, 24 July, 5, 18 August 2018. Student cards Reginald Belcher 1891, Form II, 1892, Form III; Frederick 1891 Form I, 1892, Form II; Musgrave 1891, Form I. The Belchers were withdrawn from St Peter's at the end of first term, 1892. The records indicate that Frederick was not as bright as Reginald; he was put in the same class as Musgrave who was three years younger.

14   Ludwig Bruch (ed.), *Australasian Medical Directory and Handbook*, 1892, 3rd ed., p.54, Augustus Dickenson, doctor at Booleroo, late medical officer, Swan Hill Hospital, Victoria, former Demonstrator in Anatomy, Carmichael School of Medicine, Dublin; *South Australian Chronicle*, 25 June 1892, p.23.

15   Victorian BMD, Births in the District of Drouin, 446/28655/1894.

16   Robert Caldwell, *Advertiser*, 23 March 1903, p.6.

17   P. Horton, A. Black, and B. Blaylock, 'Ornithology at the South Australian Museum, Adelaide, 1866 to 1939', pp.241–457 in *Contributions to the History of Australasian Ornithology*, vol.iv, W.E. Davis, Jr., W.E. Boles and H.F. Rechter (eds), *Memoirs of the Nuttall Ornithological Club No.23*.

18   South Australia Parliament, *Parliamentary Paper* 45/1893; David Lindsay, *Journal of the Elder Expedition*, 2 May 1891, p.16; 'Elder Scientific Exploration Expedition', Royal Geographical Society of South Australia, rgssa.org.au/Exploration.htm

19   R.J. Noye, *Dictionary of South Australian Photography*, Adelaide: Art Gallery of South Australia, 2007, p.83.

20   'The Wreck of the *Phasis*. Experiences of an apprentice', Letter from Mrs Edith M. Dickenson, Maitland, Yorke's Peninsula, Adelaide *Observer*, 30 October 1897, p.29.

21   UK Royal Navy Records, Belcher, Musgrave Vanneck Gordon, no.201654.

22   *South Australian Register*, 28 October 1898, p.4; 'Passengers Mrs Dickenson for Calcutta. Palawan left London 21 October to Calcutta and Ceylon', *Times*, 3 October 1898, p.4.

23   Edith C.M. Dickenson, 'What I Saw in India and the East', [I], *Advertiser*, 23 September 1899, p.10; 'The Sonapur Fair', II, *Advertiser*, 7 October 1899, p.10; 'Country Quarters' [Siwan, Suddowah, Bihar], III, *Advertiser*, 14 October 1899, p.11; 'Sport in Bihar', IV, *Advertiser*, 21 October 1899, p.9.

24 Patricia Clarke, 'Edith Dickenson at the Boer War', *Reporting from the Wars 1850-2015: The Origins and Evolution of the War Correspondent*, Barry Turner, Daniel Barredo Ibanez and Steven James Grattan (eds), Wilmington (USA), Malaga (Spain): Vernon Press, Series in *Communication*, 2018.

25 *Advertiser*, 12 May 1900, p.6.

26 Mrs E.C.M. Dickenson, 'Provisioning Ladysmith. A Stream of Soldiers. Kindness of Sir George White. Sympathy with Boers', Durban, *Advertiser*, 12 May 1900, p.10.

27 Mrs E.C.M. Dickenson, 'What War Means', *Advertiser*, 2 June 1900, p.15; 'Battle Horrors', 9 June, p.11; 'Over Battlefields', 12 June, p.5.

28 Dickenson, 'In Ladysmith. Difficulties Overcome. Brother Fighting Brother. Sound of Distant Guns', *Advertiser*, 8 June 1900, p.6.

29 Dickenson, 'What War Means', *Advertiser*, 2 June 1900, p.15.

30 Dickenson, 'Over Battlefields. Risk of Boer Raids. Not as Black as Painted. A Soldier's Monument', Frere, *Advertiser*, 12 June 1900, p.5.

31 Mrs E.C.M. Dickenson, 'In Ladysmith', *Advertiser*, 8 June 1900, p.6.

32 Dickenson, 'Provisioning Ladysmith', *Advertiser*, 12 May 1900, p.10.

33 Stephen Badsey, 'War Correspondents in the Boer War' in John Gooch (ed.), *The Boer War*, London: Taylor and Francis, 2013, p.188; Miles Hudson and John Stonier, *War and the Media: A Random Searchlight*, New York: New York University Press, 1998, p.31.

34 Badsey, 'War Correspondents in the Boer War', pp.199, 202.

35 Emily Hobhouse, *The Brunt of the War*, p.305; Dickenson, 'The Orange River Colony: A Fortified Village: Bethulie Camp', Bethulie, *Advertiser*, 12 April 1902, p.4.

36 Dickenson, 'Attempted Invasion of Zululand. Original Orders to Joubert and Cronje. Durban and Cape Town Menaced', Durban, *Advertiser*, 13 November 1901, p.6.

37 Peter Putnis, 'News, Time and Imagined Community in Colonial Australia', *Media History*, 2010, vol.16, no.2, pp.4-15.

38 John Hirst, 'Empire, State, Nation', in D.M. Schreuder and Stuart Ward (eds), *Australia's Empire*, Oxford (UK): Oxford University Press, 2008, pp.155-6.

39 *Argus*, 21 May 1900, p.7; *Age*, 24 May 1900, p.5.

40 *Southern Cross*, 15 June 1900, p.7.

41 Fay Anderson and Richard Trembath, *Witnesses to War: The History of Australian Conflict Reporting*, Carlton (Vic.): Melbourne University Press, 2011, pp.33-4.

42 Adelaide *Express and Telegraph*, 17 July 1900, p.2.

43   'Paris Exhibition. Back in the Dark Ages. Ascending the Eiffel Tower', *Advertiser*, 31 December 1900, p.9.

44   *Advertiser*, 7 November 1900, p.9; the article was published in papers in Rockhampton, Hillston, Queanbeyan, Muswellbrook, Grenfell, Taree, Maclean and probably many others.

45   Dickenson, Letter to the Editor, *Register*, 16 April 1901, p.6.

46   *Yorke's Peninsula Advertiser*, 3 May 1901, p.2.

47   *Advertiser*, 26 June 1901, p.7; *Register*, 3 July 1901, p.9; *Laura Standard*, 2 August 1901, p.2; *Advertiser*, 2 September 1901, p.3.

48   'British Concentration Camps', geni.com/projects/Anglo-Boere-Oorlog-Boer-War-1899-1902-British-Concentration-Camps/854; Elizabeth van Heyningen, *The Concentration Camps of the Anglo-Boer War: A Social History*, Auckland Park (South Africa): Jacana, 2000, p.ix.

49   Hobhouse, *The Brunt of the War and Where It Fell*, London: Methuen and Co., 1902.

50   Dickenson, 'Boer Women and Children. Life in "Refugee Camps". Really Prisons. A Pathetic Account', Durban, *Advertiser*, 8 November 1901, p.6; Hobhouse, *The Brunt of the War*, pp.204–8; Dickenson, 'A Refugee Camp. Pitiful Stories. The Transvaal Still Closed', Howich, 30 November 1901, p.4; Hobhouse, *The Brunt of the War*, pp.208–12. There are many other examples.

51   Dickenson, 'Boer Women and Children. Life in "Refugee Camps". Really Prisons. A Pathetic Account', Durban, *Advertiser*, 8 November 1901, p.6; Hobhouse, *The Brunt of the War*, pp.204–8.

52   Dickenson, 'A Refugee Camp. Pitiful Stories. The Transvaal Still Closed', Howich, 30 November 1901, p.4; Hobhouse, *The Brunt of the War*, pp.208–12.

53   Dickenson, 'Pretoria. An Interesting Journey. A Refugee Camp Visited [Irene camp]. Dutch Relief Committee. Military Law', *Advertiser*, 25 December 1901, p.6; Hobhouse, *The Brunt of the War*, pp.189–90.

54   Dickenson, 'The Orange River Colony. A Fortified Village. Bethulie Camp', Bethulie, *Advertiser*, 12 April 1902, p.4.

55   Dickenson, 'Bloemfontein. The Refugee Camp. Kaffirs Garrisoning Blockhouses', *Advertiser*, 26 April 1902, p.9; Hobhouse, *The Brunt of the War*, pp.304–5.

56   *Advertiser*, 9 April 1902, p.3.

57   *Advertiser*, 22 September 1902, p.7; Dickenson, 'Johannesburg. Low Wages for White Men. High Cost of Living', *Advertiser*, 5 December 1902, p.6; *Advertiser*, 25 March 1903, p.6.

58   'The Week', *Chronicle*, 28 March 1903, p.25.

59   *Southern Cross*, 22 November 1901, p.7; personal correspondence and research.

60   Jeannine Baker, *Australian Women War Reporters: Boer War to Vietnam*, Sydney: NewSouth Publishing, 2015, pp.19–25.

61   *Catholic Press*, 21 September 1901, p.19; 13 September 1928, p.1.

Alice Henry

1   Alice Henry and S.M. Franklin, 'Why 50,000 Refuse to Sew', *Englishwoman*, June 1911, pp.297–308.

2   Alice Henry, *The Trade Union Woman*, New York: D. Appleton Co., 1915, pp.113–4.

3   *Life and Labor*, January 1913, pp.6–11; Alice Henry, *Women and the Labor Movement*, New York: George Doran Co., 1923, p.118.

4   *Life and Labor*, March 1911, pp.88–9; June 1912, pp.170–2.

5   Patricia Clarke, 'Australian Influence on the American Women's Labor Movement in the First Decades of the Twentieth Century: Alice Henry and Miles Franklin, Editors of *Life and Labor*', *The Independent Scholar*, vol.5, August 2019, pp.45–59, ncis.org/sites/default/files/TIS%20Vol.5%20 Aug2019_CLARKE_Australian_influence_on_women%27s_labor_ movement_twentieth_century_Alice_Henry_Miles_Franklin_editors_Life_ and_Labor.pdf

6   Henry, *The Trade Union Woman*, pp.74–5.

7   *Life and Labor*, Editorial, January 1911, p.1.

8   Alice Henry, *Memoirs of Alice Henry*, ed. Nettie Palmer with a postscript, Melbourne, 1944, pp.5–6.

9   Patricia Clarke, *Pen Portraits: Women Writers and Journalists in Nineteenth Century Australia*, Sydney: Allen & Unwin, 1988, p.186.

10   Henry, *Memoirs*, p.14.

11   Jeanne Young, *Catherine Helen Spence*, Melbourne: Lothian Publishing Co., 1939, p.132.

12   'Cleo', *Bulletin*, 14 November 1896.

13   *Australasian*, 28 November 1903, p.49; *Evening Journal*, 30 December 1903, p.2.

14   *Advertiser*, 1 December 1903, p.7.

15   Henry, *Memoirs*, p.15.

16   Henry, 'Teaching the Unteachables', *Argus*, 25 December 1897, p.8, 8 January 1898, p.14; 'Industrial Farm Colonies for Epileptics': Paper to Australasian Science Congress, *Tasmanian News*, 17 December 1901, p.3, repeated in many Australian papers.

17   *Argus*, 19 January 1898, p.7; *Age*, 6 May 1902, p.4; 11 July 1902, p.3; *Town and Country Journal*, 18 May 1904, p.40.

18 *Age*, 15 April, p.12; 19 April 1905, p.10.

19 Henry, *Memoirs*, p.41.

20 Henry, 'Industrial Democracy: The Australian Labor Movement', *The Outlook*, 3 November 1906, pp.566–70.

21 Diane Kirkby, '"Those Knights of Pen and Pencil": Women Journalists and Cultural Leadership of the Women's Movement in Australia and the United States', in *Labour History*, May 2013, pp.82–4.

22 Henry, *Memoirs*, p.89.

23 Diane Kirkby, *Alice Henry: The Power of Pen and Voice: The Life of an Australian-American Labor Reformer*, Cambridge: Cambridge University Press, 1991, p.118.

24 Clare Wright, theconversation.com/birth-of-a-nation-how-australia-empowering-women-taught-the-world-a-lesson-52492.

25 Stella Miles Franklin to Aunt Annie (Mrs Thomas Franklin), Brindabella station, via Canberra, *Life and Labor*, Room 901, 127 Dearborn Street, Chicago, 21 November 1913 (copy with author).

26 *Life and Labor*, September 1914, pp.260–3.

27 *Life and Labor*, December 1914, pp.357–9.

28 Henry, 'The Living Wage', *Life and Labor*, July 1913, p.195; 'Wages Boards in Australia', June 1914, pp.79–81; Margaret Dreier Robins, 'The Minimum Wage', June 1913, pp.168–72.

29 Henry, 'The Chicago Waitresses', *Life and Labor*, April 1914, pp.100–03.

30 Henry, 'The Vice Problem from Various Angles', *Life and Labor*, May 1913, pp.141–4; 'Municipal Mastery of Vice,' December 1912, pp.363–4.

31 *Life and Labor,* February 1915, p.1.

32 Jill Roe, *Stella Miles Franklin*, Fourth Estate, Pymble NSW, 2008, pp.153–4.

33 Kirkby, *The Power of Pen and Voice*, pp.121–3; Roe, *Stella Miles Franklin*, p.154.

34 Kirkby, *The Power of Pen and Voice*, pp.123–4.

35 Clarke, *Pen Portraits*, pp.160–71.

36 Patricia Clarke, 'Women in the Media', in Bridget Griffen-Foley (ed.), *A Companion to the Australian Media*, Melbourne: Australian Scholarly Publishing, 2014, p.496.

37 National Library of Australia, MS1006, Papers of Alice Henry, box 2, *Evening World*, 11 February 1925.

38 National Library of Australia, MS1924, Herbert and Ivy Brookes correspondence.

39 Henry to Brookes, Brookes correspondence, box 84, 25/4990-2, 22, 31 October 1930, 31 August 1931.

40 Henry, 'Marching Towards Citizenship', in Francis Fraser and Nettie Palmer (eds), *Centenary Gift Book*, Melbourne: Robertson and Mullins, 1934, pp.101–7.

41 Henry to Brookes, Brookes correspondence, box 112, 39/191, 6 February 1938, 39/195, 8 April 1938, 39/279/280, 29 June 1939. Henry's bibliography is now available at SLNSW Mitchell Library QA820.3/H.

42 Henry to Brookes, Brookes correspondence, box 91, 26/321-2, 30 May, 1 June 1936.

43 Kirkby, *The Power of Pen and Voice*, p.221.

44 D.J. Jordan, 'Palmer, Janet Gertrude (Nettie) (1885–1964)', *Australian Dictionary of Biography*, vol.11, 1988; NLA MS3942, Papers of Vance and Nettie Palmer.

45 Nettie Palmer, 'Postscript' in Henry, *Memoirs of Alice Henry*, Melbourne: 1944.

46 ibid., pp.96–9; *Woman Today*, December 1936, p.4; Nettie Palmer, 'Pathfinders: Who was Alice Henry?', *Australian Women's Digest*, April 1945, pp.19–20.

47 Alice Henry's entry in The Australian Media Hall of Fame, halloffame. melbournepressclub.com/article/alice-henry.

Jennie Scott Griffiths

1 Patricia Clarke, 'Jennie Scott Griffiths: How a Conservative Texan Became a Radical Socialist and Feminist in World War I Australia', *ISAA Review*, vol.15, no.2, 2016, pp.31–51; 'Jennie Scott Griffiths: A Texas-born 'Red-ragger', *Unbound*, NLA Magazine, June 2017.

2 National Library of Australia, MS1071/1, Papers of Jennie Scott Griffiths (JSG), memoir.

3 JSG papers, Acc 02.050/1/1, cuttings Texas.

4 Ciwa Griffiths, *One of Ten*, Laguna Hills (USA): Wide Range Press, 1993, p.30. Copy in JSG papers, Acc 08.058/3.

5 Ciwa Griffiths, *One of Ten*, p.13.

6 JSG papers, MS1071/1; JSG papers, Acc 02.050/1/1, cuttings Texas.

7 JSG papers, Acc 02.050/1/1, cuttings Texas; JSG papers, Acc 02.050/3/16, cuttings Texas Farmer, 28 December 1895.

8 JSG papers, MS1071/1; JSG papers, Acc 02.050/1/1, cuttings Texas.

9 *Sacramento Daily Union*, 30 June 1894, p.1.

10 JSG papers, Acc 02.050/3/17, JSG diary.

11 Bruce Knapman, *Fiji's Economic History 1874–1939*, RSSS, ANU, 1987, p.1.

12 Ciwa Griffiths, *One of Ten*, p.19; JSG papers, MS1071/1.

13 Ciwa Griffiths, *One of Ten*, pp.23–112.

14 JSG papers, Acc 11.064/25.

15 JSG papers, Acc 11.064, JSG memoirs, pp.75–6.

16 ibid., p.75.

17 ibid., p.75.

18 L.G. Usher, *Brief History of the Fiji Times*, paper read to the Fiji Society, 15 October 1962. Copy in JSG papers, Acc 10.211.

19 JSG papers, MS 1071/1.

20 *The Fiji Times Our First 100 Years 1869–1969 Centennial Supplement*, p.3; several extracts throughout publication. Copy in JSG papers, Acc 10.211.

21 JSG papers, MS 1071/1.

22 JSG papers, Acc 11.064, Arthur Griffiths 'Recollections of Fiji', p.16.

23 *Fiji Times Centennial*, pp.4, 9, 25.

24 Pers. comm., Gerry Whitmont, 22 February 2016; Ciwa Griffiths, p.27.

25 NSW BDM 135161912; JSG papers, Acc 08.058, 18 July 1912.

26 Joy Damousi, *Women Come Rally: Socialism, Communism and Gender in Australia 1890–1955*, Oxford University Press, Melbourne, 1994, pp.20–1.

27 JSG papers, Acc 11.064/7, correspondence Mary Gilmore, 16 December 1912.

28 *Australian Women's Weekly*, 18 September 1915, p.13.

29 Patricia Clarke, *Pen Portraits: Women Writers and Journalists in Nineteenth Century Australia*, Sydney: Allen & Unwin, 1988, pp.160–71.

30 *Australian Woman's Weekly*, 1 April 1916, p.13.

31 JSG papers, Acc 02.050/1/4. The series was published regularly for about a year from July 1913; including on 6 September, 18 October, 15, 22 November 1913.

32 *Australian Woman's Weekly*, 20 March 1915, p.27; 20 May 1915, p.25; 6 November 1915, p.30.

33 *Australian Woman's Weekly*, 29 May 1915, pp.1–2.

34 *Australian Woman's Weekly*, 20 March 1915, pp.19–20.

35 *Australian Woman's Weekly*, 18 September 1915, p.1; 29 May 1915, pp.26, 30.

36 *Australian Woman's Weekly*, 18 September 1915, p.1.

37 *Australian Woman's Weekly*, 6 November 1915, pp.5, 16–17, 25–8.

38 *Australian Woman's Weekly*, 1 April 1916, pp.3–5.

39 JSG papers, Acc 08.058, *Worker*, 21 September 1914.

40 JSG papers, Acc 11.064/7, 16 December 1915.

41 JSG papers, Acc 08.058, Scrapbook; 'What Women Demand', *Worker*, 5 October 1916.

42 JSG papers, Acc 08.058; *International Socialist*, undated.

43 JSG papers, Acc 08.058, 'The State and the Woman', *Sunday Times*, 28 May, 4 June, 16 July, 6 August 1916.

44 Joy Damousi, 'Universities and Conscription', in Robin Archer et al. (eds), *The Conscription Conflict and the Great War*, Clayton (Vic.): Monash University Publishing, 2016, pp.106, 95.

45 Frank Bongiorno, 'Anti-Conscriptionism in Australia', in *The Conscription Conflict and the Great War*, pp.83–4.

46 Marilyn Lake, *Getting Equal: A History of Australian Feminism*, St Leonards (NSW): Allen & Unwin, 1999, p.64.

47 JSG papers, Acc 11.064, JSG's account and Don Griffiths' memoir.

48 JSG papers, Acc 11.064, Don Griffiths' memoir.

49 Damousi, 'Universities and Conscription', p.21; Rosemary Francis, 'Women's Peace Army', *Australian Women's Register*, womenaustralia.info/biogs/AWE0542b.htm.

50 Ciwa Griffiths, *One of Ten*, p.161.

51 JSG papers, Acc 11.064, *Worker*, 14 December 1916.

52 JSG papers, Acc 11.064; *Worker*, 5 October 1916.

53 JSG papers, Acc 08.058, *Worker*, 19 April 1917.

54 Damousi, 'Universities and Conscription', p.31.

55 Catie Gilchrist, 'Socialist Opposition to World War I', in *Dictionary of Sydney*, 2014, dictionaryofsydney.org/entry/socialist_opposition_to_world_war_i.

56 Joan Beaumont, *Broken Nation: Australians in the Great War*, Sydney: Allen & Unwin, 2014, p.233.

57 *Queanbeyan Age and Queanbeyan Observer*, 23 November 1917, p.2; Patricia Clarke and Niki Francis, *Canberra Women in World War I: Community at Home, Nurses Abroad*, womenaustralia.info/exhib/cww1/essay.html.

58 JSG papers, Acc 11.064, letters dated late 1917 resigning from organisations in Sydney.

59 JSG papers, Acc 08.058 cuttings; Evans, pp.26, 93.

60 JSG papers, Acc 11.064/6.

61 Evans, pp.112, 116; *Brisbane Courier*, 24 March 1919.

62 Acc 11.064 Military Intelligence Reports; *Knowledge and Unity*, 26 July 1919; Evans, p.158.

63 JSG papers, Acc 08.058, scrapbook of newspaper cuttings on the Red Flag prisoners.

64 JSG papers, Acc 14.033, handbag presented to JSG by Red Flag prisoners.

65 JSG papers, Acc 02.050/4/5.

66   JSG papers, Acc 02.050/2/5.

67   JSG papers, Acc 02.050/3/15, 20; JSG papers, Acc 02.050/3/18.

68   JSG Papers, Acc 02.050/4; *Industrial Worker*, 6 July 1951.

69   JSG papers, Acc 11.064, Don Griffiths memoir.

70   Ciwa Griffiths, *One of Ten*, introduction.

Stella Allan

1   Stella Allan, 'Nine of Us', n.d., Canterbury Museum, ARC1990.51.

2   New South Wales Marriages Henderson/Conolly, 29 August 1859, no.1195.

3   Stella Allan, 'My Finest Teachers', *Christchurch Star-Sun*, 26 August 1958, p.2.

4   Coral Broadbent, 'Stella May Henderson 1871–1962: Feminist, University Graduate, Journalist,' *Dictionary of New Zealand Biography*, updated 22 June 2007, dnzb.govt.nz/.

5   Patricia A. Sargison, 'Christina Kirk Henderson 1861–1953: Teacher, Feminist', *Dictionary of New Zealand Biography*, updated 22 June 2007, dnzb.govt.nz/.

6   'Wellington News', *Star*, 16 May 1898, p.3.

7   'Meetings of Societies', *Star*, 27 May 1898, p.3.

8   Broadbent, dnzb.govt.nz/.

9   Allan, '*Lyttelton Times* Engaged Dominion's First Woman Political Reporter', *Christchurch Star-Sun*, 16 October 1958, p.2.

10   'Women Parliamentary Reporters', *Star*, 16 August 1898, p.4.

11   'Ladies as Reporters', Melbourne *Age*, 3 September 1898, p.13.

12   Patricia Clarke, *Pen Portraits: Women Writers and Journalists in Nineteenth-Century Australia*, Sydney: Allen & Unwin, 1988, pp.164–5.

13   Allan, *Christchurch Star-Sun*, 16 October 1958, p.2.

14   'All Sorts of People', *New Zealand Free Lance*, 6 September 1902, p.3.

15   'Personal and general', *Star*, 9 December 1898, p.4.

16   Allan, *Christchurch Star-Sun*, 16 October 1958, p.2.

17   'Death of Mr E.F. Allan', Melbourne *Argus*, 3 February 1922, p.6.

18   H.J. Gibbney, 'Lukin, Gresley 1840–1916', *ADB*, vol.5, 1974.

19   'All Sorts of People', *New Zealand Free Lance*, 11 July 1903, p.3.

20   'All Sorts of People', *New Zealand Free Lance*, 30 March 1901, p.3.

21   Jean Garner, 'Elizabeth Reid McCombs 1873–1935: Socialist, Social Worker, Politician', *Dictionary of New Zealand Biography*, dnzb.govt.nz/.

22   'All Sorts of People', *New Zealand Free Lance*, 7 December 1901, p.4.

23   Allan, *Christchurch Star-Sun*, 16 October 1958, p.2.

24 Sheila Wigmore, Dolly Baverstock, Bill Baverstock, 'Florence Baverstock—First Time President', *Ink*, no.2, ed. Hilarie Lindsay, Sydney NSW, Society of Australian Women Writers (Aust), 1977, pp.103–5.

25 Allan, *Christchurch Star-Sun*, 16 October 1958, p.2.

26 Charles Patrick Smith, 'Men Who Made the *Argus* and the *Australasian* 1846–1923', c.1923, SLV MS Box 4670/3.

27 Patricia Clarke, 'Part-time Columnists to Women's Page Editors: The Problematic Advance of Women Journalists', in *Paper Headliners: Early Australasian Press Biographies* Conference, Sydney: Macquarie University/State Library of NSW, 23 November 2010; 'The Transformation of Journalist Stella Allan: From Soap-box Socialist to Conservative Women's Page Editor', *Australian Journalism Review*, no.33 (2), December 2011, pp.41–9.

28 Patricia Clarke, 'Pioneer Woman Journalist's Career Spanned Two Continents', *Margin: Life and Letters of Early Australia*, September 2007, pp.15–26.

29 'Work of Women Journalists: Lord Northcliffe's Views', *Australian Journalist*, 21 February 1913, pp.17–18.

30 National Library of Australia, MS8363 Papers of Patricia Clarke, Mrs Douglas (Patricia) Keep, 'Address at Women's Australia Day Ceremony, Melbourne, 22 January 1976', box 15, folder 40.

31 David Dunstan, '*The Argus*: The Life, Death and Remembering of a Great Australian Newspaper' in Muriel Porter (ed.), *The Argus: The Life and Death of a Great Melbourne Newspaper 1846–1957*, Melbourne: RMIT University, 2003, pp.31, 34–5.

32 Vesta, 'Lessons of the Referendum Failure of Education', *Argus*, 15 November 1916, p.12.

33 Vesta, 'The Reinforcements Campaign: A Last Appeal', *Argus*, 19 December 1917, p.12.

34 Vesta, 'Women and the War: The Suffrage Question', *Argus*, 14 February 1917, p.12.

35 'Some Australian Women', *Illustrated Sydney News*, 11 April 1891, p.13.

36 Catherine Helen Spence, *An Autobiography*, Adelaide: W.K. Thomas, 1910, p.56.

37 Clarke, *Pen Portraits*, p.253.

38 *Bulletin*, 30 December 1912, p.22.

39 Deborah Chambers, Linda Steiner, and Carole Fleming, *Women and Journalism*, London: Routledge, 2004, pp.21–2.

40 Clarke, *Pen Portraits*, p.253.

41 Patricia Clarke, 'Women in the Media' in Bridget Griffen Foley (ed.), *Companion the Australian Media*, Australian Scholarly Publishing, 2014,

pp.495–8.

42 'Current Literature', *Argus*, 6 January 1894, p.14; *Ladies at Work: Papers on Paid Employments for Ladies by Experts in the Several Branches*, introduction by Lady Jeune, London: A.D. Innes, 1893, pp.29–39.

43 R. Warden, 'Girl Reporters: Sydney Chiefs Not Certain How Many Will Stay on After War', *Journalist*, September 1894, p.3.

44 Victorian Deaths, Edwin Frank Allan, 4 February 1922, no.1823.

45 'Death of Mr E.F. Allan', *Argus*, 3 February 1922, p.6, 4 February 1922, p.20.

46 'Mrs Allen (sic) MA LLB', *International Woman Suffrage News*, November 1924, p.19.

47 'League of Nations: Australia and Refugee Problems', *Argus*, 6 March 1925, p.33.

48 'Tribute to Woman Journalist: Mrs E.F. Allan Honoured', *Argus*, 3 May 1938, p.7.

49 Mrs Douglas Keep, Clarke Papers, NLA MS8363/15/40.

50 Jeanette Conway, 'The '50s World of an *Argus* Woman Cadet', in Jim Usher (ed.), *The Argus: Life and Death of a Newspaper*, North Melbourne (Vic.): Australian Scholarly Publishing, 2008, pp.62.

51 Patricia Keep, 'Allan, Stella May (18711962)', *ADB*, Carlton: MUP, 1969, vol.7, pp.39–40.

Frances Taylor

1 Stanley Kingsbury, 'Adventures of "The Midge"', *Barrier Miner*, 5 December 1925, p.7.

2 ibid.

3 *Victorian Congregational Year Book*, ed. Rev. J.J. Halley, Melbourne, 1903, p.155; 1906, p.151.

4 M.O. Reid, *The Ladies Came to Stay: Presbyterian Ladies College Melbourne 1875–1960*, PLC Council, 1960, p.199.

5 S.A., 'In Memoriam', *Woman's World*, February 1934, p.5.

6 Rod Kirkpatrick, *The Bold Type: A History of Victoria's Country Newspapers 1840–2010*, Ascot Vale (Vic.): Victorian Country Press Association, 2010, pp.134–5.

7 Malcom Saunders, 'Taylor, Harry Samuel 1873–1932', *Australian Dictionary of Biography*, vol.12, 1990, p.179–80; Gavin Souter, *A Peculiar People: The Australians in Paraguay*, Sydney: Angus & Robertson, 1968, pp.28, 77, 170–1.

8 *Recorder* (Port Pirie), 1 January 1934, p.4.

9 Jackie Dickenson, *Australian Women in Advertising in the Twentieth Century*, Melbourne: Palgrave Macmillan, 2016, p.27.

10 Barbara Hall and Jenni Mather, 'Ruth Hollick (1883–1977)', in *Australian Women Photographers 1840 to 1960*, Richmond (Vic.): Greenhouse, 1986, pp.64–5.

11 *Woman's World*, vol.1, no.1, December 1921.

12 Frances Taylor Diary 1916, State Library of Victoria, MS Box 985/5.

13 Further information of Frances Taylor's life see Patricia Clarke, 'Frances Taylor, Founder and Editor, Guides *Woman's World* to Success', *La Trobe Journal*, 2019, pp.40–54.

14 *The Gum Tree*, vol.4, no.13, March 1920, ed. Frances Taylor, article pp.9–13.

15 *Argus*, 27 December 1933, p.11.

16 Dickenson, *Australian Women in Advertising in the Twentieth Century*, p.28.

17 Joan Gillison, *A History of the Lyceum Club*, Melbourne: The Lyceum Club, 1975, pp.58–9.

18 Dickenson, *Australian Women in Advertising in the Twentieth Century*, pp.28–9.

19 M.V.T., 'Her Hills', *Woman's World*, February 1934, p.7.

20 Anna T. Brennan, 'Blazing the Trail', in *Centenary Gift Book*, Women's Centenary Council, Melbourne: Robertson & Mullins, 1934, p.21.

21 Betty MacMillan, Editorial, *Woman's World*, February 1934, p.8.

22 Kingsbury, 'Adventures of "The Midge"', p.7.

23 SLV, MS Box 985/5, letter accompanying Frances Taylor's diary.

24 Kingsbury, 'Adventures of "The Midge"', p.7.

25 *Woman's World*, 1 December 1921, p.18.

26 *Woman's World*, 1 December 1921, p.5.

27 Brennan, *Centenary Gift Book*, p.21.

28 M.V.T., *Woman's World*, February 1934, p.7.

29 G. Flos Greig, 'Norfolk Island', *Woman's World*, April 1922, pp.14–16; May pp.13–16; 'The New Hebrides', June, pp.23–6; July, pp.24–6; 'New Caledonia', August, pp.14–6; September, pp.31–4; October, pp.31–4.

30 Taylor, 'The Girl in the Canoe', 'How I Saw Chinatown, Rabaul', *Woman's World*, December 1923, pp.23, 47.

31 Taylor, 'Witu', *Woman's World*, March 1923, pp.155, 176.

32 Taylor, 'Mrs A.E. Wisdom: Government House, Rabaul', *Woman's World*, November, pp.13–16; 'The Home of Mrs Kaumann, Rabaul', February 1923, p.61; 'The Girl in the Canoe', 'Towards Islands of Romance, *Woman's World*, November 1922, pp.27–8.

33 Taylor's articles were published between November 1922 and November 1923.

34 Taylor, 'Drivers of Austin 7', 'Driving the Light Car', *Woman's World*,

December 1926, pp.730–31.

35 'The Hut in the Hills', *Woman's World*, December 1921, p.31.

36 M.V.T., *Woman's World*, February 1934, p.7.

37 *Sun* (Sydney), 16 August 1923, p.13.

38 Margaret Preston, 'Coloured Woodprints', *Woman's World*, January 1912, pp.64, 113.

39 E.A. Allan, 'The World's Greatest Parliament', *Woman's World*, April 1925, pp.205, 229–30.

40 Gillison, *A History of the Lyceum Club*, p.59.

41 Brennan, *Centenary Gift Book*, p.21.

42 One published by John Fairfax, one by the Empire Press Union, another by the Victorian Government and one in London by Hodder and Stoughton.

43 I.F.T., 'Where the Women of Forty Nations Met: With the Australian Delegation to the Tenth Congress of the International Suffrage Alliance', *Woman's World*, October 1926, pp.604–5.

44 'An Editor Abroad', *Observer* (Adelaide), 2 October 1926, p.54; Reid, p.200.

45 Patricia Clarke, *Pen Portraits*, Sydney: Allen & Unwin, 1988, pp.160–80.

46 Helena Studdart, 'Women's Magazines', in Martin Lyons and John Arnold (eds), *A History of the Book in Australia 1891–1945*, St Lucia (Qld): UQP, 2001, pp.277–9.

47 S.A., *Woman's World*, February 1934, pp.5–6.

48 'Girl Editor: Miss Betty MacMillan', *Telegraph* (Brisbane), 8 February 1934, p.6.

49 Studdert, *A History of the Book in Australia 1891–1945*, pp.280–1.

50 *Barrier Miner*, 5 December 1925, p.7.

51 *Australasian*, 30 December 1933, p.14; *Argus*, 27 December 1933, p.11.

52 *Argus*, 24 March 1934, p.20; *Mercury*, 27 March 1934, p.12.

Janet Mitchell

1 Janet Mitchell, *Spoils of Opportunity*, London: Methuen & Co., 1937, p.163.

2 Robert W. Desmond, *Tides of War: World News Reporting between Two Wars, 1920–1940*, Iowa City: University of Iowa Press, 1984, p.3; Rana Mitter, *China's War with Japan 1937–1945: The Struggle for Survival*, London: Penguin, 2013, pp.49–50.

3 Tomoko Akami, *Japan's News Propaganda and Reuters' News Empire in Northeast Asia, 1870–1934*, The Netherlands: Dordrecht, 2012, pp.205–6.

4 National Archives of Australia, SP369/2, Janet Mitchell 'Manchuria: An Australian Travels in the War Zone', 2 January 1933.

5   Mitchell, *Spoils of Opportunity*, p.163.

6   Paula Hamilton, 'Journalism, Gender and Workplace Culture 1900-1940', in Ann Cuthoys and Julienne Schultz (eds), *Journalism: Print, Politics and Popular Culture*, Brisbane: University of Queensland Press, 1999, p.103; Patricia Clarke, 'Women in the Media', in Bridget Griffen-Foley (ed.), *A Companion to the Australian Media*, Melbourne: Australian Scholarly Publishing, 2014, p.495; see also Patricia Clarke, 'Australian Journalist Reports from "the Storm Centre of Asia": Manzhou (Manchuria) 1931-32', *Victorian Historical Journal*, vol.87, no.2, December 2016, pp.217-36.

7   Mitchell, *Spoils of Opportunity*, p.142.

8   Mary Mitchell, *A Warning to Wantons*, 1934; Lady Mitchell, *Half a Century*, London: 1940; Nancy Adams, *Saxon Sheep*, Melbourne: 1961.

9   Mitchell, *Spoils of Opportunity*, ch.2-7.

10   ibid., pp.55-7.

11   Margaret Dunn, *The Dauntless Bunch: The Story of the YWCA in Australia*, Melbourne: YWCA, 1991, p.68.

12   Mitchell, *Spoils of Opportunity*, p.59.

13   Dunn, *The Dauntless Bunch*, pp.92-3.

14   Mitchell, *Spoils of Opportunity*, pp.60-1.

15   Fiona Paisley, *Glamour in the Pacific: Cultural Internationalism and Race Politics in the Women's Pan Pacific*, Honolulu (USA): University of Hawaii Press, 2009, p.34; Muriel Heagney, Muriel Swain and Eleanor Hinder were delegates to the Pan-Pacific Women's Association inaugural conference in Honolulu. The latter two were delegates to the IPR conference in Shanghai in 1931.

16   Mitchell, *Spoils of Opportunity*, p.60; David Walker, *Anxious Nation: Australia and the Rise of Asia, 1850-1939*, New Delhi: SSS Publications, 2009, 2nd ed., p.188.

17   Mitchell, *Spoils of Opportunity*, pp.73-4.

18   Walker, *Anxious Nation*, p.188; Mitchell, *Spoils of Opportunity*, p.67.

19   *Argus*, 1 September 1925, p.11.

20   Mitchell, *Spoils of Opportunity*, pp.81-96.

21   National Archives of Australia, SP300/1, Janet Mitchell, 'Christmas with the Roosevelts', 31 March 1945; Mitchell, *Spoils*, pp.96-8.

22   Noel Griffiths, *A History of the Government Savings Bank of New South Wales*, Sydney: W.T. Baker, 1930, p.61.

23   Marjorie Harding, *This City of Peace by 23 Australian Converts to the Catholic Church*, Melbourne: Legion of Mary, 1949, pp.114-15.

24   *Sydney Morning Herald*, 19 August 1931, p.5; NAA SP300/1, Janet Mitchell,

'Income Management—Budgeting—Planned Spending', 15 October 1941.

25 *Argus*, 4 August 1931, p.3.

26 'The United Associations of Women', womenaustralia.info/biogs/AWE1023b.
htm; Winifred Mitchell, *Fifty Years of Feminist Achievement: A History of the
United Associations of Women*, Sydney: UAW, 1979, pp.6–7.

27 NLA MS 1837/30, Watt Papers, Mitchell/Watt correspondence, 18 October
1930.

28 Francis Anderson, *'War or Peace'*, League of Nations Union, leaflet no.1, p.3.

29 *Sydney Morning Herald*, 19 August 1931, p.5.

30 Tomoko Akami, *Internationalizing the Pacific*, London: Routledge, 2002,
p.159.

31 Mitchell, *Spoils of Opportunity*, p.147.

32 National Archives of Australia, SP369/2, Mitchell, 2 January 1933.

33 Mitchell, *Spoils of Opportunity*, pp.167, 169; NAA SP369/2, 2 January 1933.

34 National Archives of Australia, SP369/2, Mitchell, 2 January 1933.

35 ibid.

36 Earle Albert Selle, *Donald of China*, New York: Harper & Bros, 1948,
p.269.

37 Jacqui Murray, *Watching the Sun Rise: Australian Reporting of Japan 1931 to the
Fall of Singapore*, Lanham (USA): Lexington Books, 2004, p.17.

38 Heather Radi (ed.), *200 Australian Women: A Redress Anthology*, Sydney,
Women's Redress Press, 1988, p.194; Jeannine Baker, *Australian Women War
Reporters: Boer War to Vietnam*, Sydney: New South, 2015, p.36.

39 *Argus*, 13 February 1932, p.9.

40 Mitchell, *Spoils of Opportunity*, p.188.

41 *Argus*, 9 July 1932, p.9.

42 ibid.

43 Selle, *Donald of China*, p.279; Mitchell, *Spoils of Opportunity*, p.222.

44 *Southern Mail*, 17 February 1933, p.2.

45 William J. Pickard, *Kathleen Rouse of Rouse Hill: The Road to Harbin*, self-
published, 1992.

46 Harding, *This City of Peace by 23 Australian Converts to the Catholic Church*,
p.116.

47 Mitchell, *Spoils of Opportunity*, p.262.

48 Guy Trantor, ABC Sydney, to author, 13 September 2013.

49 NAA SP369/2, 2 January 1933.

50 ibid.

51   NAA SP369/2, 16 January 1933.

52   NAA SP300/1, 'Japan's Colonizing Methods in Manchuria', 1941.

53   Mitchell, *Spoils of Opportunity*, pp.269–75.

54   Jacqui Murray, 'Japan: The National News Story that was Not Told', *Australian Studies in Journalism*, no.3, 1994, pp.57–8; E.M. Andrews, 'Mann, Edward Alexander (1874–1951)', *ADB*, vol.10, 1986.

55   W. Macmahon Ball, *Press, Radio and World Affairs*, Melbourne: Melbourne University Press, 1938, pp.9–16.

56   A.G. Pearson, 'The Australian Press and Japan', in *Press, Radio and World Affairs*, pp.34–55.

57   W.J. Hudson, *Australia and the League of Nations*, Sydney: Sydney University Press, 1980, pp.69, 73.

58   *Sydney Morning Herald*, 11 November 1946, p.2.

59   *Southern Mail*, 17 February 1933, p.2; *Sydney Morning Herald*, 3 May 1933, p.12.

60   *Sydney Morning Herald*, 8 March 1933, p.12.

61   *Sydney Morning Herald*, 15 March 1933, p.8.

62   *Adelaide Advertiser*, 6 January 1933, p.21; *Sydney Sun*, 25 December 1932, p.19.

63   Mitchell, *Tempest in Paradise*, London: Geoffrey Bles, 1935; Mitchell, *Spoils*, p.269.

64   Quoted in Bridget Griffen-Foley, '"The Crumbs are Better than a Feast Elsewhere": Australian Journalists on Fleet Street', in Carl Bridge, Robert Crawford and David Dunstan (eds), *Australians in Britain: The Twentieth Century Experience*, Melbourne: Monash University ePress, 2009, p.8, 11.

65   Mitchell, *Spoils of Opportunity*, pp.284–5.

66   Frank Watts, *A Paper on the ABC's Education Department and Its Work*, Background Paper, ABC, January 1974, pp.10–11; *ABC Weekly*, 11 October 1947, p.19; *Adelaide Advertiser*, 17 September 1947, p.15.

67   *Radio Active*, 5 September 1955, p.11; 16 September 1957, p.13.

68   Mitchell, *Spoils of Opportunity*, pp.262, 266.

Caroline (Lynka) Isaacson

1   Information on Caroline Isaacson's life is drawn from the following sources: Harold A. Freeman, 'The Charismatic Caroline Isaacson', *Australian Jewish Historical Society Journal*, vol.xviii, 2007, part 4, pp.506–17; Patricia Clarke, 'Caroline (Lynka) Isaacson, 1900–1962', in Michael Smith and Mark Baker (eds), *Media Legends: Journalists Who Helped Shape Australia*, Melbourne, (Vic.): Wilkinson Publishing/Melbourne Press Club, 2014, pp.120–23; Denis Warner, *The Pathfinder: In the Air—On the Ground: The Peter Isaacson Story*,

Melbourne (Vic.): Information Australia, 2000; Sally A. White, 'Isaacson, Caroline (Lynka) (1900–1962)', *Australian Dictionary of Biography*, vol.14, Melbourne University Press, 1996.

2   National Archives of Australia, Isaacson, Arnold, B2455, barcode 7368134.

3   Clarke, *Media Legends*, pp.120–21; White, *ADB*, 1996.

4   *The Leader Spare Corner Book: A Unique Collection of Home and Household Hints and Kitchen Recipes: For Australian Women*, Melbourne: David Syme & Co., published in many editions, 1929 to 1940.

5   State Library Victoria lists editions every second year from 1930 to 1940, each containing several sections named 'Parts' from 2 to 9, which may have been published each year.

6   Mrs Isaacson, 'Women in Journalism', *Australian Jewish News*, 9 May 1941, p.4.

7   Beverley Hooper, 'Steinberg, Isaac Nachman (1888–1957)', *Australian Dictionary of Biography*, vol.16, 2002.

8   S. Stedman, *A Jewish Settlement in Australia*, Melbourne: Freeland League for Jewish Territorial Colonization, 1938; Isaac N. Steinberg, *Australia: The Unpromised Land—In Search of a Home*, London: Victor Gollancz, 1946; Isaac N. Steinberg, *Plainwords to Australian Jews*, trans. I. Ripps, Melbourne: Jewish Publishing Co., 1943; Isaac N. Steinberg, *Freeland League for Jewish Territorial Colonization*, Washington DC: Anglo-American Committee on Palestine, 1946.

9   'Talk on Kimberley Scheme', *Australian Jewish Herald*, 19 November 1942, p.30

10   Critchley Parker Jnr, *Tasmania, the Jewel of the Commonwealth: An Illustrated Account of the Island State of Tasmania, Its Natural Resources and Advantages, Its Activities and Enterprises and the Opportunities It Affords, Thanks to Its Wonderful Hydro-electric System for the Establishment of Secondary Industries*, Industrial and Mining Standard for the Tasmanian Government, Hobart, 1937.

11   Freeman, *Australian Jewish Historical Society Journal*, pp.509–11; Hilary L. Rubenstein, 'Critchley Parker (1911–1942): Australian Martyr for Jewish Refugees', *Australian Jewish Historical Society Journal*, vol.x, part 1, November 1990, pp 57–64; Critchley Parker Jnr, Transcript of diary/notebook, State Library Victoria, MS Box 4128/8.

12   Critchley Parker Jnr, SLV, MS Box 4128/8, letter E. Parkes, Tasmanian Under Secretary, to Critchley Parker, 5 November 1940.

13   Isaac N. Steinberg, *Australia: The Unpromised Land*, pp.133–7; Rubenstein, pp.63–4.

14   tasmaniastories.com/2017/11/29/poynduk-the-extravagant-impossible-and-understandable-dreams-of-critchley-parker/.

15 Critchley Parker Jnr, Transcript of diary/notebook, SLV, MS Box 4128/8, 23-page description of organisation of proposed settlement.

16 Critchley Parker Jnr, SLV MS Box 4128/8, transcript of journal.

17 Freeman, *Australian Jewish Historical Society Journal*, pp.508–12; Clarke, *Media Legends*, pp.121, 123.

18 National Archives of Australia, Isaacson, Peter Stuart, 03599950, A12372, R/35959/H, barcode 30697755.

19 National Archives of Australia, Isaacson, Lynka Caroline, V388729, B884, barcode 6244809.

20 White, ADB, 1996.

21 National Archives of Australia, Isaacson, Barbara Joan, VF391191, B884, barcode 6237011.

22 Warner, *The Pathfinder*, p.68.

23 Clarke, *Media Legends*, p.123; Patricia Clarke, 'Women in the Media', in Bridget Griffen Foley (ed.), *A Companion to the Australian Media*, Melbourne: Australian Scholarly Publishing, 2014, pp.495–98.

24 *Argus*, 1 July 1948, p.5; *Australian Women's Weekly*, 31 July 1945, p.10; *Dandenong Ranges News*, 4 February 1949.

25 'Editorial Policy Outlined', *Australian Jewish Outlook*, May 1947, p.2.

26 'Our Policy', *Australian Jewish Outlook*, September 1948, p.2.

27 'Editorial: The Outlook on Israel', *Australian Jewish Outlook*, September 1948, p.3.

28 Mark Baker, 'Peter Isaacson', in *Media Legends*, pp.192–5; Warner, pp.168–9.

29 Freeman, p.507; Warner, *The Pathfinder*, p.184.

30 Clarke, *Media Legends*, p.123; Warner, pp.186–7.

31 Warner, *The Pathfinder*, pp.187–91.

Connie Robertson, Iris Dexter and Patricia Knox

1 National Archives of Australia, SP112/1, 353/3/18, 26832. Proposal to send Mrs Constance Robertson overseas to cover activities of Australian women in War Work.

2 National Archives of Australia, SP 112/1, M 101, 935116 Accredited War Correspondents, p.48.

3 "Women Will be Called Up. New Man-power Drive. Longer Work Hours', *Sydney Morning Herald*, 16 October 1942, p.5.

4 'Services Need More Women', *Examiner*, Launceston, 28 January 1943, p.3.

5 Bridget Griffen-Foley, *Changing Stations: The Story of Australian Commercial Radio*, Sydney: UNSW Press, 2009, pp.318–33.

6   Bridget Griffen-Foley, 'The Fairfax, Murdoch and Packer Dynasties in Twentieth-century Australia', *Media History*, vol.8, no.1, 2002, p.94.

7   Griffen-Foley, 'Fairfax, Murdoch and Packer', p.94.

8   Helena Studdert, 'Case-study Women's Magazines', in Martin Lyons and John Arnold (eds), *A History of the Book in Australia 1891–1945*, St Lucia (Qld): University of Queensland Press, 2001, p.281; 'The Australian Women's Weekly. Depression and the War Years. Romance and Reality', *Refractory Girl*, Winter 1973, p.9.

9   Margot Parker, 'Uniform Makes the Woman,' *Woman*, 22 March 1943, p.9.

10   Patricia Knox, 'Women Can Keep Secrets', *Argus*, 5 April 1943, p.6.

11   National Archives of Australia, Isaacson, Barbara Joan, VF391191, B884, 6237011.

12   Constance Robertson, 'WAAAFs Work in Secrecy: Locked up on the Job', *Sydney Morning Herald*, 25 February 1943, p.4.

13   Patricia Knox, 'Dust and Concerts: WAAAFs at Work and Play', *Argus*, 26 February 1943, p.6.

14   Constance Robertson, 'Girls Guard Coast: Co-operation with A-A Gun Crews,' *Sydney Morning Herald*, 31 March 1943, p.11.

15   Constance Robertson, 'Army in Blue Jeans: Servicewomen at Work and Play,' *Sydney Morning Herald*, 26 February 1943, p.7.

16   Valerie Lawson, *Connie Sweetheart: The Story of Connie Robertson*, Port Melbourne (Vic.): William Heinemann Australia, 1990, pp.46–57.

17   *The Opinion*, June–July 1935, p.18.

18   Lawson, *Connie Sweetheart*, p.100.

19   Gavin Souter, *Company of Heralds: A Century and a Half of Australian Publishing by John Fairfax Limited and Its Predecessors, 1831–1981*, Carlton (Vic.): Melbourne University Press, 1981, p.386.

20   Collen Ryan, *Fairfax: The Rise and Fall*, Carlton (Vic.): The Meigunyah Press, 2013, pp.2, 4.

21   Victor Isaacs and Rod Kilpatrick, *Two Hundred Years of Sydney Newspapers: A Short History*, North Richmond (NSW): Rural Press, 2003, pp.6, 14.

22   Montague Grover quoted in Sybil Nolan, 'Manifest Editorial Differences: *The Age* and *The Argus* in the 1920s and 1930s', in Muriel Porter (ed.), *The Argus: The Life and Death of a Great Melbourne Newspaper 1846–1957*, Melbourne: RMIT Publishing, 2003, pp.83–4.

23   Peter Knox, The Knox Family Story, knoxetal.com.

24   'Sir Errol Knox Was Dynamic Figure in Newspaper Industry', *Argus*, 18 October 1949, p.3.

25   Jim Usher (ed.), *The Argus: Life and Death of a Newspaper*, North Melbourne

(Vic.): Australian Scholarly Publishing, 2008, p.54.

26   Patricia Clarke, 'Women in the Media', in Bridget Griffen-Foley (ed.), *A Companion to the Australian Media*, Melbourne: Australian Scholarly Publishing, 2014, pp.497.

27   'Bernice May' (Zora Cross), *Australian Woman's Mirror*, 11 September 1928, p.10.

28   George Aubrey Aria, Design & Art Australia Online, daao.org.au/bio/george-aubrey-aria/.

29   'Pretty Wife Tells of Husband's Treatment. Beat Her with a Razor Strop. Judge Puzzled in Strange Case,' *Truth*, 5 May 1935; 'Dismissed: Miss Iris Dexter Loses Divorce Case', *Truth*, 23 June 1935, p.24.

30   Sybil Nolan, 'Dexter, Nancy Nugent (1923–1983)', *Australian Dictionary of Biography*, vol.17, Melbourne University Press, 2007, pp.315–6.

31   Isobel Wood, 'Margot Parker Was a Woman Ahead of her Time', *Sunday Telegraph*, 7 April 19874, p.25.

32   *Western Mail*, 7 September 1945, p.27.

33   John McLaren, 'Marshall, Alan (1902–1984)', *Australian Dictionary of Biography*, vol.18, 2012, pp.130–31.

34   'Morality the Best Safeguard', *Woman*, 15 March 1943, p.8.

35   Iris Dexter, 'Veterans Don't Giggle Now', *Woman*, 5 April 1943, p.15.

36   Iris Dexter, '"Starkie" of the WAAAFeries and the "Kids" She Commands', *Woman*, 19 April 1943, pp.16–17.

37   National Archives of Australia, Isaacson, Peter Stuart, 03599950, A12372, R/35959/H, 30697755; Iris Dexter, 'Making War a Family Affair,' *Woman*, 12 April 1943, p.15.

38   Margot Parker, 'Let's All Be Girls Together', *Woman*, 5 April 1943, p.9.

39   National Archives of Australia, B883 Howard, Frederick James, VX128412, 6210898.

40   Australian War Memorial, PRO 3644 Lt Col Fred Howard Collection, Lt Colonel FJ Howard letter, 1 March 1943.

41   Australian War Memorial, PRO 3644 Lt Col Fred Howard Collection, Diary 22 Feb to 15 March.

42   Australian War Memorial, PRO 3644 Lt Col Fred Howard, Field HQ, New Guinea Force, to Major JR (Reg) Denison, Assistant Director PRO, 3 March 1943; David Dunstan, 'Howard, Frederick James (Fred) (1904–1984)', *Australian Dictionary of Biography*, vol.17, 2000, pp.552–3.

43   awm.gov.au/collection/C141191.

44   Athole Stewart, 'First Man Back to Singapore', *Argus*, 6 September 1945, p.16.

45   *Western Mail*, 7 September 1945, p.27.

46   Fay Anderson and Richard Trembath, *Witnesses to War: The History of Australian Conflict Reporting*, Carlton (Vic.): MUP, 2011, p.118.

47   Isobel Wood, 'Margot Parker was a Woman Ahead of her Time', *Sunday Telegraph*, 7 April 19874, p.25.

48   Souter, *Company of Heralds*, p.386.

49   Patricia Clarke, 'Constance Robertson', halloffame.melbournepressclub.com/article/constance-robertson.

50   Jeannine Baker, *Australian War Reporters*, Sydney: New South, 2015, pp.111–12.

51   Clarke, 'Women in the Media', p.497.

Epilogue: General references

Patricia Clarke, 'Government Propaganda in the 1950s: The Role of the News and Information Bureau', *Media International*, July 2011, pp.64–79

Patricia Clarke, 'Women in the Australian Media', in Bridget Griffen-Foley (ed.), *A Companion to the Australian Media*, Melbourne: Australian Scholarly Publishing, 2014, pp.495–8

Women for Media report, Women's Leadership Institute Australia, 2019

Select Bibliography

Akami, Tomoko, *Japan's News Propaganda and Reuters' News Empire in Northeast Asia, 1870–1934*, The Netherlands: Dordrecht, 2012

Akami, Tomoko, *Internationalizing the Pacific*, London: Routledge, 2002

Anderson, Fay and Trembath, Richard, *Witnesses to War: The History of Australian Conflict Reporting*, Carlton (Vic.): Melbourne University Press, 2011

Archer, Robin et al. (eds), *The Conscription Conflict and the Great War*, Clayton (Vic.): Monash University Publishing, 2016

Badsey, Stephen, 'War Correspondents in the Boer War', in Peter Dennis and Jeffrey Grey (eds), *The Boer War Army, Nation and Empire*, Chief of Army/Australian War Memorial, Military History Conference, Canberra: Army History Unit, 2000

Baker, Jeannine, *Australian Women War Reporters: Boer War to Vietnam*, Sydney: NewSouth Publishing, 2015

Beaumont, Joan, *Broken Nation: Australians in the Great War*, Sydney: Allen & Unwin, 2014

Bridge, Carl, Crawford, Robert and Dunstan, David (eds), *Australians in Britain: The Twentieth Century Experience*, Melbourne: Monash University ePress, 2009

'British Concentration Camps', geni.com/projects/Anglo-Boere-Oorlog-Boer-War-1899-1902-British-Concentration-Camps

Broadbent, Coral, 'Kōrero: Henderson, Stella May', Dictionary of New Zealand Biography, teara.govt.nz/mi/biographies/2h29/henderson-stella-may

'Brook Farm', Encyclopaedia Britannica, britannica.com/topic/Brook-Farm

Callaway, Helen and Helly, Dorothy O., 'Crusader for Empire: Flora Shaw/Lady Lugard', in Deborah Chambers, Linda Steiner and Carole Fleming, *Women and Journalism*, London: Routledge, 2004

Chaudhuri, Nupur and Strobel, Margaret (eds), *Western Women and Imperialism*, Bloomington (USA): Indiana University Press, 1992

Chennells, Ellen, *Recollections of an Egyptian Princess by Her English Governess*, Edinburgh: W. Blackwood and Sons, 1893

Clarke, Patricia, 'Anna Blackwell, *Sydney Morning Herald* Correspondent in Paris (1860–1890)', Royal Australian Historical Society Journal, vol.108, part 1, June 2020

Clarke, Patricia, 'In the Days of Print: Four Women Journalists in World War II', *Australian Journal of Biography and History*, no.4, 2020

Clarke, Patricia, 'Australian Influence on the American Women's Labor Movement in the First Decades of the Twentieth Century: Alice Henry and Miles Franklin, Editors of Life and Labor', *The Independent Scholar*, vol.5, August 2019

Clarke, Patricia, 'Frances Taylor Founder and Editor Guides Woman's World to Success', *La Trobe Journal*, no.103, September 2019

Clarke, Patricia, 'Edith Dickenson at the Boer War', in Barry Turner, Daniel Barredo Ibáñez and Steven James Grattan (eds), *Reporting from the Wars 1850-2015: The Origins and Evolution of the War Correspondent*, Wilmington (USA), Malaga (Spain): Vernon Press, Series in Communication, 2018

Clarke, Patricia, 'Jennie Scott Griffiths: A Texas-born "Red-ragger"', *Unbound*, National Library of Australia's Magazine, June 2017

Clarke, Patricia, 'Flora Shaw: A "Lady from London" in 1890s Queensland', *Celebrating Independent Thought. ISAA Twenty Years On: 2015 Conference Proceedings*, Independent Scholars Association of Australia, vol.15, no.2, 2016

Clarke, Patricia, 'How a Conservative Texan Became a Radical Socialist and Feminist in World War I Australia', *ISAA Review*, vol.15, no.2, 2016

Clarke, Patricia, 'Melbourne Journalist Reports on the "Storm Centre of Asia", 1931-32: Janet Mitchell: Journalist, Internationalist, Educationalist', *Victorian Historical Journal*, vol.87, no.2, December 2016

Clarke, Patricia, 'Caroline (Lynka) Isaacson (1900-1962)', in Michael Smith and Mark Baker (eds), *Media Legends: Journalists Who Helped Shape Australia*, Melbourne: Wilkinson Publishing, 2014

Clarke, Patricia, 'The Transformation of Journalist Stella Allan: From Soap-box Socialist to Conservative Women's Page Editor', *Australian Journalism Review*, no.33(2), December 2011

Clarke, Patricia, 'Pioneer Woman Journalist's Career Spanned Two Countries: Stella Allan in Wellington and Melbourne', in *Margin: Life and Letters of Early Australia*, April 2007

Clarke, Patricia, *Pen Portraits: Women Writers and Journalists in Nineteenth Century Australia*, Sydney: Allen & Unwin, 1988

Clarke, Patricia, *Tasma's Diaries with Another by Her Young Sister Edith Huybers*, Canberra: Mulini Press, 1995

Clarke, Patricia, *Tasma: The Life of Jessie Couvreur*, Sydney: Allen & Unwin, 1994

Cunningham, Gail, *The New Woman and the Victorian Novel*, London: Macmillan, 1978

Curthoys, Ann and Schultz, Julianne (eds), *Journalism: Print, Politics and Popular Culture*, St Lucia (Qld): University of Queensland Press, 1999

Damousi, Joy, *Women Come Rally: Socialism, Communism and Gender in Australia 1890-1955*, Melbourne: Oxford University Press, 1994

Desmond, Robert W., *Tides of War: World News Reporting between Two Wars, 1920-1940*, Iowa City (USA): University of Iowa Press, 1984

Dickenson, Edith C.M., *What I Saw in India and the East*, Adelaide: J.L. Bonython and Company, 1900

Dickenson, Jackie, *Australian Women in Advertising in the Twentieth Century*, Melbourne: Palgrave Macmillan, 2016

Dunn, Margaret, *The Dauntless Bunch: The Story of the YWCA in Australia*, Melbourne: YWCA, 1991

'Franco-German War', Encyclopaedia Britannica, britannica.com/event/Franco-German-War

Fraser, Frances and Palmer, Nettie (eds), *Centenary Gift Book*, Melbourne: Women's Centenary Council, Robertson and Mullins, 1934

Freeman, Harold A., 'The Charismatic Caroline Isaacson', *Australian Jewish Historical Society Journal*, vol.XVIII, part 4, 2007

Gillison, Joan, *A History of the Lyceum Club*, Melbourne: The Lyceum Club, 1975

Griffen-Foley, Bridget, *Changing Stations: The Story of Australian Commercial Radio*, Sydney: UNSW Press, 2009

Griffen-Foley, Bridget, 'The Fairfax, Murdoch and Packer Dynasties in Twentieth-century Australia', *Media History*, vol.8, no.1, 2002

Griffiths, Ciwa, *One of Ten*, Laguna Hills (USA): Wide Range Press, 1993

Griffiths, Noel, *A History of the Government Savings Bank of New South Wales*, Sydney: W.T. Baker, 1930

Hall, Barbara and Mather, Jenni, *Australian Women Photographers 1840 to 1960*, Richmond (Vic.): Greenhouse Publications, 1986

Harding, Marjorie, *This City of Peace by 23 Australian Converts to the Catholic Church*, Melbourne: Legion of Mary, 1949

Hays, Elinor Rice, *Those Extraordinary Blackwells: The Story of a Journey to a Better World*, New York: Harcourt, Brace & World, 1967

Henry, Alice, *Memoirs of Alice Henry*, ed. by Nettie Palmer with a postscript, Melbourne: 1944

Henry, Alice, *Women and the Labor Movement*, New York: George Doran Co., 1923

Henry, Alice, *The Trade Union Woman*, New York: D. Appleton Co., 1915

Henry, Alice and Franklin, S.M., 'Why 50,000 Refused to Sew', *Englishwoman*, June 1911

van Heyningen, Elizabeth, *The Concentration Camps of the Anglo-Boer War: A Social History*, Auckland Park (South Africa): Jacana, 2000

Hirst, John, 'Empire, State, Nation', in D.M. Schreuder and Stuart Ward (eds), *Australia's Empire*, Oxford: Oxford University Press, 2008

The History of The Times: The Twentieth Century Test 1884–1912, London: The Times, 1947

Hobhouse, Emily, *The Brunt of the War and Where It Fell*, London: Methuen and Co., 1902

Hopkins, F.R.C. (ed.), *The Australian Ladies' Annual*, Melbourne: McCarron Bird & Co., 1876

Horne, Alistair, *The Fall of Paris: The Siege and the Commune 1870–1*, London: Macmillan, 1965

Horton, P., Black, A. and Blaylock, B., 'Ornithology at the South Australian Museum, Adelaide, 1866 to 1939', in W.E. Davis, Jr., W.E. Boles and H.F. Rechter (eds), *Contributions to the History of Australasian Ornithology*, vol.iv

Howard, Michael, *The Franco-Prussian War: The German Invasion of France 1870–1871*, London: Rupert Hart-Davis, 1962

Hudson, Miles and Stonier, John, *War and the Media: A Random Searchlight*, New York: New York University Press, 1998

Hudson, W.J., *Australia and the League of Nations*, Sydney University Press: Sydney, 1980

Isaacs, Victor and Kilpatrick, Rod, *Two Hundred Years of Sydney Newspapers: A Short History*, North Richmond (NSW): Rural Press, 2003

Isaacson, Peter, *As I Remember Them: Men and Women Who Shaped a Life*, Melbourne: Red Dog Books, 2012

Kirkby, Diane, '"Those Knights of Pen and Pencil": Woman Journalists and Cultural Leadership of the Women's Movement in Australia and the United States', *Labour History*, May 2013

Kirkby, Diane, *Alice Henry: The Power of Pen and Voice. The Life of an Australian-American Labor Reformer*, Cambridge (UK): Cambridge University Press, 1991

Kirkpatrick, Rod, *The Bold Type: A History of Victoria's Country Newspapers 1840–2010*, Ascot Vale (Vic.), Victorian Country Press Association, 2010

Knapman, Bruce, *Fiji's Economic History 1874–1939*, Canberra: RSSS, ANU, 1987

Lake, Marilyn, *Getting Equal: A History of Australian Feminism*, St Leonards (NSW): Allen and Unwin, 1999

Lawson, Valerie, *Connie Sweetheart: The story of Connie Robertson*, Port Melbourne (Vic.): Heinemann Australia, 1990

Lee, Janet, *Fallen among Reformers. Miles Franklin, Modernity and the New Woman*, Sydney: Sydney University Press, 2020

Lindsay, David, 'Elder Scientific Exploration Expedition', *Journal of the Elder Expedition*, 2 May 1891, Royal Geographical Society of South Australia, rgssa.org.au/Exploration

Lowry, Donal, *The South African War Reappraised*, Manchester (UK): Manchester University Press, 2000

Macmahon Ball, W., *Press, Radio and World Affairs*, Carlton (Vic.), Melbourne University Press, 1938

Mennell, Phillip, *In Australian Wilds, and Other Colonial Tales and Sketches*, London: Hutchinson, 1889

Mitchell, Janet, *Spoils of Opportunity*, London: Methuen & Co., 1937

Mitchell, Janet, *Tempest in Paradise*, London: Geoffrey Bles, 1935

Mitchell, Winifred, *Fifty Years of Feminist Achievement: A History of the United Associations of Women*, Sydney: UAW, 1979

Mitter, Rana, *China's War with Japan 1937–1945: The Struggle for Survival*, London: Penguin, 2013

Moberly Bell, E., *Flora Shaw (Lady Lugard, DBE)*, London: Constable, 1947

Modjeska, Drusilla, *Exiles at Home: Australian Women Writers 1925–1945*, Sydney, Sirius Books, 1981

Murray, Jacqui, *Watching the Sun Rise: Australian Reporting of Japan 1931 to the Fall of Singapore*, Lanham (USA): Lexington Books, 2004

Noye, R.J., *Dictionary of South Australian Photography*, Adelaide: Art Gallery of South Australia, 2007

Paisley, Fiona, *Glamour in the Pacific: Cultural Internationalism and Race Politics in the Women's Pan Pacific*, Honolulu (USA): University of Hawaii Press, 2009

Palmer, Nettie, 'Pathfinders: Who Was Alice Henry?', *Australian Women's Digest*, April 1945

Parker, Critchley Jnr, *Tasmania, the Jewel of the Commonwealth: An Illustrated Account of the Island State of Tasmania, Its Natural Resources and Advantages*, Hobart: Industrial and Mining Standard for the Tasmanian Government, 1937

Pickard, William J., *Kathleen Rouse of Rouse Hill: The Road to Harbin*, Sydney: W.J. Pickerd, 1992

Porter, Muriel (ed.), *The Argus: The Life and Death of a Great Melbourne Newspaper 1846–1957*, Melbourne: Royal Melbourne Institute of Technology University, 2003

Putnis, Peter, 'News, Time and Imagined Community in Colonial Australia', *Media History*, vol.16, no.2, 2010

Radi, Heather (ed.), *200 Australian Women: A Redress Anthology*, Sydney: Women's Redress Press, 1988

Reid, M.O., *The Ladies Came to Stay: Presbyterian Ladies College Melbourne 1875–1960*, Melbourne: PLC Council, 1960

Roe, Jill, *Stella Miles Franklin: A Biography*, Pymble (NSW): Fourth Estate, 2008

Rubenstein, Hilary L., 'Critchley Parker (1911-1942): Australian Martyr for Jewish Refugees', *Australian Jewish Historical Society Journal*, vol.x, part 1, November 1990

Ryan, Collen, *Fairfax. The Rise and Fall*, Carlton (Vic.), The Meigunyah Press, 2013

Sand, George, *Jacques*, 1831, translated by Anna Blackwell 1847

Scharrer, Jos, *The Journalist: The Jameson Raid, The Klondike Gold Rush, The Anglo Boer War, The Founding of Nigeria, Flora Shaw Was There*, North Charleston (USA): CreateSpace, 2014

Selle, Earl Albert, *Donald of China*, New York: Harper & Bros, 1948

Shaw, Flora, *Castle Blair: A Story of Youthful Days*, London: 1877

'Sixty Years of Newspaper History', *Sydney Morning Herald*, 19 June 1897

Smith, Charles Patrick, 'Men Who Made The Argus and The Australasian 1846-1923', c.1923, SLV MS Box 4670/3

Smith, Michael and Baker, Mark (eds), *Media Legends: Journalists Who Helped Shape Australia*, Melbourne: Wilkinson Publishing, 2014

Souter, Gavin, *Heralds and Angels: The House of Fairfax 1841-1992*, Ringwood (Vic.): Penguin Books, 1992

Souter, Gavin, *Company of Heralds: A Century and a Half of Australian Publishing by John Fairfax Limited and Its Predecessors, 1831-1981*, Carlton (Vic.): Melbourne University Press, 1981

Spence, Catherine Helen, *An Autobiography*, Adelaide: W.K. Thomas, 1910

Stedman, S., *A Jewish Settlement in Australia*, Melbourne: Freeland League for Jewish Territorial Colonization, 1938

Steinberg, I.N., *Freeland League for Jewish Territorial Colonization*, Washington DC (USA): Anglo-American Committee on Palestine, 1946

Steinberg, I.N., *Australia—the Unpromised Land—in Search of a Home*, London: Victor Gollancz, 1946

Steinberg, I.N., *Plainwords to Australian Jews*, trans. I. Ripps, Melbourne: Jewish Publishing Co., 1943

Studdert, Helena, 'Case-study Women's magazines', in Martin Lyons and John Arnold (eds), *A History of the Book in Australia 1891-1945*, St Lucia (Qld), University of Queensland Press, 2001

Tasma, *A Knight of the White Feather*, London: William Heinemann, 1892

The *Times* Special Correspondent [Flora Shaw], *Letters from Queensland*, London: Macmillan, 1893

Usher, Jim (ed.), *The Argus: Life & Death of a Newspaper*, North Melbourne (Vic.): Australian Scholarly Publishing, 2008

The *'Vagabond' Annual: Christmas 1877*, Sydney: Turner and Henderson, 1877

Walker, David, *Anxious Nation: Australia and the Rise of Asia, 1850–1939*, 2nd ed., New Delhi: SSS Publications, 2009

Warner, Denis, *The Pathfinder: In the Air—on the Ground: The Peter Isaacson Story*, Melbourne (Vic.): Information Australia, 2000

Wright, Andree, 'The Australian Women's Weekly. Depression and the War Years. Romance and Reality', *Refractory Girl*, Winter 1973

Young, Jeanne, *Catherine Helen Spence*, Melbourne: Lothian Publishing Co., 1939

Index